Paul's Idea of Community

PAUL'S

IDEA

OF

COMMUNITY

Revised Edition

Robert Banks

Copyright © 1994 by Hendrickson Publishers, Inc.
P. O. Box 3473
Peabody, Massachusetts 01961–3473
All rights reserved
Printed in the United States of America

ISBN 1–56563–050–5

Library of Congress Cataloging-in-Publication Data

Banks, Robert J.
    Paul's idea of community: the early house churches in their
cultural setting / Robert Banks. — Rev. ed.
     p. cm.
    Includes bibliographical references and index.
    ISBN 1–56563–050–5
    1. House churches—Rome. 2. Bible. N.T. Epistles of
Paul—Theology.   3. Church—Biblical teaching. 4. Freedom
(Theology)—Biblical teaching. I. Title.
    BS2655.H72B36   1994
    262′.009′015—dc20   94–30999
                                                    CIP

The original edition of this book was published under the same
title in 1979 by Anzea Publishers, 3-5 Richmond Road, Homebush
West, NSW 2140, Australia.

TABLE OF CONTENTS

ABBREVIATIONS

The usual abbreviations are employed for books of the Bible and literary terms.

Books of the Apocrypha

Ecclus	Ecclesiasticus (Sirach)
Jud	Judith
1 Macc	1 Maccabees
2 Macc	2 Maccabees
Wisd	Wisdom of Solomon

Pseudepigrapha

Apoc. Mos.	Apocalypse of Moses
Arist.	Letter of Aristeas
2 Bar.	2 Baruch
1 En.	1 Enoch
Jub.	Jubilees
3 Macc.	3 Maccabbees
Sib. Or.	Sibylline Oracles
Test. Lev.	Testament of Levi

Dead Sea Scrolls

CD	The Damascus Rule
1QH	The Thanksgiving Hymns

1QM	The War Scroll
1QS	The Community Rule

Mishnah

'Ab.	'Aboth
'Arak.	'Arakhin
B. M.	Baba Metzi'a
Ber.	Berakoth
Dem.	Demai
Eduy.	Eduyoth
Gitt.	Gittin
Hag.	Hagigah
Ket.	Ketuboth
Kidd.	Kiddushin
Makk.	Makkoth
M. Sh.	Ma'aser Sheni
Meg.	Megillah
Pe'a.	Pe'ah
Pes.	Pesahim
R. Sh.	Rosh-ha-Shanah
Shabb.	Shabbath
Sot.	Sotah
Sukk.	Sukkah
Ta'an.	Ta'anith
Tam.	Tamid
Yeb.	Yebamoth
Yom.	Yoma

Tosephta

Ber.	Berakoth

Miscellaneous

LXX	Septuagint
RSV	Revised Standard Version

PREFACE TO THE ORIGINAL EDITION

This is not a technical book, nor a popular one either. We already have a number of stimulating technical works on Paul's view of the church, and many popular books on church life build on aspects of Paul's view in their presentation. But the former are too linguistically daunting for most readers, while the latter are too particular in their emphasis or psychological in their orientation to be fully satisfactory as treatments of Paul. I have written this for those who find themselves caught in the middle—seeking a comprehensive account of what Paul said, yet in terms they can understand. And I am not thinking of the Christianly-inclined only. Paul's idea of community is too historically interesting and significant to be closeted among the religious.

This has affected the form of the book. It seeks not only to interpret Paul, but to set him firmly in his context. Only by comparing him with his contemporaries do the genuinely distinctive elements in his approach come into focus. For while in many respects Paul was very much a man of his times, in others he was astonishingly ahead of them. Many people today are finding that he speaks more relevantly about community than representatives of the counter-culture groups and church structures. Meanwhile the sociologists of religion are beginning to discover that Paul is someone with whom they have not yet fully come to terms. Initially this book contained additional material for those who have such interests, but I did not have enough space to carry this through properly. Still, those who wish to explore further the sociological character of Paul's ideas will find here much that is helpful. And those seeking a more precise identification of the culturally conditioned and permanently relevant aspects of his thought will discover much to help them. At a later stage I hope to give more concentrated attention to these two areas.

Though this is not a technical work, it is based on a thorough investigation of the relevant primary and secondary sources, and suggests a number of new interpretations of the material involved. My first inquiries were made more than fifteen years ago and in varying degrees the subject has preoccupied me ever since. Almost five years have passed since a first draft of part of this book was completed and it has gone through many revisions before reaching its present form. For me, interest in Paul's view has been stimulated not only by reading and thinking about it at an academic level, but also by involvement in groups which feel what Paul said still has continuing relevance for their community life. We learn about the past not just by rational reflection upon it, but also by personal involvement in those aspects of our present which have common links with it. This is true not only for people in general but for those of us who are historians as well. It sharpens the questions we ask of the past and deepens our empathy with it. Since the book does contain several new lines of thought, sets Paul's ideas in a broader historical context than is customary and approaches him as a social thinker rather than a systematic theologian, I hope it will be read by some biblical scholars, ancient historians and historians of ideas, as well as those for whom it is chiefly designed.

In setting out the footnotes and bibliography I have borne in mind those who will mainly use them. References to secondary works have been excluded from footnotes to avoid unnecessarily weighting the presentation. Instead I have provided a carefully chosen bibliography, geared around the main themes of the book. This includes works supporting in more detail many lines of argument within it, broader treatments of various aspects of Paul's view and alternative views to those I have advocated. Certain references to primary sources will be found for convenience in the text but longer sets of references will generally be found in the footnotes. Citations are comprehensive as far as

Paul's writings are concerned. Other contemporary documents are cited representatively, since here I am summarizing bodies of evidence rather than treating them exhaustively. In view of the relative inaccessibility of some sources, e.g. collections of Greek papyri and inscriptions and some rabbinic commentaries and codes, I have referred only to those which the general reader will find more readily available. Those specialists who wish to consult the more technical sources should not have any difficulty finding the required references. These are in the books mentioned in the bibliography accompanying each chapter. However, where more inaccessible items have been gathered into anthologies such as C. K. Barrett's collection of background documents to the New Testament, I have included reference to them. At the close of the book there is also a glossary containing descriptions of the main figures, works and movements cited in the text and footnotes for those who may be unfamiliar with them.

I have appreciated the encouragement of various people in the writing of this book, too many unfortunately to name. But I must thank Donald Robinson, now Archbishop of Sydney, who in his lectures some years ago first opened my eyes to some of the distinctive features of Paul's view of church; and my good friend Geoffrey Moon who, in countless discussions, has stimulated and sharpened my thinking on many issues involved. Thanks are also due to John Waterhouse, at the time Manager of Anzea Publishers, for convincing me of the need for a more general work on the subject rather than yet another technical monograph, and also for carefully editing the original manuscript. I have also valued the way in which Mr. B. Howard Mudditt, until lately the Managing Director of Paternoster Press, maintained constant interest in the project. The editors of *Interchange* and the *Journal of Christian Education* freely agreed to my using some paragraphs from articles on 'Paul and Women's Liberation' (*Interchange*, Number 18. 1975, pages 81–105) and 'Freedom and Authority in Education—I: Paul's View of Freedom; II: Paul's View of Authority' (*Journal of Christian Education*, Number 55, 1976, pages 40–48 and Number 56, 1976, pages 17–24). Edwin A. Judge, Professor of Ancient History at Macquarie University, and James D. G. Dunn, Lecturer in New Testament at Nottingham University, kindly read the final draft and made a number of helpful suggestions.

I am also grateful to Stephen Barton and Peter Marshall, two of my postgraduate students, for correcting the initial typescript, and to Dr. Robert Withycombe, Warden of St. Mark's Institute,

Canberra and to the Rev. David Durie, Principal of the College of Ministry, Canberra, for helping me check the final proofs. Encouragement and help of a more personal kind was given by Audrey Duncan throughout the years it took to write. My wife Julie helped me clarify many basic ideas in our frequent discussions of the book's contents and also assisted me in checking the manuscript. Our children Mark and Simon patiently bore with it all and will, I hope, one day understand more fully how Paul could so grip one's imagination—as for me he does.

A NOTE ON THE
SECOND EDITION

Although it is fifteen years since this book appeared, there seems to be a continuing demand for it. This has provided the opportunity for me to work through the text again and make various improvements. I have wanted to do this for some time.

This second edition is the result of a thoroughgoing revision. Only a few paragraphs remain completely untouched. One consequence of this is that the text reads more easily and clearly. I have also refined some of its interpretations and viewpoints so as to take into account more recent scholarly investigations of Paul's writings and my own ongoing reflections. The bibliography has been extended and fully updated, and an index of ancient sources has been added. Indispensable in all this has been the help of Shirley A. Decker-Lucke, Assistant Academic Editor at Hendrickson Publishers. She has been everything one could hope for in an editor, and I am deeply grateful to her.

I am gratified by the continued interest in the book and trust that readers will now find it more current and accessible. The topic remains an important one and the need to translate Paul's views into contemporary practice is as urgent as ever.

INTRODUCTION

The Christian writings of the first century reflect a variety of attitudes towards the meaning and practice of community. But it is the earliest among them, Paul's letters, that contain the most detailed information. The remainder deal with the matter only intermittently, or in an indirect way, or are too brief to yield any rounded portrait. Though virtually all of them were composed later than Paul's writings, they sometimes preserve traces of an approach to community that precedes these. Paul was not the first to formulate a Christian idea of community. But there can be no doubt that he gave more attention to this than anyone else during the first century. In every one of his writings, aspects of community life come in for discussion, and in a few it emerges as the main issue for consideration.

It is not merely the extent of Paul's contribution that sets it apart from others in the first century, but its quality. We find here the most clearly developed and profound understanding of community in all the early Christian writings. Not that he provides any systematic treatment of the idea. For the most part he worked out his views in response to the problems of particular communities. Only a few of his writings were designed for a wider audience and deal with the subject in more general terms. Even these do not display a strictly systematic mind at work. But they do reveal an energetic and creative thinker who has the ability to engage in both theoretical reflection and the subtleties of argument. His writings also reveal someone unfailingly concerned with the practical consequences of his viewpoint and personally involved in the actual outcome of his recommendations.

Until the last century, and in some conservative circles up to the present time, the dogmatic approach to the NT tended to result in a monochrome treatment of its contents. This meant that the views of even highly individual authors like Paul were too often interpreted by statements contained in the writings of other early Christian figures. It also meant that the possibility of development in his views over a period of time was rarely given serious consideration. The emergence of a more historical approach to the NT rightly queried both of these procedures. But the first reassessments of Paul produced by it severed him too drastically from his first-century Christian contemporaries and reduced too arbitrarily the number of writings alleged to come from his hand. These initial experiments in the revaluation of Paul have been generally rejected as unsound, in both their methodology and their conclusions. More moderate assessments have come to prevail, recognizing the links between Paul's interpretation of Christianity and that of others in the NT and extending the number of letters felt to come from his pen.

The distinctiveness of Paul's contribution is encountered nowhere more so, I would argue, than in his idea of community. In the detailed exploration of his writings that follows, we will look at key aspects of his approach, taking care to note how he arrives at and argues from the basic principles that underlie his understanding. Two comments should be made here. First, it is the internal dynamics of Paul's communities that we are chiefly concerned with investigating, not the external responsibilities of their members to the world around them. The latter would require a full-scale treatment of its own. In any case, for Paul it is not as a community but as individuals, families, and small groups that Christians undertake and fulfill these responsibilities. Second, since all the different aspects of his approach are based on what for him is the fundamental reality that everything, his own life included, revolves around—the gospel—certain themes are bound to reappear at regular intervals throughout this study. It could not be otherwise. Paul's thinking about community cannot be compared to an argument that proceeds logically from one point to another, each stage containing the seeds of the next and unfolding naturally into it. It is more like a composition built upon a single underlying motif, each section providing a variation of this basic theme, with the motif itself resurfacing at various points in the work. We shall encounter this pattern many times in the following pages.

This investigation is primarily based on Paul's letters. Although some uncertainty surrounds the genuineness of "Ephesians," actually a general letter addressed to a broad group of Christians rather than a communication to a specific church, I have decided to include it in the discussion that follows and treat it as if originally coming from the apostle. But I have generally indicated when I am using it to make a point not found in the other letters, so that readers can judge for themselves whether or not it is consistent with them. The Pastoral letters (1 and 2 Timothy, Titus) present a more difficult problem, since the question of their authenticity continues to be decided more uniformly in a negative direction, even by some conservative scholars. No one doubts that they emanated from circles deeply influenced by Paul's thought. But there are also a number of uncharacteristic features in them and perhaps they are later compositions that, like Luke's reconstructions of Paul's speeches in Acts, were compiled to preserve some of his instructions for the next generation. Since for me too their place is uncertain, and yet it is unwise to be too dogmatic on the issue, I have discussed them separately at the close of the book, where their compatibility or incompatibility with what is drawn from the other writings is left for the reader to gauge. Material from Acts that relates to Paul's activities in founding communities is included in the main text. Luke's work contains valuable historical information on such matters, though this must always be checked against his tendency to idealize the earlier situation and also against his occasional anachronisms. I take the probable order of composition of Paul's letters to be 1 and 2 Thessalonians, Galatians, 1 and 2 Corinthians, Romans, Philippians, Colossians, Philemon, followed by "Ephesians"[1]—all of them written within a comparatively short period of time, ca. AD 50/51 to 61/62.

---

[1]Scripture references in footnotes are normally cited in this order.

1

—ꝏ—

THE SOCIAL AND RELIGIOUS SETTING

PAUL: A MAN OF HIS TIMES

It is not possible to understand a person and his activities apart from the times in which he lived. This is especially the case with Paul. In responding to the call of Jesus he did not withdraw from the world about him; rather, he found himself thrown more violently into it. As a consequence he crisscrossed vast tracts of the Mediterranean region several times over in the course of the next thirty years. In doing so he met people from a variety of racial and national backgrounds, among them Jews from the Dispersion; homeland and immigrant Greeks; Romans at the heart of the Empire and in some of its distant outposts; Cypriots, Macedonians, and the inhabitants of local districts in different parts of Asia Minor; even small groups from Egypt, Crete, Malta, and apparently, Scythia. On these travels he encountered competing philosophical schools, in particular Stoicism and Epicureanism, and alternative religious movements, especially traditional Greek city-state cults and imported Oriental mystery religions. At different points in his journeyings he also came into conflict with a wide range of civil and political authorities and experienced first hand the ramifications of a variety of legal processes and decisions. So Paul was extensively involved in, and affected by, many of the significant tendencies and tensions of his day and cannot be studied in isolation from them.

There is a further reason for insisting that Paul be approached in this way. He did not merely encounter the ideas and institutions of the people amongst whom he moved; he adopted a deliberate policy of accommodation to them. This comes out most clearly in his first letter to the Christians at Corinth. "I have become all things to all men," he says, "that I might by all means save some" (1 Cor 9:22, RSV). This does not mean that Paul compromises his beliefs and practices by simply conforming them to those he happens to be addressing at any particular time. It means that he is always taking such beliefs and practices into account and making them the starting point for his own message and behavior. Wherever he can do so, he acknowledges the validity of other approaches and incorporates them into his own (Acts 17:22–34). Where he cannot, he asserts the superiority of his approach over others and argues that it fulfills the aspirations that have been misguidedly invested in the other approaches (Col 2:8–23). Either way the things he is saying and doing cannot be properly appreciated without reference to the context in which he is speaking and acting.

Another reason Paul should be studied in the context of his culture is his frequently expressed concern with the social attitudes and structures of his day. On some occasions he calls these into question and contradicts them by his own statements or behavior (1 Cor 6:1–6); on others he insists they be carefully noted and followed (11:14–15). Where accepted conventions come into conflict with a basic implication of the gospel message, there is no doubt in his mind as to which has to give way (10:14–22). Where less central implications of the gospel are concerned and where there is the likelihood of causing offense among those outside the Christian group, there should be a willing avoidance of practices that, all things being equal, are quite legitimate in themselves (8:7–13; 10:23–30). This means that in some measure the activities of Christians in his communities were conditioned by the values and patterns of the society around them and cannot be rightly understood unless considered in relation to them.

Many treatments of Paul's view of community are inadequate in this respect. Instead of seeing Paul's views in their historical setting they discuss them independently of the wider

context in which they emerged. This results in a primarily doctrinal study of Paul's outlook, unrelated to many of the circumstances that played a part in its development. Yet it was through
interaction with the society about him, as well as involvement
with his communities, that Paul came to hold the views expressed
in his letters, not through theological contemplation removed
from the cut and thrust of daily life. This is why they have the
stamp of reality about them and are so full of life and creativity. He
was constantly being forced to justify conclusions he had already
reached and to demonstrate their relevance in situations that had
arisen. He was also frequently under pressure to deepen his convictions in order to deal with new difficulties that had appeared.
Paul's understanding of community is never static or frozen into
a theological system. It is a living thing, always open to development and in touch with the practicalities of the moment.

THE GRAECO-ROMAN WORLD:
CHANGING CONCEPTIONS OF COMMUNITY

The Graeco-Roman world in the middle of the first century
was characterized by great variety and vitality. Although Rome
now dominated the whole of the Mediterranean region and Greek
culture had penetrated to the furthest reaches of the Empire, not
only did local patterns of rule and ways of life continue to survive,
but relatively new trends in social organization began to flourish
and attract an increasing number of people. Traditionally there
had been two main types of community with which people might
associate themselves: *politeia*, the public life of the city or nation
state to which people belonged; and *oikonomia*, the household
order into which they were born or to which they were attached.
For some, involvement in communities of both types could be a
very full and satisfying affair. The Greek citizen in fifth-century BC
Athens played a vocal part in the *polis*, the city-state where he
lived, as well as a leading role in the *oikos*, the family unit that he
headed. His Jewish counterpart in eighth-century BC Israel, as an
elder in his local town or village, made a real contribution to civic
affairs and had important obligations to fulfill within the extended family that he was responsible for. But there were always
others who were unable to participate in the life of either of these

two kinds of communities in a freely-chosen or meaningful way. Among them were the majority of slaves, dependents of various kinds, adults who remained unmarried, and outcasts of society.

By the first century, even those who had previously played an influential part in their respective civil and household communities found their freedom to do so dwindling in the face of changes that were overtaking both institutions in society. Well before the rise of Rome, but accelerated by the growth of the Empire, political power tended to become concentrated in fewer and fewer hands and to remain in those hands for longer and longer periods. This was so even in Rome itself. In the wake of the victorious legions, traditional republics were still often created, but independence was never fully granted to them, and authority was generally vested in an aristocratic, often self-advancing, minority. Disenchantment with the *polis* not only took place among the politically disadvantaged sections of society but also increased among those who, in earlier days, had found their identity partly within it. To some extent the household community was the beneficiary of this exclusion from the real bodies where civil power resided. What people could not find in the wider community to which they belonged they sought in the smaller community in which they lived. Its breadth of membership and intimacy of relationship lent itself well to this. Yet the desires of many could not long be satisfied within so narrow a sphere, while the hopes of others were forever being frustrated by the subordinate position they occupied within the household framework. For these reasons people's aspirations and allegiances tended to drift away from the *oikos* in another direction.

Some of the more thoughtful and devout members of society began to look beyond the public life of their *polis* towards a cosmopolitan order that would encompass all people. They wrote or dreamt of a universal commonwealth, an international brotherhood, in which the basic divisions that recently separated people had been, or were to be, resolved. Whether this was viewed as a Stoic commonwealth governed by reason or as an international theocracy ruled from Jerusalem by the Messiah, this idea maintained a powerful grip on the minds of many Greeks, Romans, and Jews.

However, for others these expectations proved too abstract and elitist on the one hand, or too violent and utopian on the other. In increasingly greater numbers people began to find their desires fulfilled in a variety of voluntary associations that multiplied in cities all over the ancient world, especially in Greek centers. Though these associations had their precursors in groups formed for various purposes among the social elite in earlier centuries, it was in the late Hellenistic period that they came into their own and attracted a wide following—in part from the socially disadvantaged members of society. The novel feature of these groups was their basis in something other than the principles of *politeia* or *oikonomia*. They bound together people from dissimilar backgrounds on a different basis than that of geography and race, or natural and legal ties. Their principle was *koinonia*, i.e., voluntary partnership.

This does not mean that every such association was open to all who wished to join it. Many restricted entry to a certain nationality, family, class, or gender in society and excluded all others. Only a few appear to have opened their doors, in some respects at least, to all. I say "in some respects," for the majority were in any case established around a particular interest, vocation, or commitment. These were extremely varied: political, military, and sporting concerns; professional and commercial guilds; artisans and members of crafts; philosophical schools and religious societies. Although only some were purely religious in character (a religious dimension was present in nearly all such organizations, generally through the patronage of a deity and attachment to a shrine), the bulk were primarily designed to meet the social, charitable, and funerary needs of their members. It was in such voluntary fraternities, which could number anything between ten and one hundred members but mostly averaged around thirty to thirty-five, that many people in the Hellenistic world began to find their personal point of reference and to experience a level of community that was denied to them elsewhere. In this proliferation of small clubs or associations, and in the significance they possessed for those who belonged to them, there is an interesting link between the first century and our own.

DISENCHANTMENT WITH TRADITIONAL RELIGION

The Jews

Bearing in mind the wide range of associations that existed during this period, we need to look more closely at those which were predominantly religious in nature. A word first, however, about the religious scene in general during this time. Among the

Jews there was widespread dissatisfaction with the priestly hierarchy in Jerusalem, particularly in view of its collaboration with
the Roman authorities and its absorption of Greek culture. In
reaction against this, brotherhoods were formed to preserve the
purity of the traditional faith, maintain the vigor of their messianic hope, and promote adherence to the ethical code enshrined
in their sacred books. To ensure this they developed an extensive
network of regulations to protect their members against the en-
croachment of foreign influences or the relaxation of their religious
obligations. For some, so apostate were the religious leaders and
their cultic practices, and so impure the society around them, that
they withdrew into monastic communities on the fringes of civi-
lization or as conclaves within urban life. This was the course of
action adopted by the Qumran community on the shores of the
Dead Sea, and by the associated "Essene" communities scattered
throughout Jewish cities and colonies. Others formed fraternities
within the flux of everyday affairs to educate and encourage their
members in ways to live a holy life in the midst of the world about
them. Such, among others, was the practice of the "Pharisees," a
term that probably embraces a number of like-minded, though
not identical, puritan groups in Jewish society. These formed
themselves into *haburoth* in order to maintain rigid standards of
purity and celebrate religious meals together.

Apart from the brotherhoods, there was another institution
within Judaism that became a center of religious and communal
life, namely, the synagogue. Its origin lay several centuries in the
past and is partly clouded in obscurity. With the dissolution of the
Israelite monarchies in the late seventh and early fifth centuries
BC and the consequent exile of the people from the land and
Temple, the need for a new framework for preserving and nurtur-
ing the Jewish faith became evident. It was probably at this time
that local gatherings of Jews began to take place where the Law
could be read and expounded and prayer made. It is not clear
which of these two elements, the educational or liturgical, was
primary or whether both were inseparable from the beginning.
After the return of the exiles from Babylon these gatherings seem
to have continued, at least outside Jerusalem. In the capital,
except for foreign residents, the rebuilt Temple provided a focus
for worship and instruction.[1] Elsewhere, in northern districts like

---

[1] Josephus, *The Antiquities of the Jews*, 15.380–425.

Galilee,[2] Hellenistic centers like Caesarea,[3] and in cities throughout the Diaspora, synagogues (or "prayer-houses" as they were
often called outside Judaea) multiplied, particularly during the
second and first centuries BC.[4] The term *sunagoge* at first referred
to the gathering itself (Acts 13:43), then by association to the
community who met together,[5] and finally, as mostly in the NT, to
the buildings that were provided especially for this purpose.[6]
There is evidence to suggest that near the synagogue other buildings were sometimes constructed, e.g., a guest house, baths,
rooms, etc., that could be used in association with it, especially
by travelers.[7] While Pharisees were warmly welcomed by such
groups because of their pious, thoughtful, and practical approach
to religion, they were not chiefly responsible for the proliferation
of synagogues—although they frequently made use of the synagogues to disseminate their teachings.

The Greeks and Romans

Disenchantment with traditional religions also existed among
Greeks and Romans. The reality or relevance of the official gods
had been queried by the philosophers, and the ritual associated
with their worship failed to satisfy the needs of those who were
being awakened to greater individuality. Into the vacuum that was
created stepped two main claimants for people's allegiance. First
were the various philosophies of the day, which provided both an
all-embracing world view and practical advice on the well-ordered
life. These appealed to more thoughtful Greeks and Romans, their
religious overtones strengthening their capacity to satisfy other
aspects of the personality. Far and away the most influential of
these in Paul's time, and the one that most seriously grappled
with the communal tendencies within human beings, was Stoi-

[2] Matt 4:23; 9:35; Luke 4:15.
[3] Josephus, *Jewish War* 2.285, 289; cf. *Antiquities* 19.300.
[4] Philo, *On the Embassy to Gaius* 156, 311; *On the Life of Moses* 2.215;
Flaccus 45.
[5] *Corpus Inscriptionum Graecarum*, 9909, in C. K. Barrett, *The New Testament
Background: Selected Documents* (rev. and exp.; San Francisco: Harper & Row,
1989) 56. Acts 6:9; 9:2; Rev 2:9; 3:9.
[6] Philo, *Every Good Man is Free* 81. Josephus, *Antiquities* 19.305. Acts
13–19 passim.
[7] Theodotus Inscription, in Barrett, *Background*, 53–54.

cism. This had its origins in the late fourth century. However, it was Posidonius in the first century BC who did much to revitalize Stoic thought, giving it a more transcendental thrust and deeper religious character than it had previously possessed. This so-called Middle Stoicism can be found in the writings of Paul's contemporary, the Roman philosopher-statesman Seneca. Representatives of a more traditional approach were also active, for example, Musonius Rufus and later Epictetus. There were other philosophical outlooks but, unlike Stoicism, these had either failed to grip popular imagination—the fate of Epicureanism—or had not yet filtered down to the general educated conscious-ness—as with the revival of Platonism. Mention should also be made of the Cynics, those nonconformist itinerants who often shocked their contemporaries by their message and manner of life and who had an influence on Stoic ideas and practice. So much did these share in common in the first century AD that Cynicism may be aptly described as a kind of "radical Stoicism."

For some, these philosophies were too cerebral a solution. A quest for an assurance of immortality and a place in the scheme of things led some individuals to investigate the promises made by the various "mystery" or secretive religions that poured into the Western Mediterranean world from the Eastern provinces. These had a long history, some originating in Greek folk-religions that persisted alongside the setting up of the official cults. At an early stage Eleusinian mysteries were integrated into the city cult at Athens, but for the most part mysteries continued alongside the official worship and did not demand withdrawal from it as a prerequisite for membership. One thinks here of the Dionysiac festivals or, a very different phenomenon, of the Orphic brother-hoods. Particularly from the third century BC a variety of Near Eastern local religions—Egyptian,[8] Phrygian,[9] Persian,[10] and oth-ers—spread throughout the Hellenistic world. They were brought by emigrants, merchants, soldiers, even slaves, but by the second century AD were being promoted by some intellectuals and rulers as well. They established themselves as *thiasoi*, private cultic asso-ciations, though again participation in the official worship, or for that matter other mystery cults, was not forbidden. So it was that

---

[8] Plutarch, Isis and Osiris passim.
[9] Eusebius, Praeparatio Evangelica 2.2.22ff.
[10] Mithras Liturgy, in Barrett, Background, 132–33.

the rites associated with such foreign deities as Cybele, Attis, Isis and Serapis, Adonis, and, at a later date, the figure of Mithras, spread throughout the Empire. These catered to the psychological needs of people in a much more substantial way than the philosophical schools, chiefly through various dramatic rituals in which adherents participated and vivid mystical experiences to which they aspired.[11] Since such religions possessed a democratic tendency—they opened their doors to people of all nationalities, and to women and slaves as well—and maintained firm secrecy about their activities, they held a powerful attraction and fascination for many.

PAUL'S CONTACT WITH THE NEW RELIGIONS

How much contact did Paul have with these different groups? It is unlikely that he had been himself a member of anything but a *haburah*, a Pharisaic fellowship, and an attender of anything but the synagogue and Temple. He came to Jerusalem from Tarsus (the capital of Cilicia) at a young age, probably undergoing all his formal education there (Acts 22:3; 26:4). His Pharisaic training in Jerusalem would not have permitted him to belong to any other association. His Diaspora origin also brought him into contact with synagogue life in Jerusalem, certainly with the synagogue of those from Cilicia and Asia, mentioned by Luke (6:9; cf. 24:19). He was converted journeying to Damascus with an official commission to seek out Christians in the synagogues there, but he proceeded to preach the gospel in these instead (Acts 9:2, 20). Later he preached to the Hellenistic Jews in Jerusalem, probably in their synagogues (v. 29). When he subsequently returned to Tarsus (and perhaps also initially at Antioch)[12] he presumably moved in synagogue circles. Once his wider missionary work had begun in earnest, synagogues consistently provided the contact point with potential converts (Acts 17:2), e.g., at Salamis (13:5), Pisidian Antioch (13:14), Iconium (14:1), Philippi (where no building existed but simply a place of prayer, 16:13), Thessalonica (17:1), Berea (17:10), Athens (17:17), Corinth (18:4), and Ephesus (18:19;

---

[11]Apuleius, *Metamorphoses* 11 passim.
[12]Acts 9:30, 11:25, 26. Cf. Josephus, *Jewish War* 7.44.

19:8). There can be no doubt about Paul's wide acquaintance with synagogue practice.

It is more difficult to judge how much he knew about other voluntary associations in these areas, including the mystery cults. He certainly came into conflict with them on occasions, directly with the guild of silversmiths at Ephesus (Acts 19:24–27), and indirectly through his injunctions to the Corinthians about banquets in idols' temples and through other references to the ecstatic and sensual character of cultic worship.[13] The widespread existence of such associations and the increasing penetration of the cults throughout the whole Mediterranean region suggests that Paul had other opportunities to learn about them, even if the secrecy imposed upon members of the mysteries made their affairs less public. The polemical use of their terminology at various points in his letters suggests this, e.g., mystery,[14] knowledge,[15] visions (2 Cor 12:1; Col 2:18), though it is just possible that such language was in more general use. His encounters with members of the philosophical schools were probably less frequent, if for no other reason than their small following. Alongside his well-known meeting with the Stoics and Epicureans at Athens (Acts 17:18), contacts with such people can probably be deduced from his use of their venues, e.g., the hall of Tyrannus in Ephesus (Acts 19:9), reference to their activities (1 Cor 1:20; 2:4–5), and echoes of their teaching (e.g., Acts 17:28; 1 Cor 15:33). While we should not overlook the possibility that some acquaintance with the teachings of these groups formed part of Paul's education in Jerusalem, it seems likely that most of his information would have been gathered on his travels in a rather ad hoc fashion, supplemented by occasional debates with their representatives and discussions with converts from their way of life.

THE CHRISTIAN COMMUNITIES

The presence of different voluntary religious associations in the ancient world during this period means that, from one point

---

[13] 1 Cor 8:7–13, 10:14–22; 12:1–3; 13:1.
[14] Rom 16:25; Col 1:26–27; Eph 3:3–4, 9; 5:32.
[15] See pp. 70–71.

of view, there was nothing particularly novel about the appearance of Christian communities alongside them. Judaism had its parties and, in the early days at least, the Nazarenes were regarded as an additional sect within Israel, not as a heretical departure from it. Hellenism had its cults and in the initial stage of their development Christians had their private gatherings. Because it centered around an Eastern divinity, Christianity may well have been regarded by some in terms of the mysteries, though the absence of normal cult-practices within it might have led others to view it as primarily a social rather than religious phenomenon or perhaps as a new philosophical school. In retrospect, quite apart from the way in which they were perceived at the time, Paul's communities must be seen as part of a wider movement towards the spontaneous association of individuals in society and as a parallel development to the religious fellowships that were growing in popularity within Judaism and Hellenism during that period. While, in view of Paul's preconversion background and missionary environment, it is the synagogue and mystery cult that must be brought into closest comparison with his idea of community, the monastic fraternities and philosophical schools form part of the wider background to his approach. How far was it removed from the monastic order established at Qumran and how much does it have in common with the Stoic expectation of a universal commonwealth? How largely did it draw upon patterns of authority, worship, and organization characteristic of the synagogue, and how extensively did it accommodate itself to the practices and structures of the mystery cults? In other words, how genuinely distinctive was it? These are questions that we must now examine.

2

—∽∞∽—

THE ARRIVAL OF
RADICAL FREEDOM

THE THEOLOGICAL BASIS:
FREEDOM THROUGH CHRIST

Along with a description of its historical setting, a proper introduction to Paul's idea of community must include consideration
of the theological basis upon which it rests. This will involve
drawing together relevant statements of Paul from all over his
writings rather than following the development of his thoughts in
successive letters. Here we are still dealing with preliminaries—a
more sequential treatment would take too long to complete.
Although the grounds on which Paul's view of community rests
are generally investigated in terms of his understanding of "salvation," I prefer to group his various statements on the subject
around the notion of "freedom." Paul uses the term *eleutheria*,
freedom, or one of its cognates frequently throughout his writings, some twenty-nine times in all—only a little less often than
soteria, salvation, and its allied terms. What is more, the notion of
eleutheria carries over into his approach to community. Our examination of it here will provide the background for references to it
later in this study. In fact, most of the different aspects of Paul's

idea of community are related in some way to his understanding
of freedom.

We turn first to those passages where he is talking about the
common predicament of individuals in this life. Though they are
made for a relationship with God and are intended to be integrated persons, they are in reality divided beings who have generally lost sight of their way.[1] Drawing upon terms with a long
history in Greek legal and political thought and alluding to ob-
servable patterns of behavior as empirical support, Paul asserts
that people are so "enslaved" by their baser inclinations that they
are no longer "free" to properly know or pursue their real potential
and destiny. This takes place in three main ways:

1. They find themselves under an inner compulsion to "sin,"[2]
and to put their confidence in "works" and the "flesh."[3] That is to
say, they are overly preoccupied with their own concerns and
aspirations and regard their own heritage or traditions as the
ground of their future expectations.

2. They are hampered, if Jews, from responding rightly to the
moral regulations in the Mosaic law (Rom 2:23; 7:7–12) or, if
Gentiles, to those moral demands of God inscribed upon their
wills (1:32). This can take two forms. If they rebel against the
revealed or implanted "law" of God, they drift into an amoral and
unnatural way of life (Rom 1:24ff.). If they focus all their energies
on the Law, it deceives them and becomes merely another chan-
nel for their self-centered natures (Rom 10:1–3).

3. They are in bondage to certain realities outside themselves,
whether supernatural "powers" that they allow to influence and
affect their lives;[4] the "god of this world"—Satan himself—by
whom they are misled and manipulated (2 Cor 4:4; Eph 2:2); or
"death" that experienced spiritually now and physically later ultimately brings all their aspirations, relationships, and achievements to an end.[5] Thus people are not as "free" as they would like
to think, but are "in bondage" to baser inclinations, moral obligations, and alien forces. These largely shape their characters and
dominate their lives.

---

[1] Acts 17:27–30; Rom 3:9–18; 7:15–24.
[2] Rom 6:17, 20; 7:14, 25.
[3] Gal 3:10; Rom 2:17ff.; 3:20; Phil 3:3ff.
[4] Gal 4:3; Col 2:8; Eph 6:12.
[5] Rom 1:32; 6:13, 16, 21, 23; 7:5; Eph 2:2.

Although all are constrained in these various ways, this does not mean that they are completely unfree. Paul allows that up to a point people are able to know the truth about God and do what is right,[6] just as those in authority over them are able to govern society in a morally responsible fashion (Rom 13:1ff.). But their capacity to do these things is limited.[7] So it is that every person—beginning with "the first man," whose failure allowed sin to begin to exert its power in human affairs, required law to contain sin, and gave death its abnormal significance—experiences a solidarity with their fellows in "Adam." However, a second community has now come into existence through the achievement of that other person, whom Paul terms "the second Man." Through his obedience the trend initiated by the first member of the human race has been reversed (Rom 5:12ff.). Although the full impact of sin fell upon him, it gained no control over him and was defeated (2 Cor 5:21; Rom 8:3). Although he experienced the condemnation meted out to the lawless, his behavior transcended the law and terminated it (Gal 3:13; Rom 10:4). Although death unjustly made its claim upon him, he triumphed over it and the alien powers as well (Rom 1:4; Col 2:15). Since he did this not for his own sake but for the sake of all people as their representative,[8] he is the foundation of a new community, humanity, or creation.[9]

Already we see how closely Paul's understanding of freedom, or salvation, is bound up with his idea of community. He does not view salvation as simply a transaction between the individual and God. Prior to their encounter with Christ people belong to a community, however much their actions incline them to pursue their own (or their immediate circle's) self-interest. And it is into a *new* community that their reconciliation with God in Christ brings them, however much they experience that event as an individual affair. Correlatively, the salvation effected by Christ follows from his being not just an individual but a corporate personality, the "second" and "last" Adam (or, as it has been so strikingly expressed, "Adam—at last!"). This means not only that Christ's actions impinge upon the lives of others and are decisive

---

[6] Acts 17:28; Rom 1:19–21; 2:14–15; cf. Phil 4:8.
[7] 1 Cor 11:32–33; Rom 1:21–23.
[8] 2 Cor 5:14ff.; Rom 6:3ff.; Col 3:3.
[9] 1 Cor 15:20ff.; 2 Cor 4:6; 5:17; Col 3:10; Eph 2:14–15.

for them but, as we shall now go on to see, that his very life enters into them, enabling theirs to enter into his.

THE FREEDOM OF CHRIST: THE ROLE OF THE SPIRIT

Those who acknowledge Jesus as having gained this victory on their behalf and who receive his Spirit into their lives are liberated from those things by which they were inexorably gripped beforehand.[10] They are free from the compulsion to sin and from the tendency to rely on their own moral and religious achievements. They are free from the obligation to regulate their lives by reference to an instinctive or external moral code.[11] They are free from the bonds that death irrevocably puts around them (Rom 6:23; 8:21) and from those supernatural agencies that blinded their former judgment and influenced their former choices (Rom 8:38–39; Gal 4:8–11). Experience of the Spirit has the reverse effect. Instead of blinding and tyrannizing them, it has, since its gift is truth and its power love, released them and for the first time granted them freedom to choose a way of life for themselves (Rom 5:5; 1 Cor 2:10–11). This does not mean that they are altogether released from the pull of the old way of life. Far from it. In a frankly autobiographical passage Paul acknowledges:

> I am a divided being. In my innermost self, the thinking and reasoning part of me, I wholeheartedly endorse God's principles. But I am also aware of a different principle within me. This is in continual conflict with both my conscious mind and conscience, and makes me an unwilling prisoner to the power of sin which has such a grip on my personality. It is an agonizing situation to be in—to be torn by a conflict from which there is (as yet) no solution. (Rom 7:21ff.)

According to Paul it is only in the resurrection at the Last Day that the final resolution of the conflict between the mind and the conscience will take place.[12] In the meantime one must live in the tension between them, conscious of the fact that in Christ the issue has already been decided and that through the Spirit this can now in part be experienced (Rom 7:25b—9:11).

---

[10]Rom 6:7, 22; 8:10–11; Eph 2:1–7.
[11]Gal 2:19–20; Rom 7:4–6; 8:1–4; Col 2:16–23.
[12]Rom 7:24–25a; cf. 1 Cor 15:53–57.

This fundamental freedom is not merely an independence *from* certain things, but also an independence *for* others. As Paul says to the Galatians, "It is for freedom that Christ has set us free," to which he adds the corollary, "Stand fast therefore and do not fall back into slavery again" (Gal 5:1). He goes on to explain that the positive expression of this independence leads, paradoxically, to a new form of "service" (on a few occasions he even uses the term "slavery"), though service of a qualitatively different kind to that experienced before. Instead of the compulsory service of sin, there is now the voluntary service of what Paul broadly terms "righteousness" (Rom 7:17–18). Instead of conformity to a moral code of life, there is now conformity to what he calls the "law" of Christ, that is the compassionate character and sacrificial behavior of Jesus (1 Cor 9:21; Gal 6:2). Instead of the experience of spiritual and ultimately physical death, there is now the experience of "life," a life which, even in suffering, will eventually liberate believers and the cosmos itself from its bondage to decay.[13]

Quite apart from all these things, there is a new liberty towards God, which dispels fear and leads to freedom in the divine presence of a most intimate kind (Rom 8:15–18; Gal 4:1–7). (At this point Paul tends to drop the language of service and slavery in favor of that of family relationships.) This intimacy results in service to God that is quite free in character (Rom 1:9). It also leads to a new freedom towards others, which includes freedom from the fear of others' judgments as well as from one's own attempts to manipulate them.[14] This also includes freedom in the communication of one's thoughts, expression of one's emotions, the opening up of one's life, and the sharing of one's possessions.[15] Indeed, the free service of others, the voluntary giving of oneself in love to them, is at the very heart of this conception of freedom (1 Cor 9:19; 1 Thess 2:8). It also entails a more liberated attitude to the created things of this world. Since there is nothing in existence that is in principle out of bounds— "All things are yours," Paul insists, and, "To the pure all things are pure"—this opens up a freer, nonidolatrous use of possessions.[16]

So this freedom granted by God not only transfers men and women out of a broken relationship with God and a defective

---

[13]Rom 8:18–23; 2 Cor 4:11–18.
[14]1 Cor 4:3; 9:19; 2 Cor 11:20–21.
[15]2 Cor 3:12; 6:11; 7:4; 8:2; 9:13.
[16]1 Cor 3:21–22; Tit 1:15, RSV.

solidarity with others into a new community with God and others but also inclines them to live the kind of life that will extend and deepen that new community itself. The integral connection between freedom and community in Paul's thinking once again becomes transparently clear.

ALTERNATIVE FIRST-CENTURY VIEWS OF FREEDOM

In the Pharisaic and Qumran writings, as in Jewish literature generally, there are no formal discussions of the subject of freedom. This has led some commentators to suggest that it is a purely Greek conception. But this is highly questionable.

The Pharisaic and the Qumran communities

The Old Testament, under such terms as "redemption" and "salvation," speaks frequently enough of the national freedom granted to Israel at the Exodus,[17] and occasionally of personal deliverances (e.g., Ps 66:2 and 89:26) and the liberty experienced by obeying the Law (Ps 119:45). It also looks forward to the time when a greater spiritual and moral freedom will be granted to the individual by God (e.g., Is 61:1; Jer 31:33–34). In the rabbinic writings there is a reiteration of the Old Testament ideas of national freedom.[18] More personal freedom is also occasionally talked about[19] and expressed in the Law (though ritual and moral regulations at times encroach upon it);[20] it is attained as much from religious endeavor as graceful response.[21]

At Qumran the emphasis is on the Exodus events' fulfillment in the community's present deliverance from association with false worshippers[22] and its longed-for future deliverance from its enemies,[23] rather than on the deliverance of Israel as a past event. At the individual level, a more strict adherence to

---

[17] E.g., Ps 77:15; 111:9.
[18] m. Pes. 10.5–6.
[19] m. 'Ab. 2.7; 3.15–16; m. Pe'a. 1.1.
[20] m. 'Ab. 1.1; m. Shabb. 7.1f.
[21] m. Makk. 3.16.
[22] CD 3.5–21.
[23] 1QM 11.9–10.

legal traditions[24] is combined with a stronger insistence upon the necessity of divine grace for their observance.[25] Paul shares with Pharisaism the recognition of an historical event as the foundation of freedom, but this is located for him in the history of a person instead of in certain national events and is based more decisively on God's free will. He shares with Qumran the celebration of God's grace as the source of freedom, but for him this is active through the presence of the Spirit in a way that the Qumran community could not envisage until the arrival of the Messianic Age.

In all three: the OT, Pharisaic writings, and Qumran writings, service of God and others is a central concern. Paul centers less on a codified religious and moral way of life than on certain basic attitudes and principles. All three systems lead to the formation of communities in which the members possess a strong sense of responsibility for one another, though varying in the intensity of their common existence. Pharisaism, which tended to be an association of a religious elite, centered around the fulfillment of particular obligations of an occasional character; the Qumran sect established an isolated monastic order, with a self-contained life; while the Pauline communities possessed a more open and "everyday" character than either of these approaches.

The Stoic philosophers

So strong and pervasive is Paul's emphasis upon liberty in comparison with preceding and contemporary writings that many have regarded him as indebted directly to Hellenistic, principally Stoic, thought. The Stoics were certainly interested in freedom. Epictetus, the freeman philosopher, talks about the subject in his surviving writings about four times as frequently as Paul. There is in both Paul and the Stoics, unlike earlier Greek thought, a preoccupation with the question at the personal rather than legal or political level. Both agree that freedom comes not through subservience to an external law but by conformity to certain norms that are internal in character. They share the belief that it can be attained only through freeing oneself from the many false beliefs that bind people's thoughts and actions. The two stress the necessity for liberation from certain passions, in particular the fear

---

[24]E.g., 1QS 5–7; CD 10–11.
[25]1QS 9.14–15; 11.2–22.

of death. There is also, as part of this whole process, a submission to the divine and a quest for unity with other persons.

Closer inspection reveals that, despite these apparent convergences, resemblances between the two are of a formal nature. While both quest for freedom apart from adherence to an external law, for the Stoic freedom is discovered through self-understanding,[26] whereas for Paul it is discovered by possessing, through the Spirit, the "mind of Christ" (2 Cor 6:16). Although both require an awareness of the illusory value of many received beliefs and external objects, for Paul it is precisely the ascetic response that Stoicism endorsed[27] that is to be left behind (Col 2:16–23). True, both the Stoics[28] and Paul required the renunciation of certain passions, but for the latter it is only baser desires that are to be sublimated, not the emotions as a whole. (This is why Paul can call his readers to show an increase in such things as affection, grief, earnestness, eagerness, indignation, zeal, and so on [2 Cor 6:11–12; 7:2; 9:11] and also speak constructively of his own anguish, fear, sorrow, restlessness, and longing—quite apart from emotions of a more "positive" character.[29]) For Paul freedom also involves liberty for humanity's body and environment, i.e., resurrection of the body and the creation of a new universe; it is not restricted to the intellectual and spiritual faculties.[30]

Whereas commitment to the divine is by no means absent from the Stoic approach, for all its new transcendental emphasis there is a strong pantheist element in the Stoic notion of divinity: since the inner self is also basically divine, the individual's self is more firmly anchored.[31] For Paul the ego must genuinely surrender itself to a personal God, not to become a divine automaton but in order to find and become its true self.[32] In addition, although the Stoics recognized a common bond between people and sought to develop it, for them the bond had its basis in the rational harmony of all things. The sympathetic integration to which this led frequently possessed an elitist character. Paul's view of community, with its foundation in a historical event and

---

[26] Epictetus, *Dissertationes* 4.1.52, 63.
[27] Epictetus, *Encheiridion* 15.
[28] Epictetus, *Encheiridion* 12, 16, 20; *Dissertationes* 3.26, 39.
[29] 2 Cor 1:8–9; 2:3–4, 12–13; 5:3–5; 7:5; 11:28–29.
[30] Epictetus, *Dissertationes* 4.1:97ff., *Encheiridion* 1.
[31] Epictetus, *Dissertationes* 1.12.26–35.
[32] Phil 2:15–16; Col 3:10; Eph 4:23–24.

its emphasis upon sacrificial service, reconciliation, and special regard for the least qualified members, is a very different affair.

The mystery cults

Paul may have had to deal with another view of freedom that was carried over into some of his communities from the mystery cults. Freedom was regarded in these circles as primarily freedom from things such as fate[33] and, ultimately, freedom from the body.[34] There was also freedom from uncleanness, but this was mainly considered to be a ritual affair.[35] The positive freedom that was enjoyed was limited through adherence to various ceremonial and ascetic practices.[36] This tended to become an end in itself, only minimally subject to external law or inner self-control.

How did Paul's view of freedom differ from that of the mystery cults? The concept of fate was foreign to Paul. For him freedom was ultimately "for" and not "from" the body and was explicitly other-directed rather than designed essentially for the individual's enjoyment. Also, the freedom that the cults promised came through a secret and mystical experience, overwhelming the individual and, temporarily at least, fusing that person with the divine power.[37] However, according to Paul, God comes to a person through the Spirit and not merely as a power. Since the individual is addressed by Christ rather than absorbed into him, the real identity of each is retained. Both approaches certainly possessed a corporate dimension, but the cults were fundamentally based on a community of interest rather than responsibility and were characterized by shared ritual rather than mutual service. (The mysteries clearly differed from one another in emphasis here, and some, such as the Isis cult in its late forms, attained a more personal conception of deity and an increased moral understanding of obligation.)

---

[33]Apuleius, Metamorphoses 11.6, 12, 15, 25.

[34]Mithras Liturgy 3–7, in Barrett, Background, 132–33. Cf. Plutarch, Isis and Osiris 78–79.

[35]Apuleius, Metamorphoses 11.23.

[36]Tibullus, Elegy 1.23–32. Apuleius, Metamorphoses 11.27ff. Plutarch, Isis and Osiris 6–8.

[37]Plutarch, Isis and Osiris 35, 68, 77–78. Apuleius, Metamorphoses 11.24.

THE DISTINCTIVENESS OF PAUL'S VIEW

Thus, despite his Greek terminology and the presence of certain formal parallels with Stoicism, Paul's view of freedom is built on essentially Hebrew foundations but differs from the freedom characteristic of the Pharisaic and Essene groups in his day. The versatility of love, rather than a covenantal set of requirements or the exercise of self-control, tends to distinguish his concept of freedom from that of Judaism and Hellenism. To clarify this relationship between love and freedom would lead us into a full-scale study of Paul's ethical views. We are not able to undertake that here. But the centrality of love does mean that freedom is experienced not only as the content of the Christian life, but also as the process that determines its texture. For when Paul elaborates upon the nature and implications of love, he does not draw up an ethical code in which all its practical consequences are explored and established in advance. He draws attention instead to certain general attitudes with which love is associated or through which it is exhibited (Gal 5:13–23; 1 Cor 13:2–11). Since discernment is required to know which of these is appropriate in any particular situation, freedom is very much involved in deciding what is or is not fitting "in the Lord" in a certain set of circumstances.[38] Although in his writings Paul goes on to formulate broad principles of conduct that arise from these attitudes (Col 3:8–4:5; Eph 5:21–6:9) as well as to give on occasion very specific injunctions to particular individuals or churches, these principles often require fresh application "in the Spirit" to fit the changing contexts that people are involved in. The specific injunctions are not always able to be generalized into universal rules (though they may rest on principles that have a more general application). All this indicates the flexibility in Paul's approach to decision making and the extent that freedom permeates his understanding of it. He gives clearest expression to this in his assertion: "For though I am free with respect to all, I have made myself a slave to all . . . I have become all things to all people, that I might by all means save some. I do it all for the sake of the gospel, so that I may share in its blessings. " (1 Cor 9:19, 22–23, NRSV).

---

[38]Cf. 2 Cor 1:23–2:8; 13:2–11.

To summarize, freedom for Paul consists of three main components:

Independence

- from certain things, e.g., sin, the Law, death, and alien powers
- for certain things, e.g., righteousness, conformity to Jesus, and suffering
- resulting in a personal and life-giving experience of liberty.

Dependence

- upon Christ, who terminated humanity's enslavement through his death and resurrection
- upon the Spirit, who communicates Christ's life and purpose as a received divine gift rather than innate possibility.

Interdependence

- with others, since liberty leads to service and can only be practically defined in relation to their needs
- with the world, since the universe itself will experience the liberty of transformation along with those who are Christ's
- giving liberty a social and cosmic, as well as a personal and theocentric, dimension.

In the light of all this, one can understand Paul's confidence that "where the Spirit of the Lord is, there is freedom" (2 Cor 3:17, RSV). The richness of his understanding of freedom is readily apparent. As we have seen, much of his view of community is already implicit in it.

3

——m——

CHURCH AS
HOUSEHOLD GATHERING

THE GOSPEL AND COMMUNITY

In the wake of Paul's travels throughout the Mediterranean, Christian communities sprang up, consolidated, and began to multiply. This was the outcome of a deliberate policy on his part. He not only proclaimed the message about Christ and brought people into an intimate relationship with God, but he also explained the consequences of that message for the life of his converts and led them into a personal relationship with one another. As we have seen, for Paul the gospel bound believers to one another as well as to God. Acceptance by Christ necessitated acceptance of those whom he had already welcomed (Rom 15:7); reconciliation with God entailed reconciliation with others who exhibited the character of gospel preaching (Phil 4:2–3); union in the Spirit involved union with one another, for the Spirit was primarily a shared, not individual, experience.[1] The gospel is not a purely personal matter. It has a social dimension. It is a communal affair.

---

[1] 2 Cor 13:14; Phil 2:1; Eph 4:3.

To embrace the gospel, then, is to enter into community. A person cannot have one without the other. But what *sort* of a community? Where does it exist? How is it expressed? Any discussion of these questions must begin with, or quickly come to grips with, Paul's use of the term *ekklesia*, church. This word occurs some sixty times in his letters, more often than all the other occurrences of the word in the New Testament combined. It is his favorite way of referring to the communities to whom he is writing. The term itself may be found in Greek sources, including the Greek translation of the Jewish Bible, several centuries prior to its use by Paul. It is also present in Acts, where it comes early into prominence, occasionally in Matthew, Hebrews, and James—as well as in the third letter and the apocalypse of John. We must now consider its pre-Christian meaning in some detail.

THE MEANING OF EKKLESIA

Pre-Christian: any gathering of a group of people

In Greek, *ekklesia* was a familiar word. From the fifth century BC onwards it referred to the regular "assembly" of citizens in a city to decide matters affecting their welfare.[2] We have an example in the NT where *ekklesia* is used to describe just such a meeting. This occurred when Paul was staying in Ephesus during his third missionary journey (Acts 19:21–41). The silversmiths of that city feared the impact on their trade of his preaching against idolatry and provoked a demonstration of the populace against Paul and his associates. The town clerk of Ephesus, probably the chief civil officer in the city, urged the crowd to restrain themselves, advising the silversmiths to make their complaint formally before the courts or proconsuls. If the people wished to take matters further they should do so in the lawful and regular *ekklesia* where such matters were decided (Acts 19:39), not in the unconstitutional and near riotous *ekklesia* now in session (v. 41). Here we have two instances of the typical Greek use of the word in reference to an assembly of the people. The term has also been found three times in inscriptions relating to cultic societies, but in these as well the

---

[2] Compare Thucydides, *Histories* 1.187, 139; 6.8; 8.69. Philo, *On the Special Laws* 2.44; *Every Good Man* 138 et al.

sense of "meeting" or "assembly" predominates. The term does not possess an inherently religious (let alone cultic) meaning.

In Jewish circles, as the Greek translation of the Old Testament (the Septuagint or LXX) shows, *ekklesia* is generally used to translate the Hebrew word for the "assembly" of the people of Israel before God,[3] though sometimes this is rendered by *sunagoge*. It also describes less specifically religious or nonreligious assemblies, for example, the "gathering" of an army in preparation for war (1 Sam 11:47; 1 Chron 28:14) or the "coming together" of an unruly and potentially dangerous crowd (Ps 25:5; Ecclus 26:5). All in all it occurs about one hundred times in the Septuagint, though predominantly to refer to Israel's meeting before God. Sometimes the whole nation appears to be involved, as on those occasions when Moses is addressing the people prior to their entry into the promised land. At other times it is only the chief representatives that seem to be present, as with the congregation of tribal heads, or patriarchal chiefs, at Solomon's dedication of the Temple in Jerusalem. Josephus also uses the word frequently; eighteen times in LXX quotations and forty-eight times in all, always of a gathering. These vary in character; religious, political, and spontaneous assemblies are mentioned.[4] Of Philo's thirty uses, all but five occur in quotations from the LXX, and these five are in the classical Greek sense. Despite the context in which the word generally appears in these writings, it is clear that it has no intrinsically religious meaning. It simply means an assembly or gathering of people in a quite ordinary sense so that, as in Greek usage, it can refer to meetings that are quite secular in character.

Paul's use: a regular, local gathering before God

How are we to discover what Paul himself meant by *ekklesia*? Since the other occurrences of the term "church" in the NT all postdate Paul's use of the word, we cannot draw conclusions from them about the meaning he attached to it. Rather, we must approach his writings as they stand (in the order in which they were probably written) and see whether Paul follows, develops, or alters the sense that the term has in the Jewish and Greek sources.

---

[3] Deut 4:10; 9:10; 2 Chron 6:3, 12; Ps 106:32.
[4] Josephus, *Antiquities* 4.309; *The Life of Flavius Josephus* 268; *Jewish War* 1.654, 666.

Most probably the word "church" was already in Christian use before he commenced his work, at least in Hellenistic-Jewish Christian circles. This means that from the earliest times such communities distinguished their gatherings from Jewish assemblies on the one hand and Hellenistic cults on the other. With one exception, the Greek term for a Jewish community, *sunagoge*, is never used of a Christian gathering in the NT. It is found in James, though even there it accompanies the term *ekklesia*. The three usual terms that describe the Hellenistic cults (*sunados*, *thiasos*, and *koinon*) do not occur at all. The reason for the absence of these terms is probably as follows: the synagogue was so centered around the Law and the mysteries so focused on a cult, that use of either word would have resulted in a misunderstanding of what *ekklesia* was all about. This ends our discussion for now, except to mention that Paul still uses the verbal form *sunagomai* alongside *ekklesia*, and later pagan writers and church fathers refer to the Hellenistic churches as *thiasoi*.[5]

What is Paul's early usage of the term *ekklesia*, church? He first uses the term in his greeting to the Christians in Thessalonica (1 Thess 1:1). Here he is using it in the same way as in Greek and Jewish circles and yet is consciously distinguishing the "assembly" to which he is writing from others in the city. It is clear from the closing remarks of the letter that Paul has in mind either an actual gathering of the Thessalonian Christians or the Thessalonian Christians as a regularly gathering community. He earnestly requests that they "greet all the brothers and sisters with a holy kiss" and that "this letter be read to all of them" (5:26–27, NRSV). Though, like other assemblies in the city, it is described as a "gathering of the Thessalonians," it is marked off from the regular political councils by the addition of the words "in God the Father" and from the weekly synagogue meetings by both the use of the term *ekklesia* and the addition of the phrase "in the Lord Jesus Christ." The same ascription reappears in Paul's second letter to the same community (2 Thess 1:1). Elsewhere in these letters we have reference to other Christian gatherings only in the plural, viz., to "the churches of God" generally and to "the churches of God" in Judaea specifically (2 Thess 1:4; 1 Thess 2:14). This suggests that the term is applied only to *an actual gathering of*

---

[5] Cf. Lucian, *The Death of Peregrinus* 11. Origen, *Contra Celsum* 3.2, 3. Eusebius, *Ecclesiastical History* 10.1.

people or to the group that gathers as *a regularly constituted meeting* and not, as in today's usage, to a number of local assemblies conceived as part of a larger unit.

Now this does not appear to be always obvious from a casual reading of the NT writings. Indeed some statements seem to contradict it. There is, for instance, Paul's reminder early in Galatians of his original persecution of "the church of God."[6] This could be a reference to the church at Jerusalem *before* it distributed itself into a number of smaller assemblies in various parts of Judaea. It was that community that bore the brunt of Paul's vendetta against Jesus' followers; however, most probably he refers to those he persecuted as a "church" rather than as "saints" (or some similar term) because, as Acts suggests, it was as they met that arrests were made—the fact of their gathering providing evidence of their Christian associations (Acts 8:3; compare 2:46). Something like this must be in mind, since a few lines further down Paul speaks distinctively of "the churches of Judaea" in the plural (Gal 1:22).

That *ekklesia* is used for a gathering of people is supported by other literary evidence. In the greeting at the beginning of Galatians (1:2), throughout the following two letters to the Corinthians,[7] and at the end of Romans (16:4, 16), we always find the plural form when more than one church is in view. The only exceptions to this are once where the distributive expression "every church" (1 Cor 4:17) occurs, and twice where "the church of God" (1 Cor 10:32) is mentioned in a generic or, just possibly, localized sense. The plural references to "the *churches* in Galatia" (Gal 1:2; 1 Cor 16:1), "the *churches* of Asia" (1 Cor 16:19), "the *churches* in Macedonia" (2 Cor 8:1), and "the *churches* of Judaea" (Gal 1:22) demonstrate that the idea of a unified provincial or national church is as foreign to Paul's thinking as the notion of a universal church. Only if there were an occasional provincial meeting of all Christians could he have spoken of them in this way. The names of the provinces, or inhabitants, simply provide him with a convenient way of grouping them in his thinking, though sometimes he can speak more generally of "the churches of the saints" and "the churches of the Gentiles" (1 Cor 14:33; Rom 16:4). The primary sense of "gathering" is particularly clear in

---

[6] Gal 1:13; 1 Cor 15:9; Phil 3:6.
[7] 1 Cor 7:17; 11:16; 14:33–34; 2 Cor 8:19, 23–24; 11:8, 28; 12:13.

1 Corinthians 11–14, in such expressions as, "when you assemble as a church" (1 Cor 11:18) and "it is shameful for a woman to speak in church."[8] In the beginning of both letters the church is described as belonging not to the people who constitute it (as with the Thessalonians) nor to the district they belonged to (as with the Galatians) but rather to the one who brought it into existence (that is God) or to the one through whom it came into existence (that is Christ).[9]

This means that the *ekklesia* is not merely a human association, a gathering of like-minded individuals for a religious purpose, but is a divinely created affair.

THE CHRISTIAN GATHERINGS

Their location

So far as the location of these gatherings is concerned, we possess some hints in 1 Corinthians and further details in Paul's letter to the Romans. Towards the close of 1 Corinthians, probably written in Ephesus, Paul passes on greetings to his readers from Priscilla and Aquila, "together with the church in their house."[10] This is the first time in Paul's writings that we come across this expression. It could mean one of two things: the term *oikos*, house, could refer to the *quarters* that Priscilla and Aquila occupied (or possibly to a particular room within them, though this seems unlikely here) or to the *household* that was in their charge. If it is the former, then the home of Priscilla and Aquila was the meeting place for some or all Christians in Ephesus. If it is the latter, which is less likely, it was their whole household that comprised the gathering. The incidence of household baptisms in Acts[11] and the use of *oikos* to refer to the extended family, probably including slaves, in the Pastorals[12] could point in this direction. But Acts states nowhere that Priscilla and Aquila had a household of this kind, and while *oikia* does sometimes refer to slaves, it does not

---

[8] 1 Cor 14:35, RSV; cf. 14:4, 5, 12, 19, 28.
[9] 1 Cor 1:1; 2 Cor 1:1 (cf. 1 Cor 10:32; 11:22); Rom 16:16.
[10] 1 Cor 16:19; cf. Acts 18:18–19.
[11] Acts 10:48 (cf. 11:14), 16:15, 33; 18:8.
[12] 1 Tim 3:12; cf. 3:5; 5:14.

necessarily have that meaning. Therefore, the term *oikos* most probably refers to their home. We cannot tell from it whether all the Christians in Ephesus met there or only a number of them. Incidental remarks elsewhere in 1 Corinthians and Romans throw further light on the types of Christian groups in a particular city, as well as on the places in which they met.

In 1 Corinthians Paul alludes to an occasion on which "the whole church" came together (1 Cor 14:23). This implies that at other times the Christians in Corinth came together in small groups, quite possibly as "church." The reference to various groups in Corinth who owed their existence to the work of different apostles, viz., Peter, Apollos, and Paul, may be relevant here (1:12–13). In the concluding section of Romans, most probably written in Corinth, Paul includes a greeting from one Gaius whom he describes as "host to me and to the whole church" (Rom 16:23). In the Greek OT this expression consistently refers to an assembly of all Israel; thus, it must be the totality of Christians in Corinth that is in view here (e.g., Exod 12:6; Num 8:9). Gaius, like Erastus (Rom 16:23), was probably one of the more eminent men in the city. It is not surprising that his home should be used for a gathering of the whole Christian community. Ample space would be required for such a meeting and it is precisely this that a man of Gaius' status could provide. Once again the qualification "whole," unnecessary if the Christians of Corinth met only as a single group, implies that smaller groups also existed in the city.

This probability is confirmed by Paul's comments in Romans 16 about various Christian groups in the capital. There is no suggestion that Christians ever met as a whole in one place. (Indeed, as much as a century later, Justin remarks that this is still the case![13]) Presumably this is due to the size of the city. Mention is made only of smaller groups of believers. One of those named is the group associated with Priscilla and Aquila, now back in Rome. Here again we have reference to "the church in their house" (Rom 16:5). (We do not know if this refers to the same group that was at Ephesus—in which case we have here a "mobile church"— or if this couple maintained households in different centers as part of their commercial network.) The other four groups listed are not specifically described as churches, viz., "those who belong to the household of Aristobulus"; "those . . . who belong to the

---

[13] See Justin Martyr, *First Apology* 67.

household of Narcissus"; "Asyncritus, Phlegon, Hermes, Patro-bas, Hermas, and the brothers and sisters who are with them"; "Philologus, Julia, Nereus and his sister, and Olympas, and all the saints who are with them" (Rom 16:10–11, 14–16).

Their variety

What sorts of groups are in view in these four cases? There are three possibilities. They could be gatherings of the same kind as the church that met in the home of Priscilla and Aquila; yet, it is puzzling that Paul should not explicitly describe them as such, since he shows no hesitation elsewhere in this matter. This suggests that his omission of the word here is deliberate and that something other than house churches is in view. However, it is just possible that we have something like "apartment" churches, alongside the house church specifically mentioned.

Alternatively, they could be groups consisting either of slaves who are in the service of several distinguished, non-Christian patrons (e.g., Aristobulus and Narcissus) or of members of a guild who work together—neither of whom meet with other Christians in any organized way. The others mentioned in Romans 16 do not seem to have formed part of the group around Priscilla and Aquila, otherwise Paul's greeting to the church in Priscilla and Aquila's house would be superfluous (16:5). Yet Paul's injunction to "greet one another with a holy kiss" (16:16, RSV) suggests that some kind of group encounter took place. The answer may lie in the following.

The third possibility is that the groups of people addressed, belonging as they did to households and guilds and living and working in close proximity with one another, fellowshipped to-gether when they had opportunity, as part of their normal activi-ties. Since they were already in constant social contact inside and outside of working hours, they cannot strictly be said to gather, even if some lived semi-independently of the household. In any case they would not have been in a position to invite others to attend because of their pagan environment or work situation. For both these reasons, to describe such a group as an *ekklesia* was inappropriate. It could well be that in Rome, where guild life was particularly strong and frequently concentrated in certain dis-tricts, two kinds of smaller Christian groups existed—the domes-tic or work group and the house church. Corinth was unique in that, while there were smaller groups of believers assembling (e.g., "Chloe's people," 1 Cor 1:11), the meeting of the whole church probably included people from all these subcommunities.

This helps to explain an unexpected feature in the opening lines of the letter to Rome. Unlike the greetings in all five previous letters, Paul does not address himself here to "the church" or "the churches" but rather "to all God's beloved in Rome, who are called to be saints" (Rom 1:7). Since for him *ekklesia* cannot refer to a group of people scattered throughout a locality unless they all actually gather together, it is not possible for him to describe all the Christians in Rome as a "church." The "whole church" of Rome never assembled in one place. He could have called them a "church" only by giving the word a new meaning. By way of contrast the Christians in Corinth *are* an *ekklesia*. Although they, like the Romans, meet in small groups in different parts of the city, they also come together as a unit from time to time (as did the earlier believers in Jerusalem).

Their frequency and size

Concerning the time and frequency of these early Christian meetings, Paul has little to say. He does request that contributions for the Jerusalem collection be set aside "on the first day of every week" (1 Cor 16:2). But this refers to an individual rather than communal action, as the words "and store it up" indicate, and so does not necessarily allude to a weekly gathering. This expression, "on the first day of every week" recurs in Luke's account of Paul's final meeting with the Christians in Troas (when all "were gathered together to break bread," Acts 20:7). But we cannot tell for certain whether the church regularly met on that day or had chosen it because of Paul's departure the following morning. If it is the former, as is more likely, we are still not clear whether the weekly meetings were of all the Christians or of the smaller groups. Paul's rather vague way of referring to meetings of the *whole* church suggests that it met less than once a week.[14] Voluntary and cult associations met on a monthly basis; these larger Christian gatherings may well have followed suit.

The Lucan passage describes a night meeting—understandable enough in view of the obligation upon most people to work

---

[14] 1 Cor 14:23; cf. 1 Cor 11:33.

during the day. Which evening is in view then? It is generally assumed that Luke had Sunday in mind. But it is more likely that it was on Saturday night that the Christians in Troas gathered together, the "first day of the week" having begun at sunset (cf. NIV). Though in Pliny's time (first century AD) and area a Sunday night meeting took place,[15] the evidence for when early Christians met is so slender that it would be unwise to make any confident generalizations. We are much more in the dark about the question than is commonly recognized.

In these early letters of Paul, the term *ekklesia* consistently refers to actual gatherings of Christians as such, or to Christians in a local area conceived or defined as a regularly assembling community. This means that "church" has a distinctly dynamic rather than static character. It is a regular occurrence rather than an ongoing reality. The word does not describe all the Christians who live in a particular locality if they do not gather. Nor does it refer to the sum total of Christians in a region or scattered throughout the world at any particular time. And never during this period is the term applied to the building in which Christians meet. Whether we are considering the smaller gatherings of only some Christians in a city or the larger meetings involving the whole Christian population, it is in the home of one of the members that *ekklesia* is held[16]—for example in the "upper room."[17] Not until the third century do we have evidence of special buildings being constructed for Christian gatherings and, even then, they were modeled on the room for receiving guests in the typical Roman and Greek household.

This puts a limit on the numbers involved. The entertaining room in a moderately well-to-do household could hold around thirty people comfortably—perhaps half as many again in an emergency. The larger meeting in Troas, for example, was so large that Eutychus had to use the windowsill for a seat (Acts 20:9). A meeting of the "whole church" may have reached forty to forty-five people—if the meeting spilled over into the atrium then the number could have been greater, though no more than double that size—but many meetings may well have been smaller. The average membership was around thirty to thirty-five people. This

---

[15] Pliny, *Epistulae* 10.96–97.
[16] Cf. also Acts 18:7–8; 20:8.
[17] Acts 20:8; cf. Luke 22:12; Acts 1:13.

is comparable to the number of people who belonged to a voluntary association. The "house churches" and the domestic groups would have been much smaller. In any event we must not think of these various types of community groups as particularly large. Certainly there is no suggestion that, as in the synagogue, ten men had to be available before they could commence their gatherings. Even the meetings of the "whole church" were small enough for a relatively close relationship to develop between the members. So long as they preserved their household setting, this was bound to be the case.

4

—⟋ℳ⟍—

CHURCH AS
HEAVENLY REALITY

PAUL'S LATER USAGE OF EKKLESIA

Continuation of the earlier meaning

We now turn to the meaning of *ekklesia* in the later writings of Paul. To begin with, we find Paul continues to use it to mean the local gathering of Christians, as he did in his earlier correspondence. In his letter to the Philippians he reminds them that "in the beginning of the gospel, when I left Macedonia, no church entered into partnership with me in giving and receiving except you only" (Phil 4:15, RSV). Although in the letter he does not refer to the place where the church met, we can surmise from Acts that it was initially in the home of Lydia. During his time at Philippi, he stayed in her home—as he stayed in the home of Priscilla and Aquila when he was in Corinth—and it was to Lydia's home that he and Silas returned after their imprisonment in order to see "the brethren"[1] and exhort them before departing for Thessalonica (Acts 16:15, 40). We cannot tell whether there was only one

---

[1] The term *adelphoi*, "brethren," is used in the Bible and this book as an inclusive one; it refers to both women and men in the church.

Christian gathering in the city or several. If there were a number, presumably they must have also met as a whole, since the term *ekklesia* is used of them. How then do we account for the absence of the term *ekklesia* in the opening greeting in Phil 1:1 (RSV)? There is no need to look very far for this, for the reason is contained in the wording itself: "to all the saints in Christ Jesus who are at Philippi, with the *episkopoi* (bishops) and *diakonoi* (deacons)." It is because Paul wishes to specify those people who have a special contribution to make to it, that he does not simply address the letter to the gathering as a whole.

The same appears to be the case in his letter to the Colossians where it is "to the saints," the ordinary membership, and to "the faithful brethren," those who have a particular ministry to perform, that the letter is written (Col 1:2). Since Philemon was almost certainly a resident of Colossae, "the church in his house," mentioned in the brief letter sent to him by Paul, must be either the church of the Colossians or one of the smaller Christian gatherings in the city (Phlm 2). Elsewhere in the letter to the Colossians itself there is a greeting to "Nympha and the church in her house" in nearby Laodicaea, and a suggestion that the Colossians forward their letter to "the church of the Laodicaeans" so that it may be read there as well (Col 4:15). It is again unclear whether the gathering in the home of Nympha and the church of the Laodicaeans are one and the same entity, or whether smaller and larger assemblies in the one city are in view. Since the letter to the Ephesians is not addressed to a particular locality, it is not surprising that the word *ekklesia* is absent from its opening lines.

A heavenly reality to which all Christians belong

In these later writings, however, an extension of Paul's understanding of *ekklesia* takes place. This is not an altogether new development, since the foundation for it had already been laid in his earlier letters. Examine the words *en Christo*, which in a number of places accompany Paul's use of the term *ekklesia*. The "in Christ" formula is the most frequently recurring phrase in Paul's writings. It occurs 164 times and most often is found in contexts with the individual Christian, rather than the Christian community, in view. In these it refers primarily to the believer's dependence upon the work of the historical Jesus and fellowship with the risen heavenly Lord. Individuals are in relationship with Christ even when they not are "in church." Even the dead can be described as "in Christ" (1 Thess 4:16). These facts, coupled with the repeated use of *en Christo* with *ekklesia*, show that Paul hints at a wider concept of *ekklesia* than just that of the local gathering.

How are we to envisage this broader idea of *ekklesia*? Does Paul think of it as a spiritual status that is realized in practice when Christians meet together? This could provide the basis for a conception of a "universal church" that is distributed through-out various local gatherings and of an additional "eschatological church" gathered around Christ into which one passes after death. Yet this idea of a "universal church" is never developed in Paul's writings. Also, the notion of the dead being included along with the living suggests that a wider conception of the church is present here than just that of an earthly community, however broadly understood. While he does speak elsewhere of an escha-tological "gathering," this is not primarily what Paul has in view when he uses *ekklesia* in this extended sense, and entry into this gathering takes place not after death but on the Last Day (1 Thess 4:15–17). Alternatively, Paul could visualize an "invisible church" consisting of all those who are in Christ, whether living or not, to which the genuine members of "visible churches" also belong. This notion, though it has held a long and respected position in Christian thought, has no basis in Paul's teachings either. The drift of his thought in the later writings is in a different, though not altogether unrelated, direction.

The first stratum of evidence for what Paul's broadening concept of *ekklesia* is comes in Galatians, where Paul contrasts the children of the "present Jerusalem" with those who belong to the "Jerusalem above" (Gal 4:25–27). The idea is developed further in his letter to the Philippians. In this Paul affirms that Christians alive on earth are at the same time members of a heavenly community. In a highly significant passage he contrasts those who have their "minds set on earthly things" with those whose "commonwealth (*politeuma*) is in heaven," his language probably echoing the privilege of citizenship conferred upon the whole Roman colony of Philippi (Phil 3:19–20). Membership in this heavenly community, together with all the benefits that accom-pany it, was as continuing an affair as membership in the Roman commonwealth. While each membership came to expression from time to time in an assembly, participation in both their religious and political communities—the one with its focus around Christ in heaven, the other with its center in Rome on earth—went on day after day as a permanent reality. The idea reappears in Eph 2:19. (Incidentally, we have in Gal 4:25–27 a unique example of the way Paul's thinking on a particular subject was influenced by the circumstances he encountered on his mission. Though the basis for this view was already present in his earlier writings, it appears that the situation at Philippi has helped him arrive at a more definite conception.)

In the Colossian and Ephesian letters, however, the term *politeuma* (place of citizenship) is left behind and in its place the term *ekklesia* occurs. So in Colossians we are introduced to the idea of a nonlocal church of whom Christ is the head (Col 1:18, 24). This notion is generally misinterpreted as a reference to the "universal church" that is scattered throughout the world. It is not an earthly phenomenon that is being talked about here, but a supernatural one. The whole passage in which the expression occurs focuses on the victorious Christ and his kingdom of light that believers have now entered (1:9–2:7). The prospect of the End, in which the members of this *ekklesia* will be presented "holy and irreproachable and blameless" before God, is contingent upon what is viewed as a present reality (1:11, 16, 22, 28); they are described as presently existing in both a heavenly dimension and an earthly one. He reminds his readers that "you have died, and your life is hid with Christ in God" (3:3, RSV). Since "you have been raised with Christ, seek the things that are above, where Christ is, seated at the right hand of God" (3:1, RSV). It is because they live with Christ in this heavenly realm that he promises them that "when Christ who is our life appears, then you also will appear with him in glory" (3:4, RSV). The picture Paul draws here is of a *heavenly assembly* within which the Colossian Christians are *already* participating and whose culmination will take place on the Last Day.

If any hesitation remains about the possibility of under- standing *ekklesia* as a heavenly assembly in Colossians, it is dis- pelled by the language used in Ephesians. There it is explicitly said that God has "made us alive together with Christ . . . and raised us up with him, and made us sit with him in the heavenly places in Christ Jesus" (Eph 2:5–6, RSV). Compare the prayer with which the letter opens, where Paul acknowledges "the God and Father of our Lord Jesus Christ, who has blessed us in Christ with every spiritual blessing in the heavenly places" (1:3, RSV). Be- tween these two passages, at the end of a celebration of Christ's heavenly authority, reference is again made to his headship over the *ekklesia* (1:22–23). Here again we see church taking place in heaven and Christians participating in it, even as they go about the ordinary tasks of life. Metaphorically speaking they are gathered around Christ, that is, they are enjoying fellowship with him. Mention of the eschatological consummation is also present here (1:14; 2:7), but the emphasis falls upon the completed action of Christ and its immediate heavenly implications. The heavenly church idea reappears in chapter 3 where Paul says that "through the church the manifold wisdom of God might now be made known"—not to the world but "to the principalities and powers in the heavenly places" (3:10, RSV). It is probably present at the end of the chapter, especially in view of the phrases accompanying *ekklesia* (viz., "to all generations," "for ever and ever," v. 21); lies behind the reference to the community in chapter 4 (v. 2), with its talk of gifts from him who has "ascended far above all the heavens" (vv. 8–10); and is involved in the references to *ekklesia* in chapter 5, which emphasize particularly the present character of Christ's relationship with it.[2]

According to Paul therefore, Christians belong both to a heavenly church that is permanently in session and to a local church that, though it meets regularly, is intermittent in character. This means Christians are in a common relationship with Christ not only when they meet together—nor, for that matter, when they individually relate to him in thought and prayer—but at all times, wherever they are and whatever they do. Here we have an exalted conception, not easy to grasp. But it is certainly one of the most profound in the whole of Paul's writings.

THE RELATIONSHIP BETWEEN THE HEAVENLY AND THE LOCAL CHURCH

What is the relationship between these two churches—the permanent heavenly church and the local intermittent one? Paul does not spell this out in detail, but there are sufficient clues for us to move towards an answer. The language he uses indicates that the local gatherings are not *part* of the heavenly church any more than they are part of any alleged universal church. Paul

---

[2] Eph 5:23, 25, 27, 29, 32.

uniformly speaks of them as *the* church which assembles in a particular place. Even when we have a number of gatherings in a single city, the individual assemblies are regarded not as *part* of the church in that place, but as *one* of "the churches" that meet there. This suggests that each one of the various local churches is a tangible expression of the heavenly church, a manifestation in time and space of that which is essentially eternal and infinite in character.

We find no suggestion here of a visible, earthly, universal church to which local gatherings are related as the part to the whole. Nor does Paul speak of any organizational framework by which the local communities are bound together. He nowhere prescribes an ecclesiastical polity of this kind and nowhere suggests that the common life that communities share should be made visible in this way. As we have seen, he does occasionally group churches together in his letters by reference to the province in which they exist, e.g., "the churches in Galatia." But, as his consistent reference to such in the plural suggests, there is not even a hint of any idea of provincial church government. There may be parallels in the language employed to describe the informal alliances of adjacent territories in parts of the ancient world around this time. These were matters of convenience only, had only a temporary existence, and lacked any unified organizational framework.

This does not mean that links between local churches were absent. On the contrary, Paul both initiated and encouraged fellowship between them in a variety of ways. But he sought to build up enduring relationships of an organic, or only loosely organized, rather than institutional, character. This took place through the exchange of letters from their apostle (Col 4:16), the visits of individuals from one group to another (e.g., Rom 16:1), the sending of financial aid during time of need (e.g., 2 Cor 8:11–13) , the burden of prayer on each other's behalf (e.g., 2 Cor 8:14), and the passing on of greetings and news through intermediaries.[3] These scattered Christian groups expressed their unity not by fashioning a corporate organization through which they could be federated with one another, but rather in a range of organized personal contacts between people who regarded themselves as members of the same Christian family. This is so even

---

[3] 1 Cor 16:19; 2 Cor 13:13; Phil 4:22.

with respect to the foundation church in Jerusalem. Paul is eager to gain its recognition of his missionary endeavors so as to avoid any division in the Christian movement between its Jewish and Gentile wings (Gal 2:1–10), for a denominationalism of this kind would be totally abhorrent to him. He is also concerned to gain the involvement of his Gentile churches in the collection for the poor in the church at Jerusalem (Rom 15:25–27), so as to mark their acknowledgment that the gospel stemmed from them. Yet there is no sense in which his churches are subservient to the original Christian community or organizationally controlled by it. In saying this, I am anticipating the conclusions that emerge from later sections of this book—where Paul's authority and the Jerusalem collection come in for closer consideration. It would be inappropriate to discuss these in detail here since they raise issues of a wider kind as well.

THE SIGNIFICANCE OF PAUL'S LATER CONCEPT OF EKKLESIA

In the context of his age

Comparison of Paul's understanding of *ekklesia* with the intellectual and social climate of his day emphasizes both the comprehensiveness of his idea and its appropriateness for his times. Attention has already been drawn to three aspects in the contemporary scene that were particularly significant: those aspirations for a universal fraternity that captivated the minds of educated Greeks and Romans and devout Jewish leaders; the significance of the household as a place in which personal identity and intimacy could be found; the quest for community and immortality pursued through membership in various voluntary and religious associations. In a quite remarkable way, Paul's idea of *ekklesia* managed to encompass all three:

1. It is a voluntary association, with regular gatherings of a relatively small group of like-minded people. This it shares with the synagogue and cults and, although it was a more exclusive society, the Qumran community as well.

2. It has its roots in, and takes some of the character of, the household unit. Neither the pagan *thiasoi* nor the Pharisaic and

Essene *haburoth* were consciously built up on this basis; there is little concern in Stoicism with the familial group as such.

3. These small local churches were invested with a supranational and supratemporal significance. They were taught to regard themselves as the visible manifestation of a divine and eternal commonwealth in which people could become citizens. This has some overlap with the Stoic view. The communal emphasis of the local churches differs from the Stoic position[4] and is especially dissimilar to the ideals of the more individualistic Cynics.[5] Among contemporary religious groups, Qumran combined a clear view of this kind with its concrete sense of assembly, but its vision had a much more limited horizon and, in addition, retained a strong nationalistic emphasis (1QS 8.4–7, 11.3, 6–9). The mystery cults, for all their cosmopolitan character, do not appear to have thought in terms of a "communion of souls" chiefly because their anti-temporal tendencies and individualistic emphasis did not provide them with the framework for such a conception.

Only Paul's understanding of *ekklesia* embraces all three ideas of community to which people gave their commitment in the ancient world at the time. This means that, psychologically speaking, Paul's approach had a decided advantage over its first-century competitors, since it offered so much more than any of them and provided things that elsewhere could be found only by adhering to more than one religious group. Sociologically, the distinctive element in Paul's conception was its combination of all three models of community. I am not suggesting that Paul systematically related each of these models or that he consciously viewed his idea as the fulfillment of contemporary strivings. I am merely proposing that his view was conceptually richer and more socially relevant than others advanced in his day.

By his use of the quite ordinary term for assembling (*ekklesia*) and by his setting such gatherings in ordinary homes rather than cult-places, Paul shows that he does not wish to mark off his gatherings from the ordinary meetings in which others, including church members, were engaged. Paul did not see his gatherings as more religious in character than any other activity in which Christians were involved. The novelty did not stem from the

---

[4] Contrast Cicero, De Officiis 1.20–51; De Natura Deorum 2.154–165; De Finibus Bonorum et Malorum 5.65; De Legibus 22–39.
[5] See Diogenes Laertius 6.63, 72.

action of gathering itself, or from its specifically religious intention, or from the household location of the meeting; parallels exist to all of these. For example, private Hellenistic cults occasionally met in homes rather than in buildings constructed especially for the purpose. (This happened relatively rarely and the homes concerned were turned into shrines and became the center of various cultic activities.) The synagogue as well, though originating probably in open air meetings, became in time a home based institution. The first-century special buildings that were customarily reserved for its activities[6] often reflected their household antecedents in their design. The character of their gatherings and the source of their dynamic, rather than the household basis, was what distinguished Paul's communities from their first-century counterparts.

For contemporary usage and practice

Before directing our attention to certain other terms and metaphors that Paul applies to his communities, I would like to make some final comments about his use of the word *ekklesia* itself. Does it matter if Paul's understanding of it as "gathering" in a dynamic local sense and in a metaphorical heavenly sense, later fell out of use in favor of a "universal church"/"invisible church" conception? If this shift of meaning has nothing more than a semantic significance, then distinguishing Paul's view from subsequent usage has only linguistic interest and no important consequences flow from it.

Yet more than a purely semantic or linguistic question is at issue. To begin with, the later extension of the term "church" to cover not only the wider organization that binds local communities together, but also the various activities that it sponsors within the surrounding society, has created certain problems. These problems are compounded by applying those terms that truly characterize only the household gatherings and heavenly fellowship to such activities, or by requiring Christian communities to undertake responsibilities in the world that strictly belong to voluntary groups of Christians specifically called to the task. (More will be said about this later when Paul's "work" comes in for detailed inspection.) All this leads to a confusion of

---

[6] See ch. 1, n. 6.

descriptions and functions that has serious intellectual and practical repercussions.

That being said, Paul's predominant usage of *ekklesia* to refer to the actual gatherings of Christians, or the group conceived as gathering regularly, means that the word is less theologically significant than people generally assume. Its chief importance lies in the way it stresses the centrality of meeting for community life: it is through gathering that the community comes into being and is continually recreated. Although in his later writings Paul adds a new dimension to this activity—by seeing it as the expression of ongoing heavenly encounter with Christ—it is to other terms that we must turn if we are to penetrate the heart of his idea of community. The word *ekklesia* brings us to the threshold of his understanding; it does not carry us over it.

5

—⚯—

THE COMMUNITY AS
A LOVING FAMILY

SOME METAPHORS FOR COMMUNITY

Paul frequently resorts to metaphors in his discussions on community. He thinks in terms not just of the logical development of arguments but also of the illuminative significance of images. This was a characteristically Jewish way of proceeding—one that leaves its imprint everywhere in the biblical and intertestamental writings. Among the many metaphors applied to the Christian community by Paul, that of a "building" comes before us several times in his letters. Sometimes an ordinary building is in view, sometimes the Temple—the latter being the building par excellence to a Jew. The more general use of this metaphor refers either to the work of the apostles in founding local communities—Paul describing himself as the "master builder" in charge of operations[1]—or to the interdependence of the members of the community and their growth to maturity.[2] When Paul describes the community as a Temple, he is emphasizing its

---

[1] Gal 2:18; 1 Cor 3:10–14; 2 Cor 10:8; 12:19; 13:10; Rom 15:20; cf. Eph 2:20; 4:12.
[2] 1 Cor 14:5; 12, 26; Rom 14:19; Col 2:7; Eph 4:16.

relationship with God through the Spirit and, as a consequence of this, its holiness and the wholehearted service it should render to God.[3]

Once again there appears to be a difference between the earlier and later writings. In the former the whole building represents the community and it is the local community which is in view. In the latter the cornerstone of the building is said to be Christ himself and the heavenly church is under discussion. (Christ is described as the "foundation" of the building in the earlier writings, but that is not quite the same thing. In Ephesians it is the apostles and prophets who occupy that position rather than simply laying a foundation.) The metaphor can be applied to individual Christians as well as the community to which they belong. In a quite striking way they are described not merely as "stones" in God's building, but individually as "the Temple of the Holy Spirit" (1 Cor 6:19).

A further set of metaphors comes from the world of agricultural labor rather than material construction; the community is described as a "field," a "grafting" (on an olive tree), and a "planting."[4] Other metaphors, such as the comparison of the church with "dough" and of the offending member within it with "leaven," are drawn from the domestic sphere.[5] But analogies with the world of nature (like the agricultural metaphors) or inanimate objects (such as the building metaphors), despite the presence of human participants, lack the dynamic element characteristic of human and divine-human relationships. This leads Paul on several occasions to follow traditional practice and link or mix his metaphors so that the deficiencies of one may be remedied by the advantages of another.[6] Paul also shows a distinct preference for the "body" metaphor, drawn as it is from the sphere of human existence, though even then (as we shall see) he has to portray and employ the metaphor in different ways to express his views. In the long term however, the inadequacy of the organic unity of the "body" metaphor leads Paul to utilize the language of human, and especially family, relationships.

Although in recent years Paul's metaphors for community have been subjected to quite intense study, especially his de-

---

[3] 1 Cor 3:16–17; 2 Cor 6:16; Eph 2:21–22.
[4] 1 Cor 3:9; Rom 11:17–24; Col 2:7; Eph 3:17.
[5] 1 Cor 5:6–7; cf. Gal 5:9.
[6] E.g., 2 Cor 9:10; Col 2:7, 19; Eph 2:19–22; 3:17; 4:12–16.

scription of it as a "body," his application of "household" or "family" terminology has all too often been overlooked or only mentioned in passing. This presumably stems from the fact that terms like *oikeioi*, "household," occur so rarely in the Pauline writings. But, alongside this term, a number of related expressions are present that must be taken into account. So numerous are these, and so frequently do they appear, that the comparison of the Christian community with a "family" must be regarded as the most significant metaphorical usage of all. For that reason it has pride of place in this discussion. More than any of the other images utilized by Paul, it reveals the essence of his thinking about community.

A Key Image: Family

Description of membership

All Paul's "family" terminology has its basis in the relationship that exists between Christ, and the Christian as a corollary, and God. Christians are to see themselves as members of a divine family; already in his earliest letters Paul regards the head of the family as being God the Father.[7] In a unique sense Jesus is God's Son, and it is only through his identification with humans and his actions on their behalf that they are able to "receive adoption as children" (Gal 4:4–5, NRSV; cf. 1 Thess 1:10). As a result, says Paul in Galatians, "God has sent the Spirit of his Son into our hearts" so that, along with Jesus, we are able to address God in the most intimate terms as "Abba! Father!" (Gal 4:6). This privilege, he adds in Romans, confirms to our own spirit the fact that we are indeed "children of God, and if children, then heirs, heirs of God and fellow heirs with Christ" (Rom 8:16–17, RSV). This fellowship of Christians with God the Father and Jesus the Son is not at all like the calling of a royal court in which the king holds audience with his citizen subjects. Nor should we think of it in terms of the assembling of a household in which the master is surrounded by his loyal slaves. It is not even like the gathering of an ordinary family in which the head enters into relationship with his infant children. The meet-

---

[7] 1 Thess 1:1, 3; 3:11, 13; 2 Thess 1:1–2; 2:16.

ing of Christians with their God is more analogous to the encounter between adult children and their father, where they are able to relate to him, not only in the most intimate, but increasingly in the most mature fashion.[8]

Paul sees implications from this for the life of the local communities. Those who belong to them should see one another primarily as members of a common family. So in Galatians Paul encourages both himself and his readers, as they have opportunity, to "work for the good of all, and especially for those of the family of faith" (Gal 6:10, NRSV). According to Ephesians, the Christian fellowship between Jews who were members of the covenant race and Gentiles who were previously aliens to the divine promises that is experienced in the heavenly *ekklesia* is to be viewed precisely in these terms. Referring to Christ, the author points out that "through him we both have access in one Spirit to the Father. So then you are no longer strangers and sojourners, but you are fellow citizens with the saints and members of the household of God" (Eph 2:18–19, RSV). Both the local gathering and heavenly "assembly" are to be regarded as nothing less than God's family.

In addition to *oikeioi*, a whole cluster of terms from family life are applied to the Christian community. Some of these are among the most frequently used terms in Paul's vocabulary; it is their very familiarity that has led to their unfortunate neglect. Many are drawn from the business side of family affairs. For example, *oikonomos*, "steward,"[9] which Paul uses of himself and other apostles, originated as a designation for "household" personnel. It describes the responsible and accountable task that he has been given vis-à-vis his communities. We also have an occasional use of the term *doulos*, "slave,"[10] or *huperetes*, "servant" (1 Cor 4:1), underlining the kind of behavior that should govern relationships between Christians in the community, just as it does his own behavior towards them. "Slave" emphasizes the status, "servant," the function of these members of the household. But this is not Paul's most characteristic way of speaking. Most of the words Paul employs come from the intimate side of family affairs. *Adelphoi*, "brethren," is far and away Paul's favorite way of referring to the

---

[8] Gal 4:1ff.; cf. later Eph 4:13ff.
[9] 1 Cor 4:1–2; 9:17; Col 1:25; Eph 3:2.
[10] 2 Cor 4:5; Rom 1:1; Phil 1:1; Col 1:7; 4:7, 12; Eph 6:6.

members of the communities to whom he is writing. This word is often used generically of both males and females, as the word "folks" is used in American English. In spite of its frequency and its more limited reference to those who are colleagues in Paul's mission,[11] the term "brethren" has not yet lost its basic meaning and become a mere formal description. There are many passages in Paul's writings where it is clearly expressive of the real relationship that exists between Christians,[12] not least when they come together as church. Even though some of the following examples are drawn from the sphere of relationships outside the actual gathering itself, they are still pointers to the quality of relationships within it, as other passages more directly testify.

Paul, for instance, speaks movingly in 1 Corinthians of the concern that the stronger Christian should have for the weaker neighbor. The latter is described by him not only as "the brother [or sister] for whom Christ died" but quite personally as "my brother [or sister]," for whom Paul has a direct responsibility (1 Cor 8:11, 13). This kind of personal commitment to others is further illustrated by the way in which Paul talks in the warmest terms about certain fellow Christians, co-workers in his mission as well as members of local churches, with whom he had a close relationship. Tychicus, for example, is spoken of not only as a "faithful minister and fellow servant in the Lord" but as "a beloved brother" (Col 4:7; Eph 6:21). Paul refers to others such as Sosthenes, Apollos, and Quartus[13] as "our brother" in a similar fashion. He writes to Philemon, "I have derived much joy and comfort from your love, my brother." He refers to Epaphroditus in a similar way (Phlm 7, RSV; Phil 2:25).

Terms descriptive of other family-type relationships are also used by Paul in his writings. He regards Onesimus as his "child" whose "father" he has "become." Onesimus is also spoken of as "the faithful and beloved brother" (Phlm 10; Col 4:9). Of Timothy, he says "I have no one like him," reminding the Philippians "how as a son with his father he has served with me in the gospel" (Phil 2:22; Col 1:1). Elsewhere he also designates him "our brother" (1 Thess 3:22; 2 Cor 1:1). Then there are "Apphia our sister" (Phlm 2) and "our sister Phoebe," the latter being described as one who

---

[11]Gal 1:2; 1 Cor 16:20; 2 Cor 9:3, 5; Col 1:2; 4:15.
[12]Especially 1 Cor 15:58; Rom 15:14; Phil 3:1; 4:1; Eph 6:10.
[13]1 Cor 1:1; 16:12; Rom 16:23.

has been "a helper of many and of myself as well."[14] There is also that unnamed woman for whom Paul reserves one of his tenderest messages: "greet Rufus, eminent in the Lord," he begins, "also his mother and mine" (Rom 16:13). Here we are given a glimpse, all the more significant for its incidental nature, into the quality of relationship that could exist between the apostle and his acquaintances. Indeed, all of this closing section of Romans and the closing sections of many other Pauline letters witness to the strong "family" character of the relationships built up by Paul and various members of the churches he moved among. Here we also need to remember the way in which Paul speaks of his relationship to various communities as a whole by means of analogies drawn from family life, e.g., "father," "mother," "nurse," and so on.[15]

Centrality of love

An inspection of other words that spring from, or are most naturally located in, a family context confirms this conclusion. There are those, for example, whom Paul refers to as "beloved," among them Epaenetus, Ampliatus, Stachys, Persis, Tychicus, Onesimus, and Luke.[16] Even whole churches at Philippi and, surprisingly, at Corinth are sometimes addressed by him in this way. "How I yearn for you all with the affection of Christ," he exclaims to the Philippians (Phil 1:8; compare 2:12), while his closing wish to the Corinthians, that most recalcitrant of communities, is that "my love be with you all."[17] He clearly expected Christians in their various local churches to enter into the same kinds of loving relationships with one another. He prays that the Thessalonians will "increase and abound in love to one another as we do to you" (1 Thess 3:12). The Christians at Rome are reminded that in a very genuine way they should "love one another with familial affection" (*philadelphia* here possessing a more intensive meaning than in earlier usage).[18] What such love involves is spelled out in the well-known passage from his first letter to the Corinthians:

---

[14]Rom 16:2, cf. also 1 Cor 7:15; 9:5.
[15]1 Cor 4:14–15; 10:14; Phil 2:12.
[16]Rom 16:5, 8–9, 12; Col 4:7.
[17]1 Cor 16:24; cf. 1 Cor 4:21; 10:14.
[18]Rom 12:9–10 and see 2 Macc 15:14 (LXX).

[4]Love is patient and kind; love is not jealous or boastful; [5]it is not arrogant or rude. Love does not insist on its own way; it is not irritable or resentful; [6]it does not rejoice at wrong, but rejoices in the right. [7]Love bears all things, believes all things, hopes all things, endures all things. [8]Love never ends . . . (1 Cor 13:4–8a, RSV)

This description has to do with fundamental attitudes: patience, humility, tolerance, kindness, resilience, generosity, confidence, perseverance, optimism. Both here and elsewhere these attitudes detail not so much individuals' relationship with God as the interaction between Christian brothers and sisters. These attitudes should accompany their communication with one another and should also lead them into a real depth of relationship with one another.

So the Galatians, having been informed that "love" is the chief "fruit of the Spirit," are encouraged not merely to do good to those who are of the household of faith but also to "bear one another's burdens, and so fulfill the law of Christ" (Gal 5:22; 6:2, RSV). In 1 Corinthians Paul speaks of the need for the members to "have the same care for one another" as well as to suffer and rejoice with one another in their humiliations and triumphs (1 Cor 12:25–26). In Romans he urges his readers not to please themselves: "each of us must please our neighbor for the good purpose of building up the neighbor," and "live in harmony with one another, in accordance with Christ Jesus" that God might be unitedly acknowledged (Rom 15:1–2, 5–6, NRSV). In Philippians, there is to be mutual affection, sympathy, love, and harmony. Each one is told: "look not to your own interests, but to the interests of others" (Phil 2:1–4, NRSV). In Colossians, they are to "put on then, as God's chosen ones, holy and beloved, compassion, kindness, lowliness, meekness, and patience, forbearing one another and, if one has a complaint against another, forgiving each other . . . And above all these put on love, which binds everything together in perfect harmony" (Col 3:12–14, RSV). In Ephesians all this is summed up in the injunction to the brethren to "be kind to one another, tenderhearted, forgiving one another"; thus "walk[ing] in love, as Christ loved us and gave himself up for us," and to be "imitators of God as beloved children" (Eph 4:32–5:2).

The centrality of *agape* explains why Paul can sum up his understanding of Christian responsibility as "faith working through love" (Gal 5:6b) and how he can conclude that members of the community are to "owe no one anything, except to love one another" (Rom 13:8, NRSV). So basic is love that even the sacrifice of one's life is worthless unless motivated and informed by it (1 Cor 13:3). Indeed love itself is the sacrifice God really requires (Eph 5:2). Although it should govern all social relationships, it has pride of place within the community's internal life: it is the "crown" of its endeavors, for above all it is love that "binds" its members together into a true unity.[19] Far from being a human possibility, however, it has its origin in God. Only through the Spirit is it poured out into Christians' lives (Rom 5:5; 15:30). Far from being merely an attitude towards others, it involves a purposive act of will. It is, as Paul says in one passage, "a labor,"[20] and it expresses itself not in mere feeling or inclination but in concrete acts of service. While it delights in reciprocation, love gives itself to others irrespective of the reaction it receives.[21]

It is precisely at this point that *agape*, love, shows its difference from the Greek ideal of *philia*, friendship, in which reciprocity played such a central part. The concrete actions that characterize this community of love may be described as acts of identification on the one hand, or substitution on the other. Identification, the solidarity of the members with one another, goes beyond mere sociality, for each is inextricably involved in the life of the other. Substitution, bearing one another's burdens in quite tangible ways, goes beyond mere helpfulness or even compassion. Prayer made by one member of the community for another and especially suffering undergone by one member on behalf of another are just two examples of what is here in view.[22]

EARLIER USES OF FAMILY TERMINOLOGY

What, then, of the background to Paul's usage? It is not as common as might be imagined. Reference to Israel as a "household" (Amos 5:25; Jer. 38:33), and to its members as "brothers,"[23] occurs earlier in Jewish literature, but nowhere in the OT is Israel called God's *family* as such. The Greeks sporadically referred to

---

[19] 1 Cor 16:14; Col 2:8; 3:14; Eph 4:1–3.
[20] 1 Thess 1:3; cf. 2 Cor 8:24.
[21] Rom 13:10.
[22] Cf. Gal 4:19; 2 Cor 4:10–11; Rom 9:3; Col 1:24; Eph 3:13.
[23] E.g., Lev 10:4; 19:17; Deut 15:3. Philo, *Special Laws* 2.79f. Cf. Matt 5:22–24; 10:6; Acts 2:29, 36; 13:26.

members of the same political unit or to friends as "brothers."[24] At Qumran, family words are more consciously used of the community created out of the broader society but play only a minor role in comparison with other ascriptions. The Qumran community is depicted as a "household," not of God but of "truth," "holiness," and "perfection"; members are described as "sons" of "light," "truth," "righteousness," and "heaven."[25] Love of the members for one another is demanded, though only within the framework of a highly regulated life.[26] In one passage the overseer of the members is said to act as a "father" to his "children,"[27] echoing the intertestamental wisdom literature and its OT antecedents.[28] The Pharisees too have their "sons" and a rabbi is occasionally described as a "father."[29] But fraternal language does not seem to be particularly prominent and, among the Pharisees, references to love occur within the wider framework of devotion to the Law.[30] It is precisely the prominence of such language in Paul, along with personalization by means of other words such as "my," "beloved," and so on, that distinguishes his understanding of community from these others. He also breaks convention by talking, in a virtually novel way, about "sisters" as well as "brothers."[31] He can speak as intimately of them as of his "brothers" and "sons."

In the mysteries, initiates do not seem to have been described as "children" of the deities with whom they were joined, though there is talk of a father-son relationship between the initiate and priestly guardian. The Cynic philosopher is sometimes portrayed as a "father" or "nurse" to his hearers.[32] The Stoics believed that all men were the "offspring" of the gods and "brothers" of one another.[33] Since this was an abstract idea and did not

---

[24] Plato, Meno 239a. Xenophon, Anabasis 7.2.25.

[25] 1QS 1.9; 3.13, 20, 22, 25; 4.5–6, 22; 5.6; 8.5, 9; 9.6; CD 3.19. Josephus, Jewish War 2.122.

[26] 1QS 1.9; 2.24; 4.4–5; 5.25.

[27] CD 13.9.

[28] Prov 3:12; Eccl 3:1; 7:23–29.

[29] m. Makk. 2.3; m. Eduy. 1.4; m. B. M. 2.11.

[30] m. 'Ab. 1.2; m. Sot. 5.5.

[31] But see Num 25:8; Song Sol 4:9.

[32] Apuleius, Metamorphoses 11.26; Dio Chrysostom, Orationes 4.73ff., 77–78.

[33] Epictetus, Dissertationes 1.13.4. Dio Chrysostom, Orationes 3.100ff., but also Cleanthes, Fragment 537, in Barrett, Background, 67–68, and Epictetus, Dissertationes 3.22.77ff.

lead to the formation of communities even among one's Stoic neighbors, this does not have the same concrete ring about it as the Pauline conception. There are, in the papyri and inscriptions, occasional references in brotherly terms to members of the same religious society or guild. It can be concluded, however, that family terminology and the language of love nowhere occupy the central position or possess the intensive meaning that they do in Paul's writings.

Yet Paul was not the first to talk in this manner. It is Jesus who stands behind Paul's usage here: the one who looked at those sitting around him and said, "Here are my mother and my brothers! Whoever does the will of God is my brother, and sister, and mother"; the one who placed "love" at the heart of his whole teaching about personal behavior (Mark 3:34–35, RSV; 12:30–31). It is in the Spirit of Christ, then, that the early Christian communities sought to become communities of love, to become familial and familiar settings in which the art of love could be learned, to become places where the love that bound together Son and Father could be a visible, corporate reality in the lives of those who had committed themselves to the gospel.

THE RELATION BETWEEN "FAMILY" AND "FELLOWSHIP"

The metaphor of the family was a vital one to Paul. Paralleling the household *context* of community gatherings we have the use of household *language* to describe the relations between members. The correlation of the two may be accidental. Christians may not have had anywhere else to meet, especially since the synagogues soon became closed to them and the rooms attached to local temples would have possessed unsavory connotations. But just possibly the practical necessity for their use blended with a further, theologically based consideration. For, given the family character of the Christian community, the homes of its members provided the most conducive atmosphere in which they could give expression to the bond they had in common.

Before moving away from these terms, all of which in various ways stress the close relationship existing between Christians, we need to look at another word commonly believed to point in the same direction. Though not a family designation, *koinonia*, frequently mistranslated "fellowship," occupies a large place in many popular discussions of Paul's understanding of community. Paul uses the related adjectival noun *koinonos* a few times in the sense of partner in a joint activity[34] and the verb *koinoneo* five times with the meaning either of "having a share" in some external activity[35] or of "making a contribution" in a financial or other way (Rom 12:13; Gal 6:6). *Koinonia* itself occurs some thirteen times but, as with these related terms, the sense is of participation in some common object or activity, e.g., participation in the Spirit, in someone's faith, in Christ and his sufferings, in the work of the gospel, in a financial contribution[36]—not of the sharing of people concerned directly with one another.[37]

Certainly Christians do associate with one another in these activities and experiences, but in his use of *koinonia*, Paul's emphasis is upon their participation *alongside* one another in such things, not *in* one another as the term "fellowship" suggests. Paul does talk about fellowship with one another in this more personal and intensive sense, but uses words other than *koinonia* to express it—as we are about to see.

---

[34] 1 Cor 10:18ff.; 2 Cor 1:7; 8:23; Phlm 17.

[35] Rom 15:27; Phil 4:15; Eph 5:11.

[36] Phil 2:1; 2 Cor 13:13; Phlm 6; Phil 3:10; 1 Cor 1:9; Phil 1:5; Gal 2:9; Rom 15:26.

[37] 1 Cor 10:14ff. (3 times); 2 Cor 6:14; 8:4; 9:13.

6

—∽∽∽—

THE COMMUNITY AS
A FUNCTIONAL BODY

Through the description of the Christian community as a "family," Paul says something about the basis and character of the relationships within it. His comparison of the community with a *soma*, "body," however, seems more concerned with the nature and exercise of gifts present in the community and with the source from which they come. Yet it would be misleading to distinguish too sharply between the application of the metaphors, for it is one of Paul's basic convictions that the two cannot really be separated. We shall see this as we go along.

PAUL'S EARLY USAGE OF THE BODY METAPHOR

Description of the Christian community as a "body" first takes place in the latter half of 1 Corinthians, though there is earlier mention of Christians as individual "members" of Christ (1 Cor 6:15). The first two references are quite cryptic in character and occur in Paul's discussion of "the Lord's Meal." They emphasize the *unity* of the members with one another and through that their unity with Christ, rather than the *gifts* exercised for each other's welfare. "Because there is one bread," he says, "we who are many are one body, for we all partake of the one bread" (10:17, RSV).

Paul says that "all who eat and drink without discerning the body, eat and drink judgment against themselves" (11:29, NRSV). Although this has been generally interpreted as a reference to Christ's crucified body, the community itself is almost certainly in view. Members of the community need to recognize their unity and "receive" one another (this is preferable to the RSV's "wait" for one another, 11:33). The fact that there are many members of the community should lead not to the assertion of individualistic attitudes, nor to the formation of cliques within it, but instead to a continuing affirmation of its solidarity.

This problem of unity and multiplicity is given more extended and vivid consideration in the following chapter, where Paul treats the human body in parabolic, almost allegorical terms in his numerous analogies between it and the Christian community (12:12–30). In this passage, the following points deserve special notice:

1. It is the local community at Corinth that is described as the body of Christ. "You are the body of Christ," insists Paul, "and individually members of it." (1 Cor 12:27, RSV) We must avoid two possible misunderstandings here. First, it is not so much the *ekklesia*, or local gathering, that is described in these terms as it is the community. The *soma* metaphor and *ekklesia* terminology do not completely overlap, since *soma* has a wider reference. The term "body" can apply to the relations between members that take place both outside and inside the church. Yet even so, it is primarily by *assembling* that the responsibilities of members to one another are fulfilled. The "body" most clearly and fully finds expression as "church," even if it is also visible when it does not assemble. The community at Corinth is not said to be part of a wider body of Christ or to be a "body of Christ" alongside numerous others. It is *the* body of Christ" in that place. This suggests that wherever Christians are in relationship there is the body of Christ in its entirety, for Christ is truly and wholly present there through his Spirit (12:13). This is a momentous truth. We find here further confirmation of the high estimate Paul had of the local Christian community.

2. Each member of the community is granted a ministry to other members of the community. This means that no person or group of persons can discount other contributions to the "body" or impose a uniform way of operating. The community contains a

diversity of ministries, and it is precisely in the differences of function that the wholeness and unity of the body resides. God has so designed things that the involvement of every person is necessary for the proper functioning of the community (12:14–21). This means that each member has a unique role to play yet is also dependent upon everyone else.

3. It is precisely those members who render the less obviously spectacular services who should be accorded the greatest respect. The most outwardly attractive or dramatic ministries are not necessarily the most fundamental. Care must therefore be exercised in assessing the importance of certain gifts, e.g., glossolalia, for the welfare of the community. Others, less striking in character, exercised in a more private manner, may contribute more substantially to the community's well-being and growth (12:22–25).

4. So close is the link between members of the community that what affects one necessarily affects all. Paul's language must be carefully noted here. He does not say that experiences of individuals within the community, both pleasurable and sorrowful, *should* be shared by all the others who belong to it. He says instead that they *are* so shared, whether consciously experienced or not. The "body" has a common nerve. There is a common life within it in which each is identified with the other—all in one, as it were, and one in all (12:26). The interrelationship of the individuals who make up the community could scarcely be more strongly emphasized.

5. The closeness of the relationship between the community and Christ is underlined, but its character is not really specified. Although at the beginning of the passage Paul appears to identify the community totally with Christ (12:12b), at its close the community is unambiguously spoken of as his *body* (12:27). Does this mean that Christ is its head or that the community is wholly his body? The latter presumably, since no qualification is given to the contrary. This does not mean that it is his form in some literal or physical sense, as some have suggested. Paul states at the start of the passage that Christ is united to the community through the Spirit (12:13), and the relations between the members themselves are said to take place through the same agency (12:4–11; 14:12).

Reference to the community as a "body" next appears in Paul's letter to the Romans (Rom 12:4ff.). Here again it reinforces the principle of unity-in-diversity, though from a slightly different angle. Paul has in mind here not only the overvaluation of some gifts at the expense of others but also the overestimation by some members of the gift that they possess. Unlike the earlier situation, he is not reacting to an error that has already occurred but is guarding against the possibility that one might emerge (cf. Rom 1:11–13). Despite his statement that "we," rather than "you" (as in 1 Corinthians), are "one body in Christ," he is probably referring to the Roman community. The plural simply means "we Christians" (wherever we are), though just possibly he is including himself among the members of the community in view of his projected participation in it. Since, as we have already noted, the Christian community there probably gathered in different groups throughout the city, the broader use of the "body" metaphor for more than a single church is again present.

The primary application of the body metaphor to the exercise of gifts is also clear. It is precisely through the *variety* of contributions, as well as in their proportionate strength, that the unity of the community becomes manifest (Rom 12:6a, 6b). In Romans 12 Paul describes the relationship of the community to Christ in more intimate terms than in 1 Corinthians. They are not just "the body *of* Christ," but are now "one body *in* Christ" (Rom 12:5a). This way of putting it stresses the fact that Christ is the source of its unity. The means by which this takes place and the precise nature of the link between the two are not identified.

PAUL'S LATER USAGE OF THE BODY METAPHOR

In Paul's later writings certain developments in his use of the "body" metaphor may be found. These arise from the different situations encountered by the communities. Religious ideas from a number of sources—Greek, Jewish, and Oriental—have coalesced and threaten to penetrate the small Christian enclaves. According to these foreign ideas various cosmic powers, which are themselves emanations of divinity, can assist people in their contact with God. This being so, believers need to supplement their reliance upon Christ by gaining an acquaintance with such powers. In his letter to the Colossians, Paul deals with this threat by explaining that everything in creation owes its life to Christ (1:16); that he triumphed not merely over sin, the Law, and death but over these cosmic forces as well (1:20); and that he is not merely one emanation of the divinity among others but is the one in whom "all the fullness of God was pleased to dwell" (1:19). As such, he and he alone is "the image of the invisible God" and is "preeminent" over everything and everyone else (1:15). This includes his *ekklesia*. At this point Paul reintroduces the notion of the "body," describing Christ as "the head of the body, the church" (1:18). This idea is repeated three times elsewhere in the letter. A little later in this chapter he speaks of "his body, that is the church, of which I minister" (1:24). In the next he speaks of Christ as "the Head, from whom the whole body, nourished and knit together through its joints and ligaments, grows with a growth that is from God" (2:19–20, RSV). In the following chapter he speaks simply of its members as being "called in the one body" (3:15).

In Ephesians similar ideas come to the fore. The priority of Christ at every level of reality is once again reaffirmed, and his preeminence over the cosmic powers and the church are particularly singled out for mention. He is "far above all rule and authority and power and dominion" (Eph 1:21, RSV) and "head over all things for the church, which is his body, the fulness of him who fills all in all" (1:22–23, RSV). Further on in the letter, the metaphor refers to the new unity between Jews and Gentiles that exists in the church as a result of Christ's reconciling work (2:16; 3:6). Later still, it emphasizes the fact that there is only "one body" (4:4) and then goes on to note the diversity of "gifts" that exist within it, all of which have Christ as their author (4:7–8). These are given to "equip the saints for the work of ministry" (i.e., to stimulate the exercise of other gifts in the community) and to build up the body of Christ. Speaking the truth in love, "we are to grow up in every way into him who is the head, into Christ, from whom the whole body, joined and knit together by every joint with which it is supplied, when each part is working properly, makes bodily growth and upbuilds itself in love" (4:12, 15–16, RSV). This is a very compact description indeed. It employs the stark image of the body growing up into the head and suggests that the conformity of the church to Christ should become ever more complete. The final references to the metaphor in this letter occur in the list of obligations for husbands and wives. Here again Christ is spoken of as "the head of the church, his body" (5:23) and Christians as "members of his body" (5:30), which he nourishes and cherishes.

TEST, EXAMINE

1 Thess 5:21   Test everything, hold on to the good

1 Jn 4:1   Don't believe every spirit, but test them to see if they're from God

Eph 5:8-21   Find out what pleases the Lord

Acts 17:11   Examine the scriptures daily

Its development

How has usage of the "body" metaphor developed?

1. In the earlier correspondence "the body" concerns the local gathering of the church on earth. In Paul's later correspondence, it has been broadened to describe the heavenly reality that all Christians belong to: the *ekklesia*. (When the terms "body" and "church" occur together in Ephesians, it refers to "the church, his body.") There is an expanding rather than narrowing of its application, for it is the heavenly church that is brought before us in these later letters, not the local gatherings that are its earthly manifestations.

2. The relationship between the church and Christ is more fully defined in the later writings. In the early writings the community formed the whole body, head included; later Christ occupies the chief position. This signifies that he is both the source of its life and the center of its unity. Although not mentioned in Colossians, Ephesians speaks of the Spirit as the one who establishes Christ's preeminence in the church and brings this life and unity into being (Eph 2:18, 22; 4:3–4).

3. The extension of the "body" metaphor to cover the racial composition of the church, or rather the new "humanity" that has been created out of its Jewish and Gentile components, also takes place in Paul's later writings. Here we have a variation of the unity-in-diversity theme, one that focuses on the members' religious backgrounds instead of their individual gifts.

4. In talking about the mutual contributions of the members, Paul emphasizes the necessity for their corporate growth rather than on the interdependence that follows from this. This growth is defined as an ever increasing integration into Christ and as an intellectual or moral maturity for which Christ provides the standard. Growth occurs through "speaking the truth in love" (Eph 4:15).

Its limits

All these references to the "body," as well as those in Paul's earlier writings, speak only of the internal relations between Christ and the community and between the members of the community. While the heavenly "church" is viewed as the fulfillment of people's social/political aspirations, the relation between that community and the world is not directly considered by the term "body."

Though today the metaphor is frequently applied in this direction, Paul does not think of the "body" as a world oriented entity, or of Christ as dependent upon it for his visible expression in the world. The local *ekklesia* in particular has no "face" to the world as such. The world sees only Christians and sees them when they are not, as a matter of fact, in church. Nothing in Paul's writings suggests that the gathering of believers has a *direct* function vis-à-vis the world. Though the "body" metaphor also has the community of Christians in view when church is not taking place, it basically refers to the interaction of the members with one another, not with outsiders.

This does not mean that individual members of the community lack responsibilities towards the world around them but simply means that the metaphor of the "body" is never used to refer to such. Of course the church and the wider Christian community do have a function within the world, namely, the integration of the members more firmly into one another and into Christ. Since this involves their growth not only to corporate but also to individual maturity (resulting in a greater understanding and fulfillment of their wider obligations in the world), church and community do make an *indirect*, though fundamental, contribution to the life of the people around them. Indeed, if Paul's letters are any indication, much of the content of the Christians' meetings must have concerned their responsibilities to outsiders and to society in general. Some passages on the internal relations of members, for instance, stand side by side with discussions of the external obligations of individual Christians (e.g., Rom 12).

Its application

Much of what Paul says about the community as a "body" is framed in response to the possibility of disunity splitting it up. As we have seen, unity in the local church is a reality to be acknowledged, not potential to be worked towards. Paul frequently appeals for such unity to be maintained in the face of possible or existing dissensions,[1] so as to avoid the type of schism that had occurred at Corinth and threatened to take place in Rome and Colossae.[2] Rather than referring to divisions

---

[1] 1 Cor 1:10; Rom 15:5; Phil 2:1; Col 3:12–14; Eph 4:3.
[2] 1 Cor 11:18; Rom 16:17–20; Col 2:16–19.

between churches, schism for Paul designates division within a single community. It results, he says, either from a lack of agreement with one another or from a lack of care for one another (1 Cor 1:12; 11:21) and is one of the works of the "flesh" (Gal 5:20).

This does not mean that all differences of opinion within the church are to be avoided. As Paul says, "there must be different views (haireseis) among you in order that those who are genuine among you may be recognized" (1 Cor 11:19). Only when such differences are combined with a lack of acceptance of others, so that a section of the church hardens itself against the rest and behaves as if it were self-contained, does disagreement rend the body. Even doctrinal differences, e.g., whether or not the resurrection has yet taken place (15:12–58), or divergent lifestyles, e.g., the extent to which one may participate in some of the practices of the surrounding society (10:23–31), do not lead to schism within the community unless accompanied by coercive or careless attitudes on the part of some members towards others. But when something at the heart of the gospel is affected, such as insistence on an additional requirement for salvation (Gal 1:9), the infiltration of idolatrous ideas (1 Cor 10:14–22), or the exhibition of flagrantly immoral behavior (5:1–7), the controversy created by such actions must lead the church to disassociate itself from the persons involved. In order to avoid unnecessary schism, Paul does not require subscription to a detailed doctrinal confession or comprehensive moral code so much as members' expression of their common *acceptance* by God and their *quest* for a unity of purpose and love.

Its originality

How original is Paul's use of the "body" metaphor? It has no exact parallels in Jewish literature. Although the notion of "corporate personality" is present in the Hebrew Bible, it was the Greek translation of the OT that introduced the term "body" into Jewish thought for the first time (e.g., Lev 14:9; Prov 11:17). Yet neither here nor in the literature of the intertestamental period was the term used in any metaphorical way.[3] The rabbinic speculations on the grossly inflated size of Adam's body (containing all

---

[3] Cf. 2 Macc 8:11; Wisd 9:15.

of humankind in embryo) come from a later period and have a literal sense.[4]

Gnostic thought recognizes the idea of the saved community as the body of the heavenly redeemer but only in writings that are later than the NT. In any case, Paul's initial use of the metaphor, in which the community is represented by the whole body and the emphasis is upon the interdependence of its members, has no parallel in Gnostic sources.

In Stoic literature prior to the NT, we do find the cosmos (including humanity) depicted as the body of the divine world-soul[5] and society as a body in which each member has a different part to play.[6] But Paul refuses to portray the universe as Christ's body and rejects any idea of a member's wider society having priority over the Christian community. Individual and community are equally objects of his concern; neither is given priority over the other. One can be an individual only in a community and a community can function properly only when individuals are playing their distinctive roles within it. He also has a more restricted and more personal community in view than the Stoic's *polis*—one that is linked to a person and involved in his ongoing personal history. Seneca's reference to the emperor as the "soul" of the republic and the latter as his "body" provides a close parallel to this.[7] But Paul, a good Hebrew here, does not think of soul and body in these dualistic terms and therefore cannot describe the relationship between Christ and the community in this way.

While none of these usages yields an exact parallel to his ideas, they do indicate the extent to which the metaphor was "in the air" in Hellenistic circles.[8] While the term "body" did not originate with him, Paul was apparently the first to apply it to a community *within* the larger community of society and to the *personal* responsibilities of people for one another rather than their civic duties. We see again how a quite "secular" term is used by Paul to illuminate what Christian community is all about.

---

[4] Pesikta de Rab Kahana 1b.
[5] Seneca, De Ira 2.31.7–8.
[6] Epictetus, *Dissertationes* 2.10.3.
[7] Seneca, De Clementia 1.4.3–5.1; 2.2.1.
[8] See also Livy, *History* 2.32. Josephus, *Antiquities* 7.66. Dio Chrysostom, *Orationes* 17.19.

7

—⚋—

INTELLECTUAL ELEMENTS
IN GROWTH

THE GOAL: MATURITY

Paul's description of the community as a "body" indicates that its goal is not just the creation of harmony between the members—that is more the emphasis of his family terminology—but also their development towards corporate maturity. Paul stresses the need for individuals to progress towards maturity on a number of occasions,[1] though generally in contexts where the corporate maturity of the community is in view.[2] God's intention is not the fashioning merely of mature individuals but of mature communities as well. The Christian community does not exist just as a means to individual ends, though a mature community is an influential factor in shaping the individual maturity of its members.

This maturity is further defined in a number of passages throughout Paul's writings. He views it as an ever closer approximation to the "likeness" of God, so that there is an increasing

---

[1] 1 Cor 2:16ff.; 13:9–12; Phil 3:12ff.; Col 1:28.
[2] 1 Cor 1:10; 14:20; 2 Cor 1:13–14; Col 1:21–22; 4:12; Eph 4:11–16; 5:25–27.

reflection of God's attitudes, concerns, and activities.[3] Since Christ is "the image of the invisible God" in whom "all the fullness of God was pleased to dwell" (Col 1:15, 19, RSV), Paul can also describe Christian maturity as a call to the "imitation" of Christ and as a following of his "example"; as a possession of the "mind" of Christ and bearing in one's "person" the marks of Jesus; as a "clothing oneself" with Christ, allowing Christ to be "formed" within; and as a transformation into his "glory," i.e., the unique quality that characterized him.[4] It is essentially an attaining of all to "the knowledge of the Son of God, to mature adulthood, to the measure of the stature of the fullness of Christ" (Eph 4:13). Although this goal will be fully realized only in "the age to come,"[5] that is to say in God's perfected universe, we should now seek to attain it. Paul discusses this not only in passages that specifically mention the need for "progress"[6] or "growth"[7] but also, more obliquely, in metaphors drawn from athletic contests[8] and military life.[9] While he emphasizes throughout the importance of human effort,[10] it is the activity of the Spirit that alone makes this growth possible. Paul affirms this in a way that cannot be improved upon. Immediately following his statement that "the Lord is the Spirit, and where the Spirit of the Lord is, there is freedom," he adds, "We all, with unveiled face, reflecting the glory of the Lord, are being changed into his likeness from one degree of glory to another; for this comes from the Lord who is the Spirit."[11]

THE ROLE OF FAITH

How exactly does this transformation and growth take place? In what *way* does the Spirit interact with individuals in the com-

---

[3] Col 3:10; Eph 4:24; 5:1.

[4] Gal 4:19; 1 Cor 11:1; 2 Cor 3:18; Rom 13:14; 15:7; Phil 2:5.

[5] 1 Thess 2:19–20; 3:13; 5:23; 1 Cor 1:8; 15:49–57; Rom 8:28–30; Phil 1:6; 3:12–21; Col 3:1–4.

[6] Phil 1:25; cf. Rom 5:3b–4.

[7] 1 Cor 3:6–8; 2 Cor 9:10; Col 1:10; 2:19; Eph 4:16.

[8] Gal 2:2; 1 Cor 9:24–27; Phil 2:16; 3:12–14 (cf. also Col 1:29; 2:1).

[9] 1 Thess 5:8; 2 Cor 6:7; 10:3–4; Rom 13:12; Phil 1:30; Eph 6:10–17.

[10] Rom 8:5–7; Phil 2:12; Eph 6:10–20.

[11] 2 Cor 3:17–18, RSV; cf. Gal 5:16–26.

munity so that they mature? In order to understand this properly we must turn back for a moment to the beginning of Christian experience.

The key word for Paul is "faith." It is by faith, says Paul, that one embarks upon the Christian life.[12] Exertion of one's own willpower through energetic attempts at moral or spiritual reform, scrupulous observance of personal or corporate religious rituals, or involvement in various pious or mystical exercises cannot achieve this.[13] It begins only through faith, faith itself being a manifestation of the grace of God, however much human activity is engaged.[14] How does faith come? According to Paul, "Faith comes through hearing, and hearing comes through the presentation of the message about Christ."[15] This involves "persuading people" and "commending . . . the truth to every one's conscience" (2 Cor 5:11, 4:2). When this persuasion is effectual—when a genuine reception of the imparted message takes place—faith is born. Because the association between faith and knowledge is so close, Paul can even speak of his converts having "learned" Christ (Col 1:7; Eph 4:20).

So it is through faith alone that the process of becoming a Christian begins, and it is knowledge about Christ that alone makes this process possible. The crucial role knowledge plays comes through in Paul's numerous descriptions of his apostolic work—essentially he imparts knowledge or declares truth wherever he goes.[16] Yet this ministry is not simply a matter of speaking, informing, and convincing, even when we see in it the persuasive power of the Spirit rather than mere human reasoning. Paul and his companions share with the audiences "not only the gospel of God but also our own selves" (1 Thess 2:8). Their message is as much embodied in their *actions* as formulated in their words. Through both word and action their hearers learn the meaning of the message and on both model their response. The message is at its heart a message about suffering; it involves affliction for the preachers, just as it does for those who accept it.[17] Affliction is a part of life for everyone who genuinely presents and receives the gospel.

---

[12]Gal 2–3; Rom 3–5 et al.
[13]See especially Rom 10:1–10; Col 2:16–3:4.
[14]Rom 3:21–38 (cf. 4:16–20); Eph 2:8–10.
[15]Rom 10:17 (cf. Gal 3:5).
[16]See Gal 2:5; 2 Cor 2:14; 7:14; Eph 3:7–10.
[17]1 Thess 1:4–7; Gal 6:14–17; 2 Cor 1:3–8; 4:7–12; Col 1:24 et al.

Paul's ongoing work, as exemplified in his visits and let-ters,[18] continues to revolve around the communication of knowl-edge by word and life. According to Luke he does not fail to declare "the whole counsel of God" during his extended stay in Ephesus (Acts 19:27). His letters contain reminders of things already said, amplification of earlier teaching, responses to ques-tions, and instructions about problems in the communities. All are conveyed in a personal way, with an emotional openness; these are not just intellectual issues for Paul. They reveal his vulnerability (as opposed to his self-sufficiency) when his words are brushed aside. Within this, knowledge is central to the ongo-ing life of his communities, as can be illustrated in a quite striking way by simply setting out, side by side, a number of relevant statements on this theme.

THE CENTRALITY OF KNOWLEDGE

Paul says that growth takes place within the community only insofar as its members are "increased with," "enriched by," "re-newed through," and "filled with" knowledge.[19] Elsewhere he speaks of growth occurring via "the renewal of their minds,"[20] and it is on this basis that he urges them, "set your minds" on certain things, "have this mind among yourselves," and "be thus minded."[21] When they have neglected to do so he insists that they "come to their right mind"; on matters of indifference he advises "everyone to be fully convinced in his own mind"; on issues where there should be no dispute he encourages them "to be united in the same mind and in the same judgment."[22] Indeed, the mem-bers of the community are to "judge all things" and to "weigh all things," especially in church. There they should "judge for them-selves" and "weigh" what is said.[23] In all their thinking they are to "bring every thought into captivity," to "think upon whatever is" of real worth, to "fix their thoughts on things" of real value, and to "beware lest their thoughts be led astray from a sincere and

---

[18] E.g., 2 Thess 2:5; 1 Cor 14:6; Rom 15:14–15.
[19] Phil 1:9; Col 3:10; Col 1:9–10.
[20] Rom 12:2 (cf. Eph 4:22–24).
[21] Col 3:2; Phil 3:15; 2:5.
[22] 1 Cor 15:34; Rom 14:5; 1 Cor 1:10.
[23] 1 Cor 2:15; 1 Thess 5:21; 1 Cor 13; 14:29.

wholehearted commitment to Christ."[24] As regards society in general they are to be "naive towards that which is evil and wise towards that which is good," to "behave in a wise manner" towards those who are outside the Christian circle, and to have an acquaintance of God's will "in all spiritual wisdom and understanding."[25] In sum, they are to "understand" the significance of all that has been "bestowed on them by God" and to "not be childish in their understanding but mature" (1 Cor 2:12; 14:20).

This pastiche of quotations demonstrates the *frequency* with which Paul refers to rational activity of some kind, the wide *variety* of contexts in which mention is made of it, and the fundamental *place* he obviously accords it in the process of growth towards maturity. When other passages concentrating on the content of this understanding are taken into account, we find Paul using a large number of terms to bring out different aspects of what is involved, e.g., *nous*—mind (cf. *noema*—thought); *gnosis*—knowledge (cf. *epignosis*); *sophia*—wisdom; *sunesis*—understanding; *aletheia*—truth; *phronein*—to think (cf. *phren*); *logizein*—to consider (cf. *paralogizein*); *anakrinein*—to discern; *peithein*—to persuade; and *dokimazein*—to test. On occasions he can run several of these together to emphasize the importance of what he is saying. So, for example, he expresses a desire that his readers at Colossae will experience "all the wealth of the fullness of understanding (*sunesis*), the knowledge (*epignosis*) of the mystery of God, even in whom are hid all the treasures of wisdom (*sophia*) and knowledge (*gnosis*)." "This I say," he adds, "that no one may deflect your thinking (*paralogizomai*) with persuasiveness of speech" (Col 2:2–4). Throughout his writings Paul also frequently uses other terms, especially in passages where he is dealing less with the general process of growth than with specific issues encountered in its pursuit, e.g., *ginoskein*—to know; *me agnoein*—not to be ignorant or uninformed; and *anamimneskein*—to remind.

KNOWLEDGE'S RELATIONSHIP TO FAITH, LOVE, AND HOPE

The significance of knowledge for Paul can be brought into focus through further consideration of its relationship to faith,

---

[24] 2 Cor 10:5 (cf. Eph 5:6); Phil 4:8; Rom 8:6; 2 Cor 11:3.
[25] 1 Cor 14:20; Rom 16:19; Col 4:5 (cf. Eph 5:15); Col 1:9.

love, and hope, for it is these above all that are the most enduring elements in the community's experience (1 Cor 13:13). We have seen that one both begins the Christian life and makes progress in it through faith. What happens at the beginning thus sets the precedent for all that follows (Gal 3:1–5). Initially certain fundamental knowledge about God in Christ was conveyed and received. Through the aid of the Spirit people came into a new relationship with God. The way to further growth lies in the development of a deeper understanding of God and the consequent realignment of one's ways to that.

Such knowledge goes beyond the fundamental components of the gospel to matters of a more comprehensive and detailed kind, e.g., those of a doctrinal, moral, communal, social, and even political nature (e.g., Rom 9–15). Faith acknowledges and internalizes this in a wholeminded and wholehearted way (Rom 10:9–10). This results in a growing relationship with God through Christ in the Spirit. Knowledge, therefore, is the vehicle both through which faith comes into being and through which it is increased. Without knowledge there can be no genuine faith—only superstition on the one hand or speculation on the other.

Paul can summarize this ongoing Christian life in terms of "faith working through love" (Gal 5:6). Although for him love surpasses knowledge (1 Cor 13:8; Eph 3:19), and knowledge without love leads to self-centered pride rather than self-giving service (1 Cor 8:1 and 13:2), only knowledge can introduce us to love and reveal its full dimensions (Eph 3:18–19). Love must be informed by knowledge and its proper application discerned for there to be a right evaluation of what is the most loving course of action (Phil 1:9–10). On occasion this will lead to the sharing of some truth, i.e., love is sometimes best expressed through the imparting of knowledge. Paul also believes that, within the Christian community, the presence of loving relationships between the members provides the most conducive environment for fuller understanding of God to be gained—which in turn results in yet more love (1 Cor 12:31ff.; Col 2:2). Though love ultimately surpasses knowledge and lies at its source, understanding alone provides the entrance to it, comprehends its range and meaning, and directs its application.

Similarly with the communities' hope. Through "the word of the truth of the gospel,"[26] the basic elements of their hope are

---

[26]Rom 15:4; Col 1:5; Eph 1:18.

well-known to them. Nevertheless, further instruction about aspects of their hope that they should not be ignorant of is still in order.[27] In view of the threat posed by those who are pressing contrary versions of this hope upon them, Paul urges them to "remember" the content of his initial teaching and to "be not quickly shaken from (their) mind."[28] While it is only through the "enlightenment" of the Spirit that a person can have knowledge of this hope, it should be the aim of all seeking maturity to strive for it, remembering that "though our knowledge is partial now, then it will be complete" (1 Cor 13:9–11). Hope certainly goes beyond understanding, but understanding both introduces and flows from it. Understanding is the instrument through which further appreciation of hope takes place and false interpretations of hope are rejected.

ALTERNATIVE PATHS TO KNOWLEDGE

So far as faith, love, and hope are concerned then, knowledge occupies a central place in the life of Paul's communities. This makes the danger of false knowledge all the more real, and it is from this perspective that we must approach the treatment in his letter of various attacks upon knowledge.

Mystery cults

The mystery religions claimed to reveal the true character of the supernatural world and insisted that it could be attained only by nonrational means. Their *gnosis* had its climax in a "vision of the divine," i.e., in a mystical, indeed ecstatic, illumination in which the participant was taken quite outside his normal mind—even, it was held, outside his physical body.[29] Paul warns his hearers against being deceived by this (Col 2:4, 8a). It is a human creation and, for all its apparent piety and wisdom, is essentially specious in argument and sensual in appeal (vv. 8b, 18). The true *gnosis* for which it is searching is located "in Christ," and the genuine conviction for which it is aiming is an allegiance to him of "mind" and "heart" (i.e., will, vv. 2b–3, 7).

---

[27] 1 Thess 4:13ff.; Rom 13:11ff. et al.
[28] 2 Thess 2:2, 5; cf. Col 1:23.
[29] Apuleius, *Metamorphoses* 11.23. Plutarch, *Isis and Osiris* 77–78.

This does not mean that Paul rules out such experiences altogether. In one place he refers to a vision he had many years before (2 Cor 12:1–10). While not denying its legitimacy, (a) he draws attention to it unwillingly—it is forced upon him by his opponents' line of argument; (b) he nowhere suggests that it resulted in a significant change in his outlook; and (c) he regards it as being of secondary importance so far as his life and calling in Christ are concerned. In each of these respects Paul shows himself to be at odds with the values of the mystery religions.[30] It is true that in a number of other places he does talk openly about "receiving an illumination" or "knowing a mystery," but this has to do with understanding the full implications of Christ's death and resurrection, and he stresses the fact that God has now made this knowledge openly available to all.[31] It is in the name of genuine knowledge, then, that Paul dismisses the alleged knowledge of the mysteries.

Stoics and Cynics

This does not mean that Paul is arguing for a rationality of the Stoic or Cynic kind. He regarded that as also missing the mark concerning the understanding of divine things and as equally facile in its appeal (1 Cor 1:20–21). Over against that kind of rationality, he emphasizes revelation as the source of divine knowledge and its straightforward presentation as the means of impressing it upon his hearers (2 Cor 4:1–6). He is probably closest to the Stoics in the way he does this. One need not read very far through Paul's writings to see that they are principally given over to formal methods of argument in support of the instruction he wishes to convey. His kinship with Stoic practice becomes particularly apparent in the question and answer method that he employs from time to time (for example, Rom 6).

But Paul's continued insistence on the revealed source of all his knowledge sets him apart from his Stoic counterparts. This explains Paul's emphasis upon the need for *pistis*, faith, a notion that was fundamentally at odds with the Stoic or Cynic approach to life. Nonetheless, this should not obscure the fact that what divides them is their view of knowledge and how people receive it.

---

[30]Apuleius, *Metamorphoses* 11.22–24. Plutarch, *Isis and Osiris* 68.
[31]2 Cor 4:6; Rom 16:25–26; Col 2:2–4 (cf. 1:27); Eph 3:4–5, 9–10.

Judaism

In his view of knowledge Paul stands closer to the Jewish teachers of his day. Both he and they look to the OT, in which knowledge of God comes through neither human speculation nor mystical illumination, neither rational deductions based on God's past revelation nor present applications of it. It arises from a personal transaction between the dynamic word of the Lord and the prophet's mind, with human insight, visionary experience, scriptural exegesis, and situational discernment playing a subordinate role. Yet although the Jewish teachers of Paul's time have the advantage of possessing in the Law the very "embodiment of truth and knowledge," a "veil lies over their minds obscuring its real significance" from them (Rom 2:17–21; 2 Cor 3:14–15). They undoubtedly "have a zeal for God" but "it is not enlightened," for they are too preoccupied with the "letter" of the law at the expense of its "spirit" (Rom 10:2–3; 2 Cor 3:5–6).

He would have regarded approach to knowledge within the Qumran community as similarly misdirected. In some respects it may preserve the dynamic OT understanding of knowledge more faithfully than the Rabbis. But Qumran also contained unfamiliar elements, frequently speaking of knowledge as an esoteric affair and freely using the language of mystical enlightenment.[32] As was noted above, Paul's understanding of knowledge corresponds much more to the OT, especially the prophetic, outlook.

So then it is knowledge that the community needs for its growth—knowledge whose content is the "whole counsel of God" and whose only source is in God. Such knowledge, transmitted as much by life, especially suffering, as it is by word, can be communicated to members of the community only by the Spirit. "The Spirit," says Paul,

> searches everything, even the depths of God. For what human being knows what is truly human except the human spirit that is within? So also no one comprehends what is truly God's except the Spirit of God. Now we have received not the spirit of the world, but the Spirit that is from God, so that we may understand the gifts bestowed on us by God. (1 Cor 2:10b–12, NRSV)

---

[32] 1QS 4.6; 11.3–6; 1QH 18.19–20, 25–31.

Although intimations of that truth are revealed by God to people as they reflect on the character of their external environment (Rom 1:19–20), absorb the deepest insights of their culture (e.g., Acts 17:28; Phil 4:8), or listen to their most basic intuitions (Rom 2:14–15), it comes to clearest expression within the Christian community and most characteristically in the gathering of its people together. The way this happens will soon concern us, but first we must consider another basic element in community life.

8

---~m~---

PHYSICAL EXPRESSIONS
OF FELLOWSHIP

Paul singles out understanding and communicating as especially important for the community's progress to maturity but emphasizes that these do not involve only thinking and speaking. The members must live out their beliefs; only knowledge that has been translated into action and tested by affliction has the stamp of genuineness. Without action and affliction any claim to knowledge is only superficial or counterfeit. Paul's insistence that thoughts and words be embodied in his readers' lives springs from his belief that we are essentially physical beings—not, as the Greeks thought, an imprisoned intellect, spirit, or soul. A person does not just *have* a body, he or she *is* a body; a person does not live *in* a physical form, he or she exists *as* a physical form. This being the case, it comes as no surprise that physical actions have a place alongside verbal activities in Paul's communities.

BAPTISM

A striking example of an important physical action is baptism. Although Paul does not always personally baptize his converts (1 Cor 1:16) and regards baptism as only a secondary feature of his apostolic work (v. 17), for him baptism gives visible expression to the change from the old way of life to the new. Paul elaborates upon baptism's significance in a number of places in his letters.[1]

What does water baptism signify? Paul does not regard it as a solely symbolic action or as an inexplicably magical one. It is not an outward representation of an already concluded inner decision, i.e., God's covenantal election of the person involved[2] and the latter's individual commitment to God (Acts 16:33–34). Nor is it the mechanism by which God's benefits are automatically guaranteed to whoever undergoes it. Paul's linking of faith with baptism suggests that it was by means of baptism that the individual or family *actually committed* themselves to God.[3] It is precisely because the believer is a physical being, and because God's relations with him or her take place within a physical environment, that the whole person (not merely inner self) and water (an element of God's material creation) are involved. Baptism, therefore, is a genuinely dynamic affair. Through it a person becomes an individual in the full sense for the first time—by becoming aware of their own true position vis-à-vis God and being drawn into intimate relationship with God.

This means that baptism is something between the person, family, and God. It also has a broader dimension. A person's entrance into God's freedom or salvation, while an existential affair, also marks their introduction into a wider community. Baptism, which dynamically embodies and effects this translation from one way of life to another, necessarily involves a transferal from one community to another, from that "in Adam" to that "in Christ." But so far as the action itself is concerned, the *ekklesia*, church, does not strictly come into view. Nowhere in Luke's account of Paul's activities or in Paul's discussions of baptism do we find a hint that baptism has anything to do with the church. The context of baptism is the *preaching* of the gospel not the *gathering* of the community.

But we must be careful here. The general assumption that Paul always has water baptism in mind when he discusses baptism may be incorrect; he sometimes seems to be employing the word metaphorically to refer to conversion. Novel though this suggestion may seem, a metaphorical use of the term (or cognate expres-

---

[1] Gal 3:27; 1 Cor 12:13; 15:29; Rom 6:3–4; Col 2:11–12; Eph 4:5.
[2] Cf. Acts 16:33–34; 18:10.
[3] Cf. 1 Pet 3:21–22.

sions) already occurs in the Gospels (Mark 10:38–39; Luke 12:50), as well as in Paul's writings.[4] The passages certainly make excellent sense if interpreted along these lines. Metaphorically the word signifies an overwhelming experience of some kind, so it provides a very appropriate and vivid shorthand description of regeneration. It also explains those places where baptism is juxtaposed with other metaphors, e.g., death and burial (Rom 6:3–4), and putting on clothing (Gal 3:27). The combining of literal and metaphorical elements can be awkward, whereas the mixing of metaphors is a common (and quite Pauline) procedure. Certainly the allusion to baptism by the Spirit in 1 Cor 12 fits more naturally into this interpretation (1 Cor 12:13), and the isolated mention of baptism in Ephesians (Eph 4:5), alongside such spiritual realities as "faith," "hope," and the heavenly "body" and unaccompanied by any reference to the Lord's "meal," looks less out of place.

Yet clearly water baptism took place. Paul mentions some instances in passing (1 Cor 1:16–17) and Acts adds others in connection with his apostolic work.[5] These passages indicate that baptism was often a family occasion, signaling the introduction of a whole household into the Christian way of life (Acts 16:33; 18:8). Infants, however, were probably not involved, in view of the distinction generally drawn in the ancient world between children and household,[6] the close association between faith and baptism in both Acts and Paul,[7] and the special status accorded to children simply by birth into a family where at least one member is Christian (1 Cor 7:14). For Paul, baptism doesn't replace circumcision as the sign of community membership, circumcision is fulfilled in the *death* of Christ and perhaps the convert's death to sin (Col 2:11–12). Baptism is not the seal of the new covenant, the Spirit is.[8]

LAYING ON OF HANDS

Although, contrary to much that has been written, the giving of the Spirit is not necessarily tied to baptism itself—the giving

---

[4] 1 Cor 6:11; 10:2; cf. Eph 5:26.
[5] Acts 16:15, 33; 18:8; 19:5.
[6] Cf. 1 Tim 3:4, 12; Gen 18:19; 36:6; 47:12; 50:7; 1 Sam 1:21.
[7] Acts 8:12, 16:31; 18:8 (cf. 16:14; 19:4); Gal 3:23–25; Col 2:12; Eph 4:5.
[8] 2 Cor 1:22; Eph 1:13; 4:30.

of the Spirit may precede baptism, though more often follows it[9]—a correlation between the two naturally exists. But there is a physical action that normally accompanies the gift of the Spirit— the laying on of hands.[10] Once again we have a physical expression of fellowship that is neither a merely symbolic movement nor a quasi-magical one. As its OT background indicates (e.g., Gen 48:14ff.), the laying on of hands was essentially an enacted prayer, one that achieved what was requested. The action did not just *accompany* the prayer; it was part of the prayer itself.

As such the action lent itself to a variety of situations. According to Acts, those that Paul is involved in include commissioning of mission workers (Acts 13:3; cf. 6:6), healing of the sick,[11] and recognition of leaders,[12] as well as conveying of the Spirit. It would be a mistake to see in the third of these anything approaching "ordination" in the modern sense. Like the others it is simply an enacted prayer and does not carry any special significance beyond the content of the prayer itself. The language of Acts confirms this. There the phrase "the laying on of hands" is equated with "commending to the grace of God."[13] Even though Paul does not mention this action anywhere in his letters, there is no reason to doubt the authenticity of Luke's account. With the laying on of hands we have a physical sign that potentially involves not only the individual, as in baptism, but members of the community as well (Acts 13:1–3). It expresses the prayer of the members to God for the person before them and also expresses their fellowship with him.

THE COMMON MEAL

The most visible and profound way in which the community gives physical expression to its fellowship is the common meal. Paul writes about the common meal in only two places, and Acts associates him with it once. It is strange that so little should be

---

[9] Cf. Acts 2:38; 10:44.
[10] Acts 8:17–19; 9:17–18; 19:6.
[11] Acts 28:8 (cf. 9:17; 19:11; 20:10).
[12] Acts 14:23 (?).
[13] Cf. Acts 14:26 with Acts 13:3.

said by Paul about a practice that has been at the heart of Christianity. Especially when, apart from four brief references elsewhere (two in Acts, one in 2 Peter, and one in Jude), Paul says all that there is to say in the NT on the subject. This means that we have very little to help us in reconstructing his views on the matter, though there is sufficient evidence for us to discern the basic outline of his approach.

Sharing a meal in the Lord's name was a Christian practice before Paul's churches appeared on the scene. It is not fully clear from 1 Cor 10–11 whether the Lord's Supper accompanied every gathering of the "whole church" (1 Cor 11:18; cf. 14:23) or whether the community sometimes met especially for this purpose. The phrase, "when you come together to eat" (11:13), suggests the latter, but it is impossible to be certain. No mention is made of holding the meal in the smaller house-church meetings, but then little is said specifically about the content of these anyway. One would most naturally expect the Lord's Supper to be part of what took place, as was the custom from the beginning (Acts 2:42–46). In any case, the setting of the Lord's Supper, even in the larger gatherings, was always the home.[14]

The word *deipnon* (1 Cor 11:20), meaning "dinner," tells us that it was not a token meal (as it has become since) or part of a meal (as it is sometimes envisaged), but an entire, ordinary meal. The term indicates that this is the main (normally evening) meal, the one to which guests were invited. Its character as an ordinary meal is retained even though it has been given new significance. Paul's injunctions to the "hungry" to eat before they leave home (vv. 22, 34) do not represent the beginnings of a separation of the Lord's Supper from the meal itself. He is merely trying to avoid abuses that had entered into the meal at Corinth.

Nowhere does Paul suggest that the Lord's Supper has any cultic significance. With the exception of the words that accompany it, it was in no respect different from the customary meal for guests in a Jewish home. The breaking and distribution of the bread was the normal way of commencing such a meal, just as the taking of a cup was the usual way to bring it to a conclusion; prayers of blessing accompanied both.[15] Though commentators have generally assumed that the Christian meal included a formal

---

[14]Cf. Rom 16:23; Acts 20:8.
[15]See Jer 16:7. Cf. *m. Ber.* 6.1; 7.1.

recitation of the words uttered at the last meal Jesus shared with his disciples, this did not necessarily take place. While the recalling of the events of that night probably follows normal practice in his churches, Paul's reciting the words of institution may simply be to remind his readers of the *spirit* that the meal should be conducted in (1 Cor 11:23–26). Elsewhere in his writings similar references to sayings or actions of Jesus are introduced to recall to his audience the real nature of their responsibilities,[16] though, it must be admitted, these do not contain anything so explicit as Jesus' "do this in remembrance of me."

The character of the meal could be affirmed in ways other than reciting Jesus' words, e.g., through the prayers that commence and conclude it. No priestly celebrant is in view in any of the contexts where the meal is discussed; indeed, there is no suggestion that its management was in the hands of officials of any kind. Most probably general arrangements were in the hands of the "host" in whose home the meal was held, though the Corinthian practice of some eating before others (plus the fact that Paul addresses his remarks to the whole church) indicates that responsibility for proper conduct lay upon all. The presence of children in the regular meetings of Christians (Col 3:20; Eph 6:1–3) suggests that they participated in it. A precedent here would be the Passover Feast, also held in the home, which included education of the young in the fundamentals of their religious heritage (Exod 12:21–27).

The meal itself was a visible proclamation of the death of Christ to all who participated in it and, therefore, a call to discipleship by him. For Paul the words, "This is my body" (1 Cor 11:24) mean, "This is me, the one who gave up his life on your behalf." The words, "This cup is the *new covenant in my blood*" (v. 25—not, as in Matthew and Mark, "This is the blood of the covenant") mean, "This is the new relationship established between God and you through my death" (the term "blood" being for Paul a shorthand way of referring to Jesus' crucifixion[17]). References to the "body" and "covenant" of Christ (by means of the "bread" and "wine") are not simply two ways of referring to the same thing, viz., Jesus' death for the sake of others. The term "body" obviously describes

---

[16]E.g., 1 Cor 7:10–11; 15:1ff.; 2 Cor 8:8–10; Rom 6:1–11; 15:7–13; Phil 2:5–13.

[17]Rom 3:25; 5:9; Col 1:20; Eph 1:7; 2:13.

the death of Jesus, but the term "covenant" goes on to identify the great benefit that results from that death—a new relationship with God and one another. The taking of bread at the beginning and drinking of wine at the end of the meal (1 Cor 11:23–25) now become all the more appropriate, for between them lies the experience of that new relationship in the course of the meal itself.

This meal is vital, for as the members of the community *eat and drink together* their unity comes to visible expression. The meal is therefore a truly social occasion. The sharing of the wine at the close of the meal is appropriate for another reason. This action anticipates the time when they shall all "drink" (i.e., "fellowship") with Christ in God's kingdom in a more direct way. What could be a more fitting note to conclude the meal with? It is a truly eschatological event for those who participate in it.

Thus the meal that they shared together reminded the members of their relationship with Christ and one another and deepened those relationships in the same way that participation in an ordinary meal cements and symbolizes the bond between a family or group. This explains why Paul does not direct his criticisms against the attitudes of people towards the elements of bread and wine or against the quality of their individual relationships to God but against their attitudes and behavior *towards one another.* When these do not reflect the Christlike pouring out of their lives for each other that lies at the heart of the meal, they are "guilty of drinking the cup and eating the bread in an unworthy manner" and of "profaning the body and blood of the Lord" (1 Cor 11:27). This is the significance of Paul's warning that "all who eat and drink without discerning the body, eat and drink judgment against themselves" (v. 29, NRSV). Here, as in the previous chapter (10:17), the community is in view. The emphasis is upon participation, not the elements, and upon the unity of the community, as symbolized in the "one" loaf that is distributed among them.

A similar thought lies behind Paul's comments, a few paragraphs earlier, about the behavior of the "strong" towards the "weak." There he urges the former to "take care lest this liberty of yours somehow become a stumbling block to the weak." Being a stumbling block sins against the weak person for whom Christ died. But it does more, for "when you thus sin against members of your family, and wound their conscience when it is weak, you sin against Christ" (1 Cor 8:12, NRSV). Paul considers this a serious matter; for him a meal lacking sensitivity to the physical needs of the community is not the "Lord's meal" at all. He explains that, if unchecked, wrong attitudes between individuals will result in physical weakness, even death, among the members. This is one more indication of the way physical and spiritual factors are intertwined in Paul's thinking.

Comparison of the meals in Paul's communities with the *haburah* meals characteristic of the Pharisees is difficult, because there is little evidence to suggest what these lay fellowships did. Apart from the annual Passover festival and the celebration of the New Moon, we know only of meals where "fellowships for the observance of a commandment" took place, generally in the synagogue. These were essentially meals of obligation, such as those connected with circumcisions, betrothals, weddings, and funerals, in which participation as a paying guest was regarded as meritorious. It was different at Qumran where the members came together twice daily for a common meal. This played an integral part in their community life and was a real expression of their unity. But it was also a cultic celebration, presided over by a priest, with the members sitting and participating according to a rigidly defined order of precedence. Women were completely absent, and novices were excluded until they had completed the second year of their probation.[18]

There have been some ambitious reconstructions of meals held in the mystery cult that emphasize their similarity with the Pauline Supper. But these are really feasts held in honor of the initiate on his entry into the mysteries (or meals involving only the devotee and the god he worshipped), instead of occasions for mutual fellowship and service.[19] We know more about the common meals held under the aegis of a god by the members of a guild. Here again we are dealing with cultic, specifically sacrificial meals of a different kind than those Paul was advocating. The distinctive character of the Pauline meal, and of the idea of community embodied in it, remains even if at certain points there is overlap with other practices.

For Paul, people's physical frames were as much a part of their created glory as any other aspect of their personality. Consistent with this, Paul believed that the body itself is inhabited by, indeed is a "temple" of, the Holy Spirit (1 Cor 6:19). Also, according to Acts the laying on of hands conveyed healing, en-

---

[18] 1QS 6.20–21.

[19] Apuleius, *Metamorphoses* 11.24–25. Josephus, *Antiquities* 18.73.

dorsed ministry, commissioned workers, and even communicated the Spirit. Along with every other aspect of the personality, the body should take its part in the life of the church. This is anticipated in the action by which a person joins the community—baptism—but comes to fullest expression in the central action by which the community maintains and deepens its life—the Lord's meal.

THE EXCHANGE OF KISSES

Two final physical expressions of fellowship remain. "Greet all the brethren with a holy kiss,"[20] Paul says to his first converts in Thessalonica and to the recipients of his letters in Corinth and Rome. To interpret this action as merely a formal or secondary procedure would be to underestimate its importance. Not as significant as baptism and the Lord's Supper, it does, like the laying on of hands, play an important role in early Christian communal life. By means of this action the bond between each member of the church was given real, not merely symbolic, expression.

In itself the exchange of kisses in such a group is not particularly remarkable. While we have no direct evidence of it in the synagogue or at Qumran, it was part of the everyday life of Eastern societies, especially among relatives, friends, and those giving and receiving hospitality (compare Luke 7:45). In the mysteries it signified the type of relationship that existed between the initiate and his or her spiritual mentor or other members of the cult.[21] In Greek society it generally played much the same role as it did in the East. So it is the significance attached to it that differentiates its Christian use. The breadth of the relationship to which it gives expression—it is the kiss of Christ's peace among people of different races, classes, and families—gives it a more profound meaning than its practice in Eastern society. And its communal character marks it off from its more individualized exercise in the mysteries—in church the members are all to "greet one another."

---

[20] 1 Thess 5:26; 1 Cor 16:20; Rom 16:16; cf. Acts 20:37.
[21] Apuleius, *Metamorphoses* 7.9.

THE SHARING OF POSSESSIONS

For all his emphasis on these physical expressions of fellow-ship, Paul never suggests that the members of his communities have "all things in common," as did those at Qumran. The one-ness of Christians in the gospel does not necessarily involve the pooling of all their material resources. Not that their attitude to property stays unaffected by their commitment to Christ and one another. They are to remember "the grace of our Lord Jesus Christ, that though he was rich, yet for your sake he became poor, so that by his poverty you might become rich" (2 Cor 8:9, RSV). In practical terms this does not mean divesting themselves of all their prop-erty so much as the sharing of their "abundance" and "prosperity" with those in want (2 Cor 8:14; 1 Cor 16:2). This should lead to the situation where "the one who gathered much had nothing over, and the one who gathered little had no lack" (2 Cor 8:15, RSV). In the spirit of the gospel such sharing should spring from a "loving" and "generous" heart.[22] Indeed without this voluntary response, even the total yielding up of one's possessions is worthless, an "exaction" stemming from a "command" (2 Cor 8:8; 9:5). Paul insists that "each of you must give as you have made up your mind, not reluctantly or under compulsion, for God loves a cheer-ful giver" (2 Cor 9:7, NRSV). And this opens up the possibility of people exhibiting a "wealth of liberality," giving not only "accord-ing to their means" but "beyond their means, of their own free will" even though in a situation of extreme poverty (2 Cor 8:2–3, RSV).

Paul does not call for the abolition of private property or for its transformation into joint ownership. But neither does he talk of people possessing a right to it. Any idea of rights is foreign to Paul. It cuts across all that he stands for. The gospel is about not the claiming of a right but the offering of a present. It is no accident that at the climax of his longest discussion on the sharing of possessions he breaks off into the exclamation, "Thanks be to God for his inexpressible gift" (2 Cor 9:15, RSV). All that the believer owns has to be viewed through the cross, feel its imprint, and become the basis for service to others. In some instances that will mean parting with things, particularly when there is more than enough; in others it will mean parting with some when there

---

[22] 1 Cor 13:3; 2 Cor 8:8; 9:11, 13.

is really less than enough. Just occasionally, as with Paul himself, it will mean parting with all and not even asking for recompense.

Paul's view of possessions goes beyond that characteristic of the Hellenistic associations. For Paul, the sharing of material possessions as a physical expression of fellowship was to take place voluntarily. Though the principle of mutual financial support also lay at the heart of club life, it was a carefully regulated affair and kept within calculated limits. In this respect it mirrored the general practice of philanthropy in the ancient world at this time, which was to desire reciprocal returns.[23] If other motives sometimes surfaced, these concerned the expectation of official honor being awarded to the donor.[24] Even where gifts were distributed without anything being received in return, it often took place on a quid pro quo basis, with the most worthy of the disadvantaged gaining most of what was dispersed.[25]

Unlike the Essenes,[26] Paul did not found communes as he moved around the ancient world, but this does not mean that he did not challenge common attitudes to property. Those who became members of his communities could never again look on what they owned with the same eyes.

---

[23] Cicero, De Officiis 1.15, 48. Seneca, De Beneficiis 2.35.
[24] Pliny, Epistulae 1.8, 15.
[25] Cicero, De Officiis 2.5.54. Pliny, Epistulae 9.30.
[26] Cf. 1QS 6.19ff.

9

—ɯ—

GIFTS AND MINISTRY

THE PURPOSE OF CHURCH: WORSHIP, MISSION, OR EDIFICATION?

One of the most puzzling features of Paul's understanding of *ekklesia* for his contemporaries, whether Jews or Gentiles, must have been his failure to say that a person went to church primarily to "worship." Not once in all his writings does he suggest this is the case. Indeed it could not be, for he held a view of "worship" that prevented him from doing so.

This is crystallized in his plea at the beginning of Rom 12:

> I appeal to you therefore, brothers and sisters, by the mercies of God, to present your bodies as a living sacrifice, holy and acceptable to God, which is your spiritual worship. Do not be conformed to this world, but be transformed by the renewing of your minds, so that you may discern what is the will of God — what is good and acceptable and perfect. (Rom 12:1–2, NRSV)

For Paul, worship is obedience rather than literal sacrifice and is rational or voluntary rather than ecstatic. This distinguishes Paul's view from that of the Jewish or Hellenistic cult. Paul certainly talks in the cultic language through which the Jewish worship of God was offered in the Temple. Such language would have been familiar to Gentile audiences as well, though their understanding of these terms would not generally have possessed the same moral dimension. The striking feature of Paul's statement, however, is his noncultic use of this language, that is, its metaphorical application to the sphere of everyday behavior. The spiritual or rational "worship" (*latreia*) that Christians are called upon to make requires them to offer (*parastesai*) their whole selves, bodies included, to God as a living sacrifice (*thusia*), dedicated (*hagia*) and acceptable to him. In practice this means behaving in such a way that all their actions are determined by God's will, which is by definition good and perfect, rather than by the characteristics of the times in which they live.

So worship involves the whole of one's life, every word and action, and knows no special place or time. The remainder of this section in Romans brings this out most forcibly. In turn, and without marking them off from one another, Paul discusses behavior in the Christian community, among other social circles, and at the political level (Rom 12:3–13:4). Since all places and times have now become the venue for worship, Paul cannot speak of Christians assembling in church *distinctively* for this purpose. They are already worshipping God, acceptably or unacceptably, in whatever they are doing. While this means that when they are in church they are worshipping as well, it is not worship per se but something else that marks off their coming together from everything else that they are doing.

This "something else" has in the past often been defined as "mission." According to this way of looking at things, the primary purpose of church is evangelism and/or social action. Paul does say a good deal about the importance of these, but he never suggests that they provide the basic rationale for church as such. He insists that Christians should "conduct themselves wisely towards outsiders, making the most of the time," and that this involves both their conversation with such people and their behavior towards them. They are to "do good to all," providing food and drink even for their enemies and are to "hold fast the word of life" by their uncomplaining and unargumentative way of life.[1] He envisages these things as taking place outside church, as there is "time" and "opportunity" among the contacts and circumstances of everyday life.

---

[1] Col 4:6; cf. Gal 6:10; Rom 12:14–21; Phil 2:14–16.

This does not rule out the possibility that evangelism and/or social action may occasionally happen within the gathering itself, but when it does so it is only as a by-product. He gives an illustration of this in 1 Cor 14. Having already defined prophecy as something that "edifies the church" (1 Cor 14:4) and as a gift for believers, not unbelievers (14:22), Paul says that "if all prophesy, an unbeliever or outsider who enters is reproved by all and called to account by all. After the secrets of the unbeliever's heart are disclosed, that person will bow down before God and worship him, declaring, 'God is really among you.' " (vv. 24–25, NRSV). All this is a consequence of Christians sharing the word of God *with one another* (not directly with the outsider)! We shall have more to say about this later, for the church indirectly involves itself in mission to the world outside its meetings in a variety of ways. But not in the first instance. The main reason for its activities lies elsewhere.

The purpose of church is the growth and edification of its members into Christ and into a common life through their God-given ministry to one another (1 Cor 14:12, 19, 26). We have seen that this takes place as they participate in a meal and share gifts with one another through the Spirit. These two activities probably led into each other (e.g., Acts 20:7–12), or the two were merged into a whole. The disciplinary meeting described in 1 Cor 5 appears to be simply part of the regular gathering (1 Cor 5:4–5), as does that involving the settling of disputes between Christians foreshadowed in the following chapter (1 Cor 6:5ff.). This is not to say that other occasional meetings never took place, for example, gatherings for prayer during a crisis situation (compare Acts 12:5) or gatherings of leaders when the calling together of the whole community was impracticable (Acts 20:17ff.). The most general form of meeting, however, centered around the eating of a meal and the exercise of ministry for each others' benefit.

THE DYNAMICS OF CHURCH: GIFTS AND MINISTRIES

This brings us to a consideration of Paul's understanding of *charisma*, "gift." This is the main, though not the only, term by which Paul refers to the Spirit's work through mutual ministry. His use of it has little precedent in the ancient world of his time. Though it occurs twice in an apocryphal[2] and once in a pseudepigraphical work,[3] the textual tradition underlying the first is not very secure and the second is almost certainly a post-Pauline reference. Paul's near contemporary, Philo of Alexandria, uses it twice in one passage. For all these the word means simply a "token of favor" in quite an ordinary sense.[4] In classical Greek literature the term *charisma* does not occur at all, while in the papyri there are only a few occurrences, all of them dating later than the NT. In these it also means "present" in the most general sense, without any religious significance attached. Though the word probably did not originate with Paul, he does appear to have been the first to give a technical meaning to it. Here, as with *ekklesia* and *soma*, we have a further example of Paul's utilizing a common term to describe some aspect of community life. But in the case of *charisma*, the term is given a more distinctive twist. This is something for which there does not appear to be any real parallel in the rest of his writings.

This term "gift" is important because it expresses the basic principle involved in Paul's approach to the dynamics of church. For a long time this was neglected or minimized in scholarly treatments of Paul's view of the church. Only in the last generation has its significance for Paul's thinking on this subject come to the forefront. But the term is not confined to passages in which the life of the Christian community is under discussion. The word has a wider reference, which gives a basic insight into its meaning and also provides the proper framework for understanding its other use.

"Gift" describes those privileges that Israel received at God's hands and rejected.[5] It refers to the saving work of Christ and the acquittal from condemnation that has been extended to many as a result (Rom 5:15–17). It also designates the gift of eternal life that can be experienced now as the alternative to sin's "wages" of death (6:23). Paul's use of *dorea* and *dorema* as synonyms for *charisma* in Romans 5:15–17 suggests we can include in this the reference to Christ himself (as "God's inexpressible gift,"[6]) and to

---

[2] Ecclus 7:33 (Codex B); 38:30 (Codex S).
[3] Sib. Or. 2:54.
[4] Philo, *Allegorical Interpretation* 3.78.
[5] Rom 11:29 (cf. 9:4–5).
[6] 2 Cor 9:15 (cf. Rom 9:5b).

faith, "which is God's gift" (Eph 2:8). So Paul can comprehend virtually the whole of God's saving activities vis-à-vis humanity in terms of gift: the sonship, the glory, the covenants, the giving of the Law, the worship and the promises, justification, faith, eternal life—even Christ himself. Paul could do this because the word stressed for him, at one and the same time, the freedom of God, the generous nature of God's dealings and, as a consequence, a person's grateful dependence upon God for all that he or she enjoys. These *charismata* are the fundamental gifts of God and undergird whatever other presents may be given to those who are in Christ.

Other gifts Paul mentions are also explicitly said to have God,[7] or alternatively Christ,[8] as their author. The Spirit's task is to "apportion" (1 Cor 12:11) them to every one and "manifest" (12:7; 14:12) them through individuals for the common good. Paul's prepositions indicate that the gifts are given "in accordance with," "by means of," "through" the Spirit, not "by" him. To talk of the "gifts of the Spirit," as if the Spirit were their source, is misleading. The gifts are derived not from the Spirit, *pneuma*, but from God's grace, *charis*.[9] They are its concrete expression.

The different terms used to describe the gifts bring to the fore different facets of their character, e.g., their revelatory character (*phanerosis*: manifestation), their dynamic quality (*energema*: effectual operation), and their social purpose (*diakonia*: service—1 Cor 12:4–6). They are thus said to be specific and effective ways in which God communicates to believers so that they may be corporately strengthened. Perhaps the words *charisma* or *charismata* themselves might be more appropriately translated as "grace" or "graces," thinking of these in a particular rather than general sense. The word "graces," for all its old-fashioned associations, does catch more of the flavor of the term than our overused and somewhat colorless word "gifts." Clearly the *charismata* are not temporary in character but ongoing features of the community's life. They are not given merely to help the churches get started but are intended as the main constituents of their gatherings so long as they continue to meet. According to Paul it is only when "that which is perfect is come" (13:10), when all communications

---

[7] 1 Cor 12:6, 28; Rom 12:3; Eph 3:7.
[8] 1 Cor 12:5; Eph 4:7, 8, 11.
[9] 1 Cor 1:4ff.; Rom 12:6; Eph 4:7.

of an intermediary character between God and humanity are abolished, that these gifts will come to an end.

Paul provides us with four main lists of the *charismata*, two within the same chapter. The word is also used in some isolated references to life outside the Christian community. We will leave these to one side for the moment.[10] We also have two other references—Paul's desire to share an undefined *charisma* with the Christians in Rome when he visits them ("undefined" because, until he has arrived, he does not know what contribution will be relevant, Rom 1:11) and his acknowledgment that the community in Corinth did not lack in *charisma* (1 Cor 1:7). The first of the four main lists mentions the following: the utterance of wisdom (special insight into the profundity and implications of the gospel);[11] knowledge (understanding of the OT and Christian traditions and capacity to expound them concretely); faith (with respect not to salvation but to a specific circumstance); healings (of various kinds in view of the plural, and of a nonmiraculous character in view of the distinction from the following gift); miraculous works (especially exorcisms); prophecy (knowing and speaking God's mind intuitively rather than deductively through the sacred writings); discernment of spirits (whether they are of God, are from a demonic source, or merely reflect a human opinion); glossolalia and the interpretation of glossolalia (the speaking and explaining of unknown, nonhuman languages—1 Cor 12:7–11). A reiteration of most of the items on this list occurs shortly afterwards, partly in terms of the persons to whom a gift has been given, partly in terms of the *charisma* itself. Also present are three additional *charismata*. This second list runs as follows: apostles, prophets, teachers, then miraculous works, healings, helps, administrations, various kinds of tongues, and the interpretation of tongues (1 Cor 12:28).

The remaining two lists are much briefer. One mentions prophecy, concrete acts of service, teaching, exhortation, financial aid (or the sharing of possessions), the ministry of guiding, and the carrying out of merciful actions to those in need (perhaps including the giving of financial aid—Rom 12:6–8). The other list talks about *domata* rather than *charismata*, and the persons who possess ministries appear to be themselves described as gifts.

---

[10] 1 Cor 7:7; 2 Cor 1:11; perhaps 1 Cor 7:17ff. (cf. Rom 11:29).
[11] Cf. Rom 11:33–35; 1 Cor 2:6–10.

Here we have apostles, prophets, evangelists, and pastors and teachers. The last two are bracketed together and probably refer to the one activity, as we shall see later (Eph 4:11). Two of these items, viz., apostleship[12] and financial aid,[13] are mentioned elsewhere as independently related to God's grace. Other gifts are referred to in different places in the NT but are not designated specifically as gifts. These are: apostleship,[14] prophecy,[15] evangelism (2 Cor 8:18), oversight (Phil 1:1), teaching (Gal 6:6; 2 Cor 8:7), exhortation (1 Thess 5:14), service,[16] miracles (Gal 3:1), faith (1 Cor 13:2; 2 Cor 8:7), and merciful actions (Gal 6:10; 1 Thess 5:14).

This last point raises the question of consistency in Paul's use of the term *charisma*. We can, in fact, detect a development in the understanding of "gifts" and his employment of the word. This idea is present in the earliest of his writings, but the terminology is absent. Thus, already in the Thessalonian letters we find reference to the activity of the Spirit in fellowship, the importance of prophecy, the obligation upon all to contribute, the need to test ministries, and so on. It is not until First Corinthians that Paul offers any extended teaching on the subject or uses the term *charisma* itself. Perhaps he is prompted by the particular situation that had arisen there. After that he discusses the matter in his most systematic letters, Romans and Ephesians. (Although *doma* rather than *charisma* is used in Ephesians, this probably arises from its presence in the LXX quotation of Ps 67:19[17] and not from any disinclination on the writer's part to use the word *charisma*.)

THE NATURE OF THE CHARISMATA

On the basis of these various lists, isolated references, and accompanying remarks, the following conclusions may be drawn about the nature of the *charismata*.

---

[12] Eph 3:7 (*dorea*).
[13] Phil 4:17 (*doma*).
[14] 1 Cor 3:5; Rom 16:17; Phil 2:25; Eph 2:20.
[15] 1 Thess 5:19–20; 1 Cor 13:2, 14 passim; Eph 2:20.
[16] 1 Cor 16:15; Rom 16:1; Phil 1:1; Col 4:7, 12, 17; Eph 6:21.
[17] Ps 68:18 in English translations.

Open-ended in character

To begin with, these lists contain *charismata* of both word and deed and are clearly intended to be open-ended. Neither individually nor as a group do they exhaust the possibilities for spoken and practical ministry within the community. The mention of particular *charismata* within the lists springs from the nature of the audience and the type of group to whom Paul is writing. The Corinthian community, we are told elsewhere, met as a "whole" church and in house groups. They favored the more extraordinary gifts—-both of these factors are reflected in the wide range and specific items in the lists given in chapter 12. In Romans we have a briefer list. At first this list appears to be more random in character, but perhaps it corresponds to the kinds of gifts most frequently exercised in the smaller house church (or domestic groups) in which Christians largely gathered in that city, the former being familiar to Paul through his previous association with Aquila and Priscilla. In Ephesians we have an even more restricted and structured list which, in accordance with the circular nature of the letter, mainly concerns itself with the itinerant and significant local ministries. Thus Paul nowhere attempts to provide a systematic or full description of the gifts available to the Christian community. Indeed it is reasonable to assume on the basis of the gifts included in these lists, that any instructive contribution of a constant nature from any member of the community would be recognized by Paul as a gift.

Individually, but not evenly, distributed

Each person within the community receives at least one *charisma* for the benefit of his or her fellows.[18] But not all have the same gift,[19] and some have obviously been granted more gifts than others. The *charismata* are not distributed equally by the Spirit. Paul himself exercises a very large number of them—virtually all the gifts he mentions in his list.[20] Though there is a democratic element in the Spirit's way of proceeding, no egalitarian principle

---

[18] 1 Cor 12:7, 11; Rom 12:3; Eph 4:7.
[19] 1 Cor 12:29–30; Rom 12:6; Eph 4:11.
[20] E.g., Paul in 1 Thess 2:7ff.; 2 Thess 2:15; Gal 2:2; 1 Cor 1:1; 2 Cor 12:1, 6, 14, 18; Rom 15:19; Acts 20:10, 34.

is involved. Nor does Paul envisage the possession of a gift as always a static affair, so that the type of contribution each member makes to the life of the community has a fixed character about it. Paul can encourage his readers to seek after gifts that they do not as yet exercise (1 Cor 14:1).

Ranked according to their benefits

This brings us to a further point. Paul describes the gifts to which people should especially aspire as "higher" or more significant than others (1 Cor 12:31). We have already seen that in two of the four lists there is a ranking of gifts or of the ministries proceeding from them. These are not to be graded according to their form, with priority given to the most extraordinary manifestations. This was the Corinthian error. Paul's lists demonstrate that quite ordinary, practical actions are more valuable than those dramatic ones, such as glossolalia, that the Corinthians prized. He wishes to eradicate any distinction between gifts made on the basis of appearance. Rather, the gifts are graded on the basis of their effect; those that make the most profitable contribution to the community's growth are accorded the highest importance.

One of the interesting things resulting from this is that, generally speaking, certain gifts of speech predominate over those of deed. Understandably enough Paul gives first place to apostles, for without their preaching of the gospel and binding together of their converts the communities would not exist. Behind this ministry lies the possession of "wisdom," which for Paul signifies special insight into God's saving plan and its benefits for his hearers. Yet despite its preeminent position, Paul never says that his ministry is derived from a particular charisma, e.g., apostleship, but only from *charis* in general (Rom 12:3; Eph 3:7). The reason for this could be that the apostle exercises all the basic gifts (see footnote 19). These form a necessary part of his equipment if his communities are to be founded on the broadest possible base. His leaving them then provides the opportunity for the same range of gifts to develop within the communities themselves.

Second are the prophets, for they communicate to the community those things that it needs to hear directly from God for its concrete encouragement, admonition, and direction. Teachers come next, for they are able charismatically to draw specific insights from what God has already done or said and to extrapolate practical challenges for the present. Behind these two stand the gifts of communicating "revelation" and "knowledge" respectively. But to some extent the importance of these "higher" gifts is relative. A "lower" gift, such as glossolalia, when complemented by another gift, the gift of interpretation for instance, can become equivalent to a "higher" one (1 Cor 14:5b). One can also infer from Paul's writings that, according to the specific needs of the community at a given time, a gift that is generally of lesser value than another, for example teaching in comparison with prophecy, may be temporarily more relevant to the situation at hand.

Regularly and occasionally contributed

The existence of these "higher" gifts reminds us that some exercise a *charisma* in a regular fashion, providing the basis for a continuing ministry, while others exercise it only in an intermittent or occasional manner. All, according to Paul, ought to and can prophesy,[21] but only some have an ongoing ministry of this kind and can therefore be regarded as "prophets" (1 Cor 12:29). Paul does not see a qualitative distinction between members on the basis of their exercise of a gift, merely a quantitative difference in the *frequency* with which they exercise it and (perhaps) the scope of the message they communicate. Both the "higher" gifts and those low on the scale of charismatic priorities can become the bases for a regular ministry, designated by Paul through a description of their function, rather than a title (12:30).

Not only new but renewed

Paul questions not only the priority of the more spectacular gifts but also any distinction between ordinary and extraordinary manifestations. In his lists both lie side by side, for example, "miraculous works" and "gifts of healing" are alongside "helpful deeds" and "practical guidance" (1 Cor 12:28). This raises a related question: to what extent are these gifts to be regarded as natural phenomena and to what extent as purely supernatural affairs?

The distinction really begs the question, for it is not one that Paul would have made. He certainly stresses the "newness" of the gifts, i.e., their distribution by the Spirit whom the Christians are

---

[21] 1 Cor 14:5a; perhaps 14:31.

now experiencing. Paul talks elsewhere about the "newness" of the whole life of the converted person: "So if anyone is in Christ, there is a new creation: everything old has passed away; see, everything has become new!" (2 Cor 5:17, NRSV). Paul does not mean that the Christian is a completely different person. He is pointing to the radical change that takes place when a person genuinely encounters God in Christ. Paul's language about "gifts" should not be taken to rule out altogether their connection with created capacities implanted by God or with social advantages conferred by God's providence. (We can see certain continuities between Paul's previous capacities and his current gifts, and later we shall call attention to links between people's social position and their Christian ministry.) Such abilities are renewed (passing through their own "crucifixion" and "resurrection"), along with all other aspects of the personality, and activated by the Spirit to achieve their full potential when there is a service to be performed.

Exercised on any appropriate occasion

In all the writings where lists of charismata occur, the primary context for Paul's discussion is not the "church" but the "body," not the gathering of the Christians together but the local Christian community itself.[22] Though gifts are certainly, even preeminently, exercised in church, they are also exercised on other occasions when Christians are in contact with one another. It follows from this that those who have continuing ministries within the community would engage in these while church is in progress, as well as at other times.

There is another aspect to this. Since Paul has the local Christian "body" in view in these passages, only when "all" are assembled can the full range of gifts given to the community become evident. This does not mean that smaller gatherings are invalid, but it does mean that in the meetings of the "house churches" there will not be as broad a representation of gifts as in the gatherings of the "whole church." On the other hand, the restrictions that Paul imposes on the number of people who can participate in the meetings of the "whole church" (1 Cor 14:27–33) would not have been necessary in the gatherings of the smaller "house church" groups.

---

[22] 1 Cor 12:12–27; Rom 12:4–6; Eph 4:4, 12–16.

10

—⚬—

CHARISMA AND ORDER

Thus far we have described the place of gifts in the community in theory. But how are they to operate in practice? To answer this we need to analyze the actual exercise of the gifts in the community and Paul's approach to *taxis*, or "order." We commence with a closer inspection of the purpose of gifts.

THE IMPORTANCE AND BREADTH OF EDIFICATION

Paul insists that gifts were granted to individuals not primarily for their own enjoyment but rather for the edification or building up of the community (1 Cor 12:7; Eph 4:12). Though he recognizes the legitimacy of a private use of *charisma*, only in a very limited way is it appropriate in church (1 Cor 14:28). There the service of others, not oneself, should be in view. In fact, it is precisely through seeking to fulfill the needs of others, rather than an individual quest for the *charismata* themselves, that various members of the community will come into a greater experience of the gifts (1 Cor 14:12). This reverses the procedure that was apparently in operation at Corinth where the charismatic aspirations of the individual were considered instead of the common good of the community. The basic principle that Paul lays down for the conduct of church is that "all things should be done for edification" (1 Cor 14:26). Only when a contribution has this as its object should it be exercised.

This idea of edification requires closer attention, for Paul has a much broader understanding of it than is generally recognized. Edification can take place in a number of different, though ultimately complementary, ways. This becomes apparent when the various aspects of community life served by the gifts are identified, even though most *charismata* fall into more than one category.

Some gifts are primarily directed towards the community's *growth of understanding* of God, the community itself, outsiders, the world. This cognitive aspect of the community's life is particularly served through the exercise of prophecy, teaching, exhortation, discernment of spirits, and interpretation, though all of these also involve personal conviction and practical action, not just intellectual appreciation. Knowledge, we have seen, is as much doing as thinking, as much commitment as reflection.

A second group of gifts is primarily directed towards the *psycho-social well-being* of the community, i.e., the integrity and harmony of the group and of its members. Important are the gifts that have a pastoral orientation, for example, practical "helps," "acts of mercy," and the pastoral gift itself. As these gifts are exercised, the psychological needs of the members are met and the social cohesion of the group sustained.

A third group is primarily directed towards the *physical welfare* of the community. Paul never suggests that the *charismata* affect only the spiritual dimension of those whom they serve. The rendering of financial assistance, the exercise of gifts of healing, and the occasional performance of miraculous works are all practical. The "body" of Christ, or the gathering of the "church," is not merely a communication of hearts, minds, or souls but a fellowship of persons physically in contact with each other as well.

A fourth group of gifts appears to be directed towards what we might call the *unconscious life* of the community. There are things, says Paul, that our spirit wishes to communicate with God and our conscious minds are unaware of (Rom 8:26–27). It is the function of speaking in tongues and singing in the Spirit to make this communication possible. The one who engages in either of these activities "utters mysteries in the Spirit" (1 Cor 14:2) and "prays with the Spirit" (1 Cor 14:15), though they should seek for an interpretation so that their mind does not remain "unfruitful" (1 Cor 14:13f.).

This means the gifts have been designed by God to encompass every aspect of the community's life. Since the individuals within it are inextricably bound up with the relationships, obligations, and structures of the world around them, the gifts must also concern these aspects of the members' activities. For that reason the content of church must sometimes have been quite "everyday" or "secular." Nor are aesthetic aspects of people's personalities excluded from this process. References made to "singing in the Spirit" (spiritual songs), "psalms" (sung teaching), and "hymns" (sung prophecy)[1] remind us that this is not left out. In addition, the passionate enthusiasm characteristic of Paul's thinking and the depth of feeling invested in Paul's ministry— from his outpouring of love at one end of the spectrum to his agonies of anxiety at the other—emphasize the emotional dimension of exercising the gifts. The breadth of charismatic activity in the community is very marked indeed, and the levels at which edification can take place are very diverse in character.

THE EXERCISE OF GIFTS

In a proportionate way

Paul consistently argues for a proportionate exercise of the gifts in the community's gatherings, though once again he does not do this based on some egalitarian principle. Because he regards some gifts as more fundamental than others, he wishes more time to be given to these. Prophecy and teaching (1 Cor 14:6) and those gifts directed towards growth of the community's understanding are for him the most important. He closely associates teaching with pastoral care (1 Thess 5:12–14), since it is through the discerning ministry of the word that personal help is frequently given. This indicates that gifts directed to the psychological and social harmony of the community are never far from view.

Paul still insists that lesser gifts should not be ignored just because others are more inherently helpful. The higher gifts should not dominate the meeting in too unbalanced a way (1 Cor 14:29). Partly for this reason he places a restriction on the number

---

[1] 1 Cor 14:26; Col 3:16; Eph 5:19.

of contributions of even the most important gifts that should be made during any gathering of the "whole church." Responsibility devolves to the individual possessors of gifts, as well as to the community as a whole, to ensure that a discerning balance of gifts is present, for only so can all aspects of church life develop in proper relation to one another.

Within an intelligible context

In view of Paul's emphasis upon gifts that deepen understanding, it comes as no surprise that one of the main criteria by which contributions are judged is their intelligibility. His view of glossolalia provides a good illustration of this principle at work. "If you speak in tongues that are unintelligible" he says, "how will anyone know what is said? For you will be speaking into the air" (1 Cor 14:9). It is the new member and interested outsider who are at a particular disadvantage here and who are likely to receive the wrong impression as to the purpose of church (14:16, 23). Paul does not wish to prohibit the *charisma* itself, for it is a genuine gift of the Spirit and is an edifying way of communicating with God (14:2, 39). In fact, the gift is not without rational content; it is just that this content is *hidden* from the mind of the person giving expression to it. That is why Paul directly encourages those who exercise the gift to pray for the ability to interpret it (14:13ff.) and speaks of others within the community who have a particular ministry of interpretation (14:27–28). The gift's incommunicability, not its irrationality, makes its presence inappropriate in the gatherings. The whole spirit of Paul's outlook is crystallized in his statement: "I thank God that I speak in tongues more than you all; nevertheless, in church I would rather speak five words with my mind, in order to instruct others, than ten thousand words in a tongue" (14:18–19).

Evoking a discerning assessment

Each member must think through to a proper estimate of the kind of contribution he or she can make to the community's life. Believers should not overestimate their abilities here, i.e., think they have a gift when they do not (Rom 12:3; Eph 4:7) or exercise one out of proportion to their possession of it (Rom 12:6). It is through discernment that the truth and value of contributions are to be gauged. The prophets particularly, but in fact all the members, should be involved in this. They are, says Paul, to "test everything" (1 Thess 5:21) and "weigh what is said" (1 Cor 14:29), even if uttered by someone claiming to be under prophetic inspiration. All is to be tested by the original gospel (Gal 1:8), the apostolic tradition (2 Thess 2:15), church practice elsewhere (1 Cor 14:33), previous experience (Phil 3:16), the spirit accompanying the gift (1 Cor 13:1ff.), and its constructive character (1 Cor 14:26). So, recognition of gifts, realization of their limits, and evaluation of others' contributions are related criteria used to determine the character of gatherings.

Under the individual's self-control

All these principles of "church order" presuppose the importance of self-control on the part of those exercising the gifts. It is a mark of the genuine operation of the *charismata* that members do not compete but follow one another in an orderly sequence (1 Cor 14:27b, 30–31, 40). This is within the control of those making contributions to the meeting, even with respect to the more spectacular gifts. Paul insists that "the spirits of the prophets are subject to the prophets" (14:32). The timing of their contributions lies within their power; they are quite able to restrain themselves if another has a more relevant contribution to make (14:30). Similarly with glossolalia. If no interpreter is present, those who have this gift are to refrain from giving expression to it (14:28). If an interpreter is present, however, two or three may exercise the gift in turn (14:27). For Paul it is clear that neither prophecy nor glossolalia are ecstatic phenomena that the speaker has no control over. On the contrary, both can be integrated in an orderly way into the gatherings.

Within a framework of love

Finally, all contributions must take place within the framework of loving behavior between the members. Here we come to the most basic principle of all, one that Paul expresses in all his discussions of gifts.[2] Exercise of one's gift, however wholehearted, is unproductive without love (1 Cor 13:1–3). Paul defines

[2] 1 Cor 13 passim; Rom 12:8–9; Eph 4:15.

love in terms of the fruit of the Spirit in his letter to the Galatians (Gal 5:22). Since love is not "rude," does not "insist on its own way," and is not "jealous or boastful," it is easy to see its relevance to some of the criteria we have already identified (1 Cor 13:4ff.). Such things as allowing others to contribute their gifts without interruption, submitting one's own revelations to the testing of others, and having a proper estimate of one's own abilities have their roots in a loving attitude towards other members of the community. The gifts and fruit of the Spirit are bound together (so inextricably in fact that the same term can occur in lists of both, though with a different emphasis, i.e., *pistis*, faith).[3] Exercise of the one without the presence of the other leads to chaos in the gatherings, unfruitfulness in understanding, and derision on the part of outsiders. Only when the two occur together is proper order and genuine edification present.

THE SPIRIT AND ORDER

Although we have thus far viewed the gifts chiefly from the perspective of those who exercise them, the sovereign control of the Spirit over the order that results from their appropriate expression should now be brought into focus. The gifts are and remain his to direct. This means that the fellowship of Christians is through and through a divine "gift" rather than a human "work." The Spirit does not allow a random or fluctuating distribution of the gifts, and there should be no uncertainty within the community as to the functions different members have. For God is "not a God of confusion but of peace" (1 Cor 14:33). The Spirit's sovereignty over the gifts results in a stable, though not inflexible, distribution within the community and in their orderly, though not fixed, interplay in the gatherings. In so working, the Spirit does not arbitrarily or coercively force gifts upon people but works through their wills in a way that safeguards their integrity and freedom. In the same way, their exercise is not signaled by an overwhelming experience over which they have no control. Throughout this whole process the Spirit respects and does not violate the wills of the persons involved.

---

[3] Cf. Gal 5:22; 1 Cor 12:9.

So then, provided certain basic principles of the Spirit's operation are kept in view: balance, intelligibility, evaluation, orderliness, and loving exercise, Paul sees no need to lay down any fixed rules for the community's proceedings. There is no one order proper for its meetings; any order is proper so long as these criteria are observed. Paul therefore has no interest in constructing a fixed liturgy. This would restrict the freedom of God's communications. Each gathering of the community will have a structure, but it will emerge naturally from the particular combination of the gifts exercised.

This structure will vary from gathering to gathering and from community to community. Within this, fixed liturgical elements such as psalms, doxologies, blessings, responses (e.g., amen, maranatha), credal statements, traditional formulae, scripture passages, and hymns have their place.[4] However, there is no suggestion that the reading aloud of the OT, as opposed to its use in charismatic evangelizing, prophesying, and teaching, was a regular element in the community's gatherings. Certain decisions on the form of the meeting obviously were sometimes made in advance.[5] So the Spirit's order was not the result of a purely spontaneous exercise of the gifts. The form and content of the early Christian gatherings were determined partly beforehand and partly during the occasion itself.

Paul's notion of *charisma* cuts across the distinction between formal and extempore contributions. All is to be governed by the Spirit, and the possibility of a fresh word from the Spirit interrupting the proceedings is always present (1 Cor 14:30). Taking all this into account, it becomes clear why the notion of order (*taxis*) could never become a central idea in Paul's understanding of community life. The word, in fact, occurs only twice in all his writings.[6] Order is important, but it is not a primary concern. If the basic principles of Christian ministry and behavior are observed, then order naturally follows. Where order is lacking, it is remedied by attending more seriously to those principles that have been transgressed.

---

[4] 1 Cor 14:26; Col 3:16; Eph 5:19; also Rom 15:9ff.; 16:25–27; 2 Cor 13:13; 1 Cor 16:22; Gal 6:18; Rom 1:3–4; Gal 6:4; Eph 4:8; Phil 2:6–11.
[5] Cf. Acts 20:7–11.
[6] 1 Cor 14:40; (in a different sense) Col 2:5.

OTHER CONTEMPORARY APPROACHES TO CHARISMA

Though Paul first gave the word *charisma* a technical meaning, both Judaism and Hellenism were familiar with aspects of the phenomenon.

The rabbinic Judaism of Paul's time was convinced that the Spirit had temporarily departed from Israel.[7] The apocalyptic Judaism at Qumran had a somewhat Hellenized view of the Spirit's operation.[8] These views tended to push charismatic concerns to the periphery. Insofar as the rabbis viewed God as still active in Israel's life[9] and Essene groups or some Galilean rabbis[10] possessed stronger charismatic interests (e.g., in prophecy, healing etc.), some common ground with Paul existed. But the centrality Paul gave to the *charismata* in the community's gatherings and the insight he demonstrated into their operation had no parallel in these circles.

A different picture presents itself in Hellenistic religious circles. Interest in the more extraordinary charismatic phenomena, particularly those of an ecstatic kind, was widespread in both the mystery cults and certain aspects of traditional religion. But these were restricted to certain individuals and were not a community experience. An excellent example of this is the philosopher-wonderworker Apollonius of Tyana, who was frequently said to prophesy and heal. Greek terms utilized by Hellenistic religions to describe such happenings include *ekstasis*, *entheos*, *empneusis*, *enthusiamos*, and probably *pneumata*, which is also mentioned by Paul in 1 Corinthians.[11] (In using that term, Paul is almost certainly echoing, not endorsing, the Corinthian view that prophecy overwhelms the person and compels them to say "Jesus be cursed" rather than "Jesus is Lord," 1 Cor 12:3.)

Paul describes these charismatic experiences outside Christianity in terms of people being manipulated by idols so that they

---

[7] *m. Sot.* 9.15.

[8] 1QS 3.17ff.; 4.18ff.

[9] Josephus, *Antiquities* 13.46–49; 15.373–379; 17.345–348.

[10] *m. Ber.* 5.5; *m. Ta'an.* 3.8; *m. Sot.* 9.5. Josephus, *Antiquities* 14.22–24; cf. 17.43 (?).

[11] 1 Cor 14:12; note especially 12:10.

have no control over what they say or do. What marks off the Christian exercise of the *charismata*, including prophecy and glossolalia, is its basis in a relationship with one whose gifts are subject to the control of those who receive them (1 Cor 12:2). Paul's desire to distinguish such gifts from their Hellenistic counterfeits leads him to avoid all the customary Greek words for ecstatic experiences and turn the Corinthians' attention away from the term *pneumata*. Instead he almost uniformly uses his own term *charisma*. Just occasionally he employs the term *pneumatikos*,[12] which he can take up because elsewhere he uses it of other aspects of Christian experience.[13]

PAUL'S IDEA OF COMMUNITY: ITS DISTINCTIVENESS

We are now in a position to identify more precisely the basic difference that marks out Paul's view of community from that of his contemporaries. We have already seen that by his integration of the notions of "commonwealth" and "household" into his understanding of "church," Paul's view is broader than its parallels. His understanding of identity and unity within the church, of the significance of the meal, and of ministry and order also possesses distinctive accents.

But there is more. For the members of Jewish religious associations, such as at Qumran and among the Pharisees, life centered primarily around a *code*, as embodied in the Torah.[14] This lay at the basis of the blessings, readings, expositions, confessions, and prayers that formed the content of the synagogue services. For the members of the Hellenistic religious associations, life centered primarily around a *cult*, with dramatic rituals, processions, and mystical experiences.[15] This cult provided the basic rationale for its activities. According to Paul's understanding,

---

[12] 1 Cor 12:1; 14:1 (cf. 14:37); Rom 1:11.
[13] E.g., 1 Cor 2:13; 9:11; 15:44; Rom 15:27; Col 3:16; Eph 1:3.
[14] Philo, *Embassy to Gaius* 156; *On Dreams* 2.127; *Life of Moses* 2.215–216. Josephus, *Jewish War* 2.301; *Antiquities* 19.300, 305. *m. Yom.* 7.1; *m. Meg.* 3–4; *m. Sot.* 7.7–8; *m. 'Ab.* 1.1–2.
[15] Apuleius, *Metamorphoses* 11 passim. Plutarch, *Isis and Osiris* 2ff.

Christian life centers primarily around *fellowship*, expressed in word and deed, of the members with God and one another. Paul's conception demonstrates concretely the already experienced reconciliation between the individual, God, and others and reveals that the gifts and fruit of the Spirit are instruments through which this reconciliation is expressed and deepened.

This means that the focal point of reference for Paul's communities is neither a book nor a rite, neither a code nor a cult, but a set of relationships. God primarily communicates to them, not through the written word and tradition or mystical experience and cultic activity, but through one another. Certainly fellowship is not altogether lacking in these other groups, and the OT scriptures and various corporate activities are present in the Pauline churches. But a real difference lies at the heart of their respective gatherings.

This makes it impossible for Paul to have derived his approach from the practice of the synagogue or of the cults. For him something quite new has broken into human experience, and this is nothing less than the "first fruits" of that community between God and the people that will be ushered in at the Last Day. Paul's view arises from his understanding of the gospel and the Spirit and has only secondary points of overlap with the synagogue and virtually nothing in common with the cults. But since even the synagogue's worship is based in an order that is "passing away" (2 Cor 3:4–11), Paul does not begin with the synagogue and "Christianize" it. Nothing in his writings suggests that the order of the synagogue service or the central features of its worship, i.e., the Shema, Eighteen Benedictions, or Priestly Blessing, played a part in the meetings of his communities. He integrates elements of synagogue practice only insofar as they are compatible with the Gospel and the Spirit, frequently altering their emphasis and presentation.

Paul's approach is revolutionary in the ancient world. In view of subsequent developments—in which Catholicism increasingly followed the path of the cults in making a rite the center of its activities, and Protestantism followed the path of the synagogue in placing a book at the center of its services—it would be true to say that in most respects it remains no less revolutionary today. Of course the Bible and communion are fundamental to what takes place in church, but church should not be reduced to "word and sacrament." There is more to the Spirit's presence and work than this.

11

—ᴍ—

UNITY IN DIVERSITY AMONG THE MEMBERS

We have seen that individual Christians come together as a church to share gifts with one another and to join in certain corporate activities. Within this each member of the gathering has his or her particular contribution to make. Since all have some thing to give, there are no mere spectators in church but only active participants. In turning now to look more closely at the participants themselves, we need to inquire whether the early churches preserved the various distinctions that were drawn between people in the ancient world at that time. In this chapter and the next, Paul's attitude towards these distinctions will occupy our attention.

THE OVERCOMING OF RACE, CLASS, AND GENDER DISTINCTIONS

Tendencies in Graeco-Roman society

In the Roman Empire of Paul's day distinctions along national, social, and gender lines existed. Those who had a common nationality, were free, male, or Roman citizens possessed real privileges, if also responsibilities.

However, a blurring of the distinctions was gradually taking place. Though social status still remained the principal criterion by which people were evaluated, many slaves occupied high managerial or bureaucratic positions and this cut across many lines of differentiation. For the most part, women were regarded as second class citizens during this time. But in some parts of the Empire, in the Eastern provinces and to a lesser extent in Rome, they were able to participate in public, commercial, and religious life, own property, and have a relatively independent existence. Public thinking and practice moved in a more tolerant direction as a result of philosophers who talked of a universal republic embracing all people.[1] People began to recognize that legal slavery and freedom had little to do with inward bondage or liberty,[2] and there were occasional pleas for more equality between men and women.[3]

The breakthrough in Paul's letters

Paul's thinking does not begin with the differences that divide people from one another but with the differences that divide all people from God. He describes the Christian community as uniting all (irrespective of nationality, social position, or gender) who acknowledge the death and resurrection of Christ, experience the power of the Spirit, and look forward to the coming of God's kingdom. These believers all share in a common salvation that has its roots in certain past events, its reality in the present experience of liberation, and its culmination in a future life of a qualitatively new kind. In all these respects no distinctions between Christians can be made. What they now have in common has been given freely as a gift to them all.

An individual's national identity or heritage gives no advantage here. "God shows no partiality" at this point, says Paul. Since "all have fallen short" of God's ideals, "no distinction" can be made between people on these grounds (e.g., Rom 3:22b–23). The fact that some belong to a nation favored by God, i.e., the Jewish nation (3:1–2a; 9:4–5), is of no account here. For those who have responded to the gospel message "there is no distinction be-

---

[1] Plutarch, De Alexandri Fortuna 1, 6. Philo, On Joseph 6.28–31. Seneca, De Otio 4.31. Cf. Marcus Aurelius, Meditations 6.44.

[2] Epictetus, Dissertationes 2.1.27; 4.1.1–5, 89. Cf. Dio Chrysostom, Orationes 14.18; 15.29–30.

[3] Especially by Musonius Rufus, Fragments III–IV.

tween Jew and Greek." "Everyone" who declares allegiance to Christ will be accepted by him and given membership into his community.[4] In fact, non-Jews who follow this course are said to inherit all that the Jews have received in the past. They have been grafted in, says Paul, to the Jewish olive tree (11:17ff.). They can claim Abraham as their ancestor and have become heirs of all that was promised to him (Gal 3:29; Rom 4:16–17). "By one Spirit we were all baptized into one body—whether Jews or Greeks . . . —and all were made to drink of the one Spirit" (1 Cor 12:13).

The same principle of common status applies despite an individual's social position. In these matters "there is neither slave nor free . . . for you are all one in Christ Jesus" (Gal 3:28, RSV), all recipients of the one Spirit (1 Cor 12:13), and consequently all members of the one community (Col 3:11). In a sense there has been a reversal of conditions, for "whoever was called as a slave is a freed person in the Lord, while whoever was free when called is a slave of Christ" (1 Cor 7:22). In fact, the free are to regard the slave "no longer as a slave, but more than a slave, . . . both in the flesh and in the Lord."[5] This principle also relates to other indicators of social prestige such as intellectual ability, political authority, or aristocratic rank. Though some people in the community possessed advantages of this kind, these did not place them in any privileged position vis-à-vis God (1 Cor 1:26–29). God's action in Christ is the real criterion of wisdom, power, and dignity (1:30). Members of the community should reject the way the world evaluates these and instead recognize that all believers are members of the one family (1:26; 2:1 et al). In the community intellectual, political, or social status are irrelevant.

This principle of equality also operates in the area of gender differences. Regarding entry into the community "there is neither male nor female; for you are all one in Christ Jesus" (Gal 3:28, RSV). If, as is most likely the case, this phrase recalls the very similar wording in Gen 1:27, it forms a climax to what precedes it. Paul is arguing that in Christ not only conventional distinctions of religious allegiance or social rank are banished, but even the primeval gender distinction has ceased to be relevant. This may have implications for the homosexual/heterosexual distinction that exists between people. Though Paul does not discuss this

---

[4] Gal 3:11; 2 Cor 5:16; Rom 10:12–13; cf. Rom 2:11.
[5] Phlm 16; cf. Col 4:9.

issue in the kind of context we are considering here, it would seem that a homosexual background was no bar to membership in the church nor grounds for being regarded in a different light (1 Cor 6:9–11). His remarks elsewhere indicate that he would not have tolerated continuing homosexual relations on the part of such a person (Rom 1:26–27). But then he does not tolerate "adulterers . . . the greedy, nor drunkards, nor revilers" in the community either.[6]

Comparisons with other religious groups

So, all are in the same position concerning their basis for membership in the community. This is an advance upon contemporary attitudes in Judaism. Only by becoming a full citizen could a non-Jew find entry into Jewish religious groups. Even the synagogue, with its open-door policy to Gentiles who embraced monotheism and the commandments but were unwilling to become circumcised, regarded these Gentiles only as second-order members of their assemblies.[7] Occasionally Gentiles were the synagogue's principal benefactors (e.g., Luke 7:5), and in these cases they did receive appreciation and formal honor. In the mystery cults a more flexible situation existed. While the initial impetus for their spread in foreign countries generally came from expatriate citizens, e.g., soldiers, tradespersons, and people involved in commerce, over a period of time the dominant positions in the cult passed into the hands of local supporters.

While slavery was not nearly as common among the Jews as elsewhere, the more wealthy and politically influential members of the population did practice it,[8] and Jewish subjects could become slaves for up to six years as a way of paying off their debts.[9] Most slaves were aliens who soon became Jewish citizens so that their masters could associate with them without infringing the law. In fact, their religious obligations were the subject of special legislation, particularly in the Temple.[10] Since they were not obliged to observe all the requirements of the Law[11] their

---

[6] 1 Cor 6:9–10; cf. Rom 1:29–32.
[7] Acts 10:28; cf. 10:22.
[8] *m. R. Sh.* 1.7. Josephus, *Antiquities* 20.205, 207.
[9] Josephus, *Antiquities* 4.273; 16.3. Cf. Exod 21:2; Deut 15:12.
[10] *m. Pes.* 8.2 and see *m. B. M.* 1.5; *m. 'Arak.* 8.4ff.; *m. M. Sh.* 4.4.
[11] *m. Ber.* 3.3; *m. Sukk.* 2.1, 8.

involvement in the synagogue may have been circumscribed. This probably did not affect their participation in corporate prayer or, if the slaves were men, hearing instruction, but would most likely have prevented them from holding any of the offices. The mystery cults appealed strongly to slaves and freepeople and welcomed them openly. Slaves could become priests of the cult alongside their social betters. But it does not appear that the higher priestly grades were open to them, and the expenses involved in becoming even an initiate must have hindered many from proceeding this far.[12] Still, they provided a group to identify with that was less class conscious than most. (It should not be forgotten that due to the increasing number of slaves born within households during this period, many were treated as members of the family and could sometimes rise to positions of considerable responsibility. On the whole they could expect to be given their freedom at a relatively early age in adult life.)

Within both Jewish and Graeco-Roman religion, women generally possessed secondary importance. Women and daughters were included within the Jewish covenant, but the basic rite of circumcision was for males only.[13] This later rabbinic prayer that was recommended for daily use, while it may not necessarily reflect first-century attitudes, does show that this inferior estimation lingered: "Blessed be God who has not made me . . . a woman."[14] Among the Cynic philosophers we do find an insistence upon equality—of race, birth, and sex—that corresponds with Paul's, but the Cynic's lack of interest in community meant that equality was viewed in highly individualistic terms.[15] While wholesale importation of the mystery cults gave women an increasingly recognized position, the records we possess nowhere contain so explicit a declaration as that in Gal 3:28: "There is neither Jew nor Greek, there is neither slave nor free, there is neither male nor female; for you are all one in Christ Jesus" (RSV).

With Gal 3:28 Paul canceled national, social, and gender distinctions that still separated individuals within the ancient world. Fellowship with God and with one another was no longer limited by these differences. But this should not lead us into a false impression of what he is asserting. Paul's stress is not so

---

[12]Apuleius, Metamorphoses 11.17, 23, 27–28.
[13]Cf. Gen 17:10ff. et al.
[14]t. Ber. 7, 18, 16.
[15]E.g., Diogenes Laertius 6.72.

much upon the equality of Jews and Greeks, free and slave, men and women as upon their unity in Christ. (The same emphasis can be found in the similar statement in Colossians 3:11, though this does not include reference to overcoming gender distinctions.[16]) This is an important point to grasp. The emphasis lies on their shared integration into Christ, not on the new status disadvantaged groups have acquired vis-à-vis others.

Also, Paul's remarks do not imply that differences between groups disappear as a result of what has now happened. As his comments elsewhere indicate,[17] even within the new community forged by Christ, Jews and Greeks continue to exist alongside one another as Jews and Greeks, as do slaves and free, men and women. He does not deny the continuing legitimacy of national, social, and gender differences—Paul is no advocate of a universal, classless, and unisex society—he merely affirms that these differences do not affect one's relationship with Christ and membership in the community. There is an egalitarian strain in Paul's pronouncement, but it is secondary. He is more interested in the unity the gospel brings than in its equality, and in this unity diversity is preserved rather than uniformity imposed.

THE REDIRECTION OF RACE, CLASS, AND GENDER DISTINCTIONS

This diversity can be demonstrated by considering ways in which the differences between each of these groups continued to play some part in the life of Paul's communities.

Jews and Gentiles in the communities

Most of Paul's communities contained a reasonable proportion of Jews. As long as Paul's preaching in the cities began in the synagogue, this was bound to be the case, though God-fearers probably responded more freely to his message and formed the numerical base of his churches. In some places, such as Philippi,

---

[16]See also Eph 2:11ff.
[17]1 Cor 1:14; 16:15; Rom 16:3ff.; Col 4:10, 11; Acts 13:43; 14:1; 16:1; 17:4, 12; 18:2, 8; 19:9.

a Gentile Christian community seems to have existed from the start, but this was the exception.[18] Although, as we have seen, the Jews possessed no special advantage so far as acceptance into the Christian community was concerned, Paul can speak of their being favored over others by virtue of their role in God's program for humanity's salvation.[19] In this respect Paul does not view the Christian community, with its predominantly Gentile membership, as altogether replacing Israel in God's purposes.

In the first place, Gentiles have only been "grafted on" to the Jewish olive tree (Rom 11:17). And though they have temporarily become the locus of God's saving work in the world, he still reserves a future role for Israel.[20] Even in the present, converted Jews play a prominent part in communicating the message of Christ, not only to other Jews but to non-Jews as well (Rom 1:1). All this lends weight to the suggestion that Jewish converts, because of their knowledge of the OT, had an important teaching function in the initial stages of church life.

More general differences also emerged between Jewish and Gentile Christians within Paul's communities. Converted Jews and Gentiles tended to carry past religious and cultural patterns of behavior into their new way of life. Jews in particular, in the dispersion as well as in Jerusalem, continued to adhere to certain revered customs, such as observance of the Sabbath day and abstinence from particular kinds of food and drink. The distinction Paul draws between the "strong" and the "weak" in Romans probably reflects this difference in lifestyle (chs. 14–15). There he distinguishes between "one who believes he may eat anything" and "esteems all days alike" and the other who "eats only vegetables" and "esteems one day as better than another." This is not to say that some Jews did not break through to a freer attitude on such matters or that on occasions Gentiles did not maintain habits adopted from the synagogue. The distinction between "strong" and "weak" does not in all respects correspond to that between "Gentile" and "Jewish" Christians, but there must have been a considerable overlap between the two.

Paul allows such cultural differences to coexist within his communities provided each person acts with integrity before God

---

[18]Acts 16:11–40; 18:4.
[19]Rom 9:4–5; 11:28–29.
[20]Rom 11:11–15, 25–27, 30–32.

and does not put pressure upon others to conform (Rom 14:20–23). The "strong"—among whom Paul counts himself—have to be particularly sensitive here (15:1). But when Jewish Christians turn what is a matter of lifestyle into a criterion of salvation by insisting that circumcision and observance of the Law are obligatory for Gentiles, the time for mutual toleration is past and legalists must be shown the error of their ways.[21] Or when the pursuit of different lifestyles prevents Jewish and Gentle believers from sharing a common meal together, a trap into which both Peter and Barnabas had fallen at Antioch, hard words must be spoken in order to restore harmony (Gal 2:11–16). Here "weakness" has turned into harshness, vulnerability into self-righteousness, and to such "Pharisaism" one must not yield. By the same token, Gentile Christians who flaunt their freedom before weaker, more vulnerable Christians, whether Jewish or sensitive Gentile converts, and put their faith at risk should voluntarily forgo their freedom (1 Cor 8:7–13). If no "weaker" person is in view, however, the "stronger" may pursue their own convictions to whatever practical conclusion they might have (1 Cor 10:23–30). In all this the basic principle is one of "peace" and "acceptance" among the believers despite their differences.[22]

The socially eminent and socially disadvantaged in the communities

Although distinctions were not to be made within the community on grounds of intellectual, political, or social prestige, Paul's writings suggest that the advantages possessed by people in such positions often led to their making a contribution to the community that others could not make. Acts attests the presence of advantaged people in many places Paul visited.[23] Even at Corinth, where "there were not many . . . wise according to worldly standards, not many . . . powerful, not many . . . of noble birth" (1 Cor 1:26), a significant number of people in the church came from the more respected levels of society. No fewer than eight or nine people named in letters to the community were members of the wealthier class, as hints about their occupation, dependents,

---

[21]Gal 1:6–8; 4:8–10; 5:1, 2; 6:12–15.
[22]Rom 15:7; cf. 14:17.
[23]Acts 16:14; 17:4, 12 , 34; 18:7.

and/or possessions demonstrate. Stephanas, Crispus, Gaius, Erastus, Aquila, Priscilla, Titius Justus, Phoebe, and perhaps Sosthenes all come into this category.[24] What is more, these are clearly the most prominent figures in the congregation. Gaius, for example, acted as "host to the whole church," i.e., placed his premises at its disposal for larger gatherings and also accommodated visiting apostles or their delegates while they worked among churches in the vicinity.

Some social differentiation probably would have occurred at the "house church" level as well. Social privileges, no longer a mark of *distinction between* members of the community, could become an occasion for *service to* them. Aquila, Priscilla, and Lydia, who were all engaged in commerce and trade, illustrate this principle at work. The owners of homes naturally had much to offer the community, given the cramped quarters in which many people lived and the subordinate position of slaves. Other men and women of similar position probably were among those able to give substantial financial help to those in need. Differentiations of a social kind were not treated as if they did not exist, nor were they subjected to an indiscriminate leveling process; they were used to benefit others.

We have seen that unity within the community transcends gender. But here too Paul envisages people functioning differently in some respects. Due to the great volume of evidence and the divergences in its interpretation—not to speak of the wide contemporary interest in this question of men's and women's contributions to the community—we must go into this in more detail. The next chapter has been set aside for that purpose.

---

[24] 1 Cor 1:14–16; 16:15–17; Rom 16:1, 2, 23; Acts 18:2–3, 6–8, 17 (?).

12

—␣␣—

THE CONTRIBUTION OF
WOMEN IN CHURCH

What part did women play in Paul's churches? This question is customarily answered by reference to those passages where Paul explicitly comments on the activities of women in church. In order to see these in proper perspective we need to look first at other details in Paul's letters that throw indirect light on the issue. These are all too often overlooked and yet they provide the necessary framework for considering his more specific remarks.

WOMEN AS FULL MEMBERS
OF THE CHRISTIAN COMMUNITY

We begin with the fact that Paul addresses his letters to all the members of the communities he was writing to, not just to the men. This includes those sections where he deals with the conduct of the churches' affairs. For example, in response to situations that had developed at Corinth, Paul outlines his views on the ordering of their meetings (1 Cor 12–14), arranging of their meals (chs. 10–11), settling of their disputes (chs. 5–6), and directs his remarks to all "the brethren"[1] rather than to any one person or group within the church. As has already been noted, use of this term does not mean that Paul speaks here to the male members of the church only, for in his writings this term embraces "the sisters" as well. It is often used in proximity to such comments as "When *you* are assembled . . . " (i.e., as a church—5:4), "When *you* come together . . . ," (cf. "When *you* come together as a church"—11:27), and, "If, therefore, the *whole* church assembles . . . " (14:23). The use of such other terms as "all,"[2] "whoever" (11:27), "everyone" (12:6), "anyone,"[3] and "each one"[4] further confirms that Paul is addressing women as well as men. Both genders participate in these aspects of the community's life and contribute to the good order and well-being of its gatherings. (For this reason, among others, it is unfortunate that some translations insert the word "men" in these passages where there is no basis in the Greek[5] or where the word *anthropos* is used generically—11:28; 14:2–3).

In his explicit remarks on the contribution of women in church, Paul underscores their freedom at a number of levels. In 1 Cor 11, for example, his opening comments indicate that women normally prayed and prophesied in the gatherings at Corinth (11:5), and his closing reference to the practice of other churches suggests that this was the custom elsewhere also (v. 16). (We have independent evidence that Paul moved amongst other churches in which women prophesied, e.g., Acts 21:19.) His mention of female prophets is most significant for, as we have seen, Paul believed that prophecy was the most important activity that could take place in church.[6] This ministry of sharing a direct word from God with others had precedence over the activity of the teacher. (The reversal of this order throughout the succeeding history of Christianity and the conviction that prophecy no longer occurs have obscured the significance of Paul's remarks here.) Since for him women have as much freedom to participate in this as men, Paul would presumably agree with Luke's view that Joel's prophecy had now become a reality: "In the last days it shall be,

---

[1] 1 Cor 11:33; 12:1; 14:6, 20, 26, 39; cf. 5:11.
[2] 1 Cor 10:17; 12:26; 14:5, 18, 23, 24, 31.
[3] 1 Cor 11:29, 34; 14:9, 16, 27, 37–38.
[4] 1 Cor 11:21; 12:7, 11, 18; 14:26.
[5] 1 Cor 5:9; 10:15; 11:33; 14:21; 16:16, 18.
[6] 1 Cor 14:1–5, 20–25, 30, 31, 39, 40; cf. 1 Thess 5:19–20; 1 Cor 12:28; Rom 12:6; Eph 4:11; Acts 13:1; 15:32.

God declares, that I will pour out my Spirit upon all flesh, and your sons and your daughters shall prophesy . . . yea, and on my menservants and my maidservants in those days I will pour out my Spirit; and they shall prophesy."[7]

RESTRICTIONS PLACED UPON WOMEN BY PAUL

Concerning dress

In spite of the freedom reflected in 1 Cor 11, Paul argues that certain restrictions apply to the way in which women appear in church. He talks about the length of hair that women should have. The wearing of veils is probably not an issue here. With the exception of one verse (1 Cor 11:10) where the word often translated "veil" is the Greek term for "authority," Paul throughout uses a word that simply means a "covering." The type of "covering" is not described in the early part of the passage but later we are told explicitly that a woman's hair is given her for a "covering" (11:15). In this matter he does not lay an obligation only upon the women. Women are to wear their hair at a certain length in church, i.e., long, and men should wear theirs at an appropriate length as well, i.e., short. This appears to be in keeping with the custom in Paul's time, as his own remarks suggest (11:14). Presumably at Corinth women in the church were tending to disregard this custom, perhaps as part of a wider movement towards liberation in their recently reconstituted and highly mobile city, perhaps as a consequence of their experience of freedom in Christ, or perhaps both.

Within marriage

It is not always clear which kind of women Paul has in mind, i.e., whether married, single, or women generally. The usual Greek terms for "men" and "women," *aner* and *gune*, serve also for "husband" and "wife." Only the context can determine which sense these words are being used in.

In 1 Cor 11 it is wives and husbands who seem to be primarily in view (v. 3), though women and men in general are also

---

[7] Acts 2:17, 18, RSV; cf. Joel 2:28, 29.

present in the background.[8] The wife's appearance marks her subordination to her husband: "For a man ought not to cover his head, since he is the image and glory of God; but woman is the glory of man" (1 Cor 11:7, RSV). Yet in some sense it also signifies her own "authority" (11:10), even if we cannot be sure exactly what Paul intended to cover by this word (or what he understood by his accompanying words that it is "because of the angels" that the wife must so appear). So the wife has a legitimate sphere of authority and ministry alongside her husband.

Paul's argument for wifely subordination stems from his interpretation of the Genesis narratives. From them he draws the conclusion that man is the source of the woman (which is why though both are stamped with the image of God, man reflects the "glory" of God while woman reflects the "glory" of her husband). He also understands that woman was made for man (11:8–9). But to prevent the male members of his audience from gaining a false sense of their own importance, Paul immediately qualifies these remarks by adding that "in the Lord woman is not independent of man *nor man of woman*; for as woman was made from man, *so man is now born of woman*." Most important of all is the fact that "All things are from God" (11:11–12, RSV). That is why, at the commencement of this whole passage, he can pronounce that "the head of every husband is Christ, the head of a wife is her husband, and the head of Christ is God" (11:3), playing on the dual sense of the term "head," which in Greek can mean both "source" and "preeminence." Supporting arguments for the way in which women (and men) should appear in church are also drawn from nature (11:14), custom (11:14), and church practice (11:16).

It is tempting at this point, as at the end of the following paragraph, to inquire into the legitimacy of the reasons given by Paul for his position on this subject. The question of interpretation or hermeneutics becomes very pressing here but, as this is a treatment of Paul's view of community, we cannot pursue it now. Yet it would not be out of place to observe that there are three kinds of arguments employed by Paul, only one of which has a fundamental significance. The argument from church practice is dependent on the other two and cannot stand without them. The arguments from nature and custom are in fact one (since Paul assumes that current practice exhibits a natural state of affairs)

---

[8] Cf. 1 Cor 11:8–9, 11–12.

and depend on customs of dress or appearance remaining the same. What some see as a fourth "argument" from christology is in fact an analogy from the Genesis narratives; its continuing force depends upon one's estimate of the historical way Paul reads them. We should also bear in mind that Paul's instruction is corrective rather than absolute. It is provoked by a particular situation in which women have exceeded their proper limits (just as men have elsewhere). We should be wary, therefore, of interpreting his remarks here in too prescriptive a fashion.

During church

At first sight, Paul's endorsement of women praying and prophesying in church seems to conflict with his statement that "the women should keep silence" in the gatherings (1 Cor 14:34). Attempts to overrule his earlier endorsement by this statement or to elide these later verses from the text should both be avoided. There is no justification for the former and scarcely any manuscript support for the latter, and an appreciation of the wider and immediate context of Paul's advice renders such solutions unnecessary. The injunction is the third in a series (14:20ff.), all of which are directed against the existence of chaos in church, first through all speaking in tongues at the same time and second through all jointly prophesying. The precise nature of the offence of the women (more strictly of the wives) becomes clear in the following verse: "If there is anything they desire to know," he says, "let them ask their husbands at home" (14:35, RSV). The wives have been interrupting the meeting with questions about things said within it. If more than that were involved, then Paul would not single out this one problem without any reference to others. The injunction to "keep silence" does not itself necessarily possess an absolute sense and must always be interpreted by the context in which it occurs.

The situation presupposed by Paul's remarks is perfectly understandable. Women for the most part did not receive any substantial education in religious matters, yet in Christian gatherings they could be present throughout the whole meeting and also contribute to it in a number of ways. Particularly in a church like that at Corinth, where Christian liberty was prized so highly, it comes as no surprise that wives felt free to query things they did not understand. In advising against this, Paul reminds them again of its contravention of prevailing custom (14:35)—in Greek cities it was only the *hetairai*, courtesans, who engaged in public discussions with men—and of the practice of other churches (14:36) and even of the OT (14:34).

PROMINENCE ACCORDED TO WOMEN BY PAUL

Alongside the corrective, and occasionally prescriptive, statements of Paul we find many important descriptive ones. At this point we can return to the mention of Phoebe in Rom 16:1 where Paul describes her as a *diakonos*, deacon. The term *prostatis* (generally translated "helper") in the following verse may explain what this means. While it could, as we will see, refer to her involvement in Paul's mission as a patroness, cognate terms from the same root are used elsewhere to describe the activities of those who exercise important functions in the churches. This could suggest that Phoebe was engaged in "teaching" and "leading" in her local church at Cenchreae.

Paul's statements elsewhere imply that women had some share in teaching and exhorting in his communities. In the first place, if Paul permitted women to prophesy in his churches and considered prophecy as more important than teaching, why should participation in the latter be denied them? It could be argued that their lack of sufficient education in the OT makes it improbable that they taught. This would certainly help to explain the apparent absence of references to such (though in Acts 18:26, Priscilla teaches in her home), but if so it means that a cultural circumstance, not a theological principle, lay behind this state of affairs. In the second place, in other passages Paul envisages that all "God's chosen ones" both should be full of the Spirit and should "let the word of Christ dwell in them richly, as (they) teach and admonish one another in all wisdom, and as (they) sing psalms and hymns and spiritual songs with thankfulness in (their) hearts to God" (Col 3:16). Paul probably has in mind the informal teaching and exhorting of one another that went on throughout the Christian meetings, rather than some formal exhortatory address. However, this does suggest that women as well as men, and women who were not necessarily deacons as well as those who were, were involved in these activities. Since these two activities

are the basic elements in "pastoral" ministry, this indicates that
for Paul all Christians function in these ways to some extent.

Paul may even refer to women involved in teaching and
leading at the fullest level. "The household of Stephanas," whom
the Corinthians were to respect, would have included women as
well as men, and his remarks may be addressed to both (1 Cor
16:15). He also mentions "Nympha, and the church in her house"
(Col 4:15). Most probably Nympha was a relatively wealthy woman
who, like Gaius at Corinth, acted as host to a local group of
believers. It seems unlikely that she, presumably a widow who
conducted her family, managed her slaves, and welcomed her
friends all week, would take an insignificant part in the proceedings in favor of socially inferior male members. To do that would
be culturally unacceptable whereas, in the absence of a husband,
it would be perfectly legitimate in the eyes of others for her to
behave in home and church *as her husband would have done* if present.
Most probably male heads of other households also belonged to
this church and had an influential role in its activities but, given
her position, Nympha would have functioned alongside them in
an equal capacity. This acts as a reminder that Paul generally talks
about the relation of wives to husbands; where no husband is in
view, quite different arrangements become possible.

THE POSITION OF WOMEN IN
OTHER RELIGIOUS COMMUNITIES

Unfortunately, little is known for certain about the position
of women in the synagogue at this time.[9] Practice was almost
certainly less rigid than the later records suggest. According to
these texts, women and girls sat separately from their menfolk
and were permitted to be present only during the liturgical part
of the service. The second part of the service involved instruction
in the Law and this they were not allowed to receive. As a result
women could not teach in the synagogue, though before the Fall
of Jerusalem they could be asked to read the Torah. In later times
they continued to be called but it was customary for them not to

---

[9] But see Philo, *Special Laws* 3.171; *On the Contemplative Life* 69. Josephus,
Antiquities 14.260–261.

respond. A synagogue itself could be constituted only by ten Jewish males coming together; women did not count for this purpose, no matter how many.[10] In the Diaspora, by reason of surrounding influences, women came to play a more prominent part in certain aspects of synagogue life, even formally occupying the position of *archisunagogos*, that is, the chief patron.

Unlike Essene groups generally, which contained at least some married people, Qumran was virtually a male society; women seem to have existed only on the margins of its community life.[11] The rites and experiences at the heart of the mystery religions, along with the rewards that they promised to their adherents, gave them a strong and widespread attraction for women, especially among the upper classes. For example, when the cult of Isis gained her consort Serapis, women participated fully in the various ceremonies.[12] They also became priestesses on their initiation and occasionally rose to considerable prominence within the cult. Even so, in the cult of Isis, and probably in many other cults as well, the proportion of men involved continued to exceed that of women. Athens and Rome are two places where female devotees may have comprised about half the membership. Normally the very highest positions within the cult of Isis were uniformly reserved for men. On the other hand, in more private household based mystery cults women do appear at times as priestess-leaders.

CONCLUSION

While the position of women in Paul's communities generally went beyond that which they possessed in Judaism, it converged more closely with their situation in the Hellenistic mystery cults. There too the distinctions between women and men were undergoing change, though they do not seem to have articulated this in as principled a way as Paul. Since participation in the cult was preeminently an individualistic affair, the impact of this

---

[10]*m. Meg.* 4.3.
[11]CD 7.6–9; 14.16; 16.10. On other Essenes, see Josephus, *Jewish War* 2.119–121, 160–161.
[12]Apuleius, *Metamorphoses* 11.6ff.

increased involvement on the personal relationships of members of the cult could not have been as marked as in the early Christian communities. For all his insistence upon equality at one level within the community, Paul does recognize the legitimacy of continuing gender differences at other levels of its operation. Equality of religious status, which in any case should be subordinated to the new unity members experience with one another, does not rule out the possibility of functional diversities within the community. This principle has further ramifications that we must now go on to explore.

13

—~m~—

PARTICIPATION AND
ITS RESPONSIBILITIES

Paul's approach to community partly abolished and partly preserved distinctions that divided people in the ancient world during his time. Yet what it preserved was also transformed. Distinctions no longer provided a way to maintain an advantage over others. Instead they provided the basis for serving others. We can now go on to see whether the new gifts individuals received and the new responsibilities they undertook introduced into the community a different set of distinctions that once again separated people on the grounds of privilege or status.

To answer this we must first discover whether any of the traditional religious distinctions maintained a place within Paul's churches. Do we find here a persistence of differentiation between priests and laity, between officials and ordinary members, between holy and common people? In considering these we will look briefly at each in turn, even though in many cases these three categories coalesced in the one person or group.

PAUL'S DISSOLUTION OF
TRADITIONAL DISTINCTIONS

Between priests and laity

One of the most noticeable features of Paul's writings is the absence of the term *hiereis*, priest. This is a strange phenomenon from the standpoint of contemporary religious practice. Certainly the term *leitourgia*, priestly service, or one of its cognates docs occur, though only seven times in all. But each time Paul uses it, it is in a metaphorical or quite noncultic sense, e.g., the service rendered to God by the apostolic preaching of the gospel (Rom 15:16) and the commitment of faith that arises out of it (Phil 2:17); the service rendered to others by sharing fellowship with those lacking it (Phil 2:25, 30) and giving financial aid to those in need (Rom 15:27; 2 Cor 9:12); and the service rendered to society at large by the Roman political authorities in the exercise of their power (Rom 13:6).

We also find the term *latreia*, worship (and verb *latreuein*). In the Septuagint this refers to not merely religious, but specifically ceremonial actions. Paul uses it in this way of both Jewish (Rom 9:4.) and Gentile (Rom 1:25) worship (compare his use of *threskeia* only of heretical worship in Col 2:18). He applies the word to the Christian community to describe the dedication of its members to God and to Christ in the Spirit (Phil 3:3), as well as the total life service of both the individual (Rom 1:9; 15:16) and the whole fellowship (12:1). He also employs such other terms as *prosphora*, priestly offering,[1] *thusia*, sacrifice,[2] *aparche*, first fruits (cf. *prosagoge*, access),[3] but here too the offerings are decidedly noncultic in character. Those who present them are Christians in general, not a selective group among them.

So, although Paul uses the language of priesthood, priestly service, and priestly cult, he never refers to a sacred caste, activity, or object. Instead, the individual believer, the community as a whole, or the secular authorities are "priests" in his sense.

---

[1] Rom 15:16; cf. Eph 5:2.
[2] Rom 12:1; Phil 2:17; 4:18; cf. Eph 5:2.
[3] 2 Thess 2:13; 1 Cor 16:15; Rom 16:5 (see also Rom 8:23); Rom 5:2; Eph 2:18b; 3:12.

"Priestly services" can be performed through religious commitment, charitable actions, and apostolic vocation. For Paul, faith, love, and the total dedication of one's life are the "cultic actions" that God now requires. This means that distinctions between priest and layperson, mediatorial and common service, cultic ritual and secular activity do not exist within the church.

Confirmation of this comes from another quarter. Paul not only transfers sacred language from its cultic domain to the sphere of everyday life but also utilizes vernacular terms to describe features of church life. We have already come across several examples of this and now we can compile them. Paul describes the coming together of Christians by such terms as *sunerchomai* and employs the word *ekklesia* for the assembly that results. He characterizes the members who belong to it by use of the terms *oikeioi* and *soma* and refers to its central activities with the words *charisma* and *deipnon*. While terms like *soma* and *ekklesia* occasionally turn up in cultic contexts outside the NT,[4] all these words are essentially noncultic. Even when they do occur in connection with a cult society, they do not necessarily have cultic significance themselves, e.g., *ekklesia* appears two or three times in inscriptions simply because a word is needed to refer to the fact of meeting. And Philo's use of *charisma* to refer to God's gifts in creation, a use that would not have been known to Paul, does not mean that the word had an inherently religious meaning; the few occasions where it turns up in the papyri suggest otherwise. Although *deipnon* does here and there signify a cultic meal, Paul's discussion of the Lord's Supper shows that he did not use the term that way. So, alongside Paul's noncultic application of specifically religious terms, we find that he consistently calls in everyday words to describe basic aspects of church life. This dramatically highlights his refusal to work with the usual sacred/ secular dichotomy.

The metaphorical use of cultic language sometimes occurs in the later prophetic books of the OT[5] and in intertestamental Judaism[6] but, apart from certain anticultic tendencies in Hellenistic Judaism and partially in Qumran, it is never associated with a fundamental rejection of the cult.[7] In Paul, however, the

---

[4] E.g., Josephus, *Antiquities* 18.73.
[5] E.g., Ps 51:17; Is 58:3ff.; Mic 6:6–8.
[6] E.g., Jud 16:16; Jub. 2:22; Apoc. Mos. 33; Test. Lev. 3.
[7] Dan 3:38–40 (LXX); 1 En. 45:3; Arist. 170, 234; and see 1QS 9.3–4.

official priesthood that exists to mediate between God and humanity is a common priesthood with no distinction between clergy and laity.

To a large extent Pharisaism and the synagogue anticipated this approach. The former was essentially a lay movement and the latter was a popular assembly of the local community, organized by it rather than by the priesthood. Yet both sought not to replace the cultic life of the Temple, as did Paul, but to supplement it. The post AD 70 practice of both, which may or may not reflect earlier practice, preserved a residual role for members of the priestly caste who associated with them. Among the ten men required to found a synagogue there had to be at least one priest. Some procedures within the synagogue required the priests' presence and validation, and certain prayers in the service were customarily reserved for them.[8]

The priestly element is stronger at Qumran. Alongside its commitment to the Law, this group saw itself as the guardian of an alternative, yet (until the Temple fell into their hands in the coming Messianic war) incomplete, cultic system. Priests were therefore essential to the conduct of its religious life and played a prominent part in its council, worship, admission procedure, common meals, and disciplinary actions.[9]

The mystery cults were hierarchically sacral in character. A clear distinction was drawn between the initiates, who automatically became priests of the cult, and all those who had not yet been favored by the god with a revelation. Between the initiates themselves there existed a graded series of priestly orders that one might ascend.[10]

Despite partial parallels with Pharisaism and the synagogue, Paul's abolition of the distinction between priest and people, sacred and profane, cult and ordinary service has no full precedent among his contemporaries. While it has a parallel in certain Stoic statements rejecting sacrifices (more often they are criticized for not springing from a moral intention), the "spiritual" worship that replaces them is more an individual than communal affair.[11] The breaking down of these distinctions has its basis in

---

[8] *m. Meg.* 4.3, 6.

[9] 1QS 5.2, 21–24; 6.2–5, 8; 8.1–4; 9.6–7; cf. 1QS 1.21; 2.11, 19–23; 7.2–3; CD 10.4–6; 14.3–6.

[10] Apuleius, *Metamorphoses* 11.10, 12, 16–17, 22. Plutarch, *Isis and Osiris* 4ff.

certain attitudes of Jesus, but Paul was the first to give explicit expression to it and work out its communal implications in the most thoroughgoing fashion.

Between officials and ordinary members

Paul also rejects any formal distinction between official figures and ordinary members in the community. Had he wished to draw attention to the existence of offices as such, there were any number of Greek terms he could have used. However, the title *arche* (compare *archon* or *archegos*)—ruler, head, or leader—often possessing in Greek a sense of legality or rank—never refers to individuals within the communities but significantly refers only to Christ himself[12] or to various subsidiary supernatural powers.[13] The term *time,* which emphasizes dignity of office, and the term *telos,* which stresses the power inherent in such, are also absent from Paul's ecclesiastical vocabulary. Instead, as a general term for the service of individuals within the church, he uses almost uniformly the word *diakonia,* "service," or one of its related forms. Paul chooses a word that is quite everyday in character and that places the issue of dignity or position in a different framework.

Diakonia occurs only twice in the Septuagint and then in a quite general and secular sense.[14] In Philo and Josephus it occasionally refers to "waiting at table" but more often to "serving" in general,[15] both meanings being present in ordinary Greek usage. This "serving" covers a whole range of activities and people. Depending on the person whom one serves, it can involve fulfilling an important task or a less important one and can accord the one carrying it out greater or lesser significance. If the servants' master is a significant person, especially God, they have a significant role to play and have significance attached to them. But they do not possess this in and of themselves. It is a derived significance and stems from whose servant they are rather than from who they themselves are or even from what they do. So Paul is not

---

[11]Seneca, *Fragment* 123.
[12]Col 1:18 (cf. Rom 15:12).
[13]1 Cor 2:6, 8; Eph 2:2; 6:12.
[14]1 Macc 11:58; Esth 6:3.
[15]Philo, *Contemplative Life* 70. Josephus, *Antiquities* 2.65; 11.163, 166.

using "servant" instead of "leadership" language to highlight inferior as opposed to superior tasks or positions. He uses it to highlight the dependent character of the work and responsibility in contrast with the independent stance that so often goes with leadership. Plato was typical of Greek philosophers when he wrote, "How can a man be happy when he has to serve someone?"[16] The main difficulty he and other Greek philosophers had with "servanthood" and "slavery" was not with the inferior nature of the work involved (often the work was at the higher educational, professional, or managerial level) but with the dependent nature of the relationship between servant or slave and master. Paul employs this term for service of any kind by any member of the community, whether insignificant or important, to any member of the community or of another community. He uses it of the service rendered by apostolic delegates (Col 4:7; Eph 6:21), including himself,[17] other prominent figures within the church,[18] including women (Rom 16:1), and all believers.[19]

Significant for understanding the meaning of *diakonia* in relation to those being served is Paul's use of the word for the work of the Spirit and Christ (2 Cor 3:8; Rom 15:8). Its association with the Spirit confirms what has already been said about the Spirit's facilitating work within the community. The work of the Spirit takes place by neither compulsion nor force. Jesus said that he did not come to be served but "to serve and give his life as a ransom for many" (Mark 10:45). Paul holds up as a model those in the church who "have devoted themselves to the service of the saints" (1 Cor 16:15). Because of this service Jesus rendered and its continuation through the Spirit, he is the *arche* (Col 1:18) of the community. With his deliberate and consistent choice of this word, Paul rejects the idea of certain people in the community possessing formal rights and powers over ordinary members.

This renunciation of offices, and of the titles and honors that belong to them, radically departs from first-century attitudes to religious organization. For example, the synagogue had many officials, beginning with the *archisunagogos*, who has already been mentioned. The *hazzan* was chiefly responsible for the conduct of

---

[16]Plato, *Gorgias* 491e.
[17]2 Cor 4:1; 6:3ff.; 11:8, 23; Rom 11:13.
[18]1 Cor 16:15; Phil 1:1; Col 1:7; 4:17.
[19]1 Cor 12:5; 2 Cor 8:4, 19–20; 9:1, 12–13; Rom 15:31; Eph 4:12.

public worship.[20] The Gospels portray the Pharisees as occupying the chief seats in the synagogue (Matt 23:6). Members of the congregation could fulfill those responsibilities that were functions, not offices,[21] such as the reciting of the prayers, the announcing of the *Shema*, the reading of the Scriptures, and the preaching of the homily (Luke 4:16–17; Acts 13:15), only when summoned to do so by its officers.

In the mystery cults various grades of officials were attached to local shrines and temples. These looked after the administrative and financial aspects of the cult's operations. Most probably those who held official positions were themselves priests who belonged to the higher orders of the sacral hierarchy.[25]

Officials also existed at Qumran and among the Essenes. The *mebaqqerim*, or guardians, distributed in the community and throughout the camps, assessed candidates applying for membership,[22] received reports about transgressions that had occurred,[23] acted as the recipients and distributors of charitable gifts, and instructed members in the maxims of the Law and the rules of the community.[24] Whether or not these were identical with the priests, whose functions we have already noted, is not altogether clear.

In the mystery cults various grades of officials were attached to local shrines and temples. These looked after the administrative and financial aspects of the cult's operations. Most probably those who held official positions were themselves priests who belonged to the higher orders of the sacral hierarchy.[25]

Between holy and common people

Paul also refuses to draw distinctions between members of the community according to the measure of "holiness" they possess. The principle that keeps Paul from having any leading caste of a priestly or official kind also extends to a rejection of any spiritual aristocracy within the community. All members of the community possess the Spirit. "Through one Spirit" they were all introduced into it (1 Cor 12:13); "in one Spirit" they all have equal access to God (Eph 2:18); "from one Spirit" they all draw the same resources (1 Cor 3:18); "by the (same) Spirit" all are to direct their lives (Gal 5:25). Since it is the same Spirit who dwells in them all,

---

[20] *m. Sot.* 7.7–8; *m. Yom.* 7.1; cf. Matt 9:18; Mark 5:35ff.; Luke 4:20; 8:41, 49; 13:14; Acts 14:15; 18:8, 17.

[21] *m. Ber.* 5.5; *m. R. Sh.* 4.9; *m. Tam.* 5.1.

[22] 1QS 6.13–14; CD 13.7–13.

[23] CD 9.16–20; 14.9–10.

[24] 1QS 6.19–20; CD 14.12–16.

[25] See n. 10.

all share in the qualities of character that the Spirit produces (Gal 5:22–23), and all participate in the gifts of ministry that the Spirit distributes (1 Cor 12:4–11). All who belong to the community, therefore, are intrinsically "spiritual."

Paul's use of the terms *laos*, people, and *hagios*, holy, confirms this. Apart from its occurrence in OT quotations[26] and in direct references to the Jewish nation (Rom 11:1–2), *laos* refers only to Christians as a whole, as those upon whom the promises of God concerning the creation of a "people" have fallen (2 Cor 6:6). Nowhere does the term refer to merely a part of the community, nor is it used in distinction from *kleros*, clergy. (It was only in the third century that the words for clergy and layperson came into Christian usage.) Nor does any one member of the community, or any group of members, possess a particular "holiness" denied to others. Because of its OT associations, Paul does sometimes use the plural of *hagios* for the Jewish Christians in Jerusalem,[27] even though elsewhere all believers in a particular region or community are referred to as "saints."[28] In so describing the Jewish Christians, Paul does not mean they possess some inherent personal quality which sets them apart from others. In OT terms he simply refers to their having been "reserved" for, "set aside" by, or "dedicated" to God. Since all share equally in this, there cannot be different grades of holiness within the community.

The presence of the Spirit was not a central theme among the Pharisees and the Essenes. Still, as we have seen, a small succession of charismatic rabbis emerged outside the main body of adherents in Jerusalem and the Essenes had a reputation for their prophetic predictions and interpretation of dreams. Apart from these, it does seem that grades of achievement existed within Pharisaism, and at Qumran the council of the community ranked its members according to their level of spiritual attainment and enforced strict rules concerning participation in the community.[29] In spite of this, there was a real participation by each person in the Qumran community since all "eat in common, bless in common, and deliberate in common," though only ac-

---

[26] 1 Cor 10:7; 14:21; Rom 9:25–26; 10:21; 15:10.
[27] 1 Cor 16:1; 2 Cor 8:4; 9:1, 12; Rom 15:25–26; Eph 2:19.
[28] 1 Cor 1:2; 14:33; 16:15; 2 Cor 1:2; 13:13; Rom 1:7; 16:2, 15; Phil 1:2; 4:22; Col 1:2, 3, 12, 26; cf. 3:12; Eph 1:2, 15, 18; 3:18; 5:3.
[29] 1QS 6.25–27; 9.12–16; *m. Hag.* 2.5–6; *m. Dem.* 2.2–3.

cording to rank and under the supervision of a smaller group of the more senior members.[30]

In Hellenism, a different atmosphere prevailed. Holy men who practiced divination and performed miracles, or socially disadvantaged but charismatically gifted individuals employed to practice their gifts for gain, existed in many places (compare Acts 16:16–18). There were also smaller groups who banded together in monastic societies and, like the Essenes, became noted for their virtuous way of life. Though Paul's view of a community of "saints" has something in common with such groups, and within it some exercised extraordinary powers, he rejects the idea that holiness involves isolation from the world or possession of unusual abilities. On the contrary, both of these can easily coexist with quite profane attitudes (1 Cor 3:1–3). He has a different and less elitist understanding of "spirituality" and "holiness." So alien to his thinking is the later Christian notion of "the saint" as an extraordinarily holy person. that reference to the apostle as "Saint" Paul is ironic indeed.

Paul has no place in his view of community for the traditional distinctions between its members along cultic, official, or religious lines. This clears the ground for a more positive appraisal of his approach to responsibility in the community. We must now investigate the extent to which the high view he has of all believers affects their carrying out of various tasks within it. Where did the responsibility lie for the organization of church, including the common meal, the care of members, discipline, and the direction of the community?

PAUL'S EMPHASIS UPON CORPORATE RESPONSIBILITY

For organization

In several places in his letters Paul talks about specific aspects of the church's meetings, clarifies the principles upon which decisions should be based, and gives concrete advice on the sorts of arrangements that follow from them. Nowhere does he address his remarks to a group of persons (or to any one

---

[30] 1QS 6.2, 6–13.

person) who alone have responsibility for dealing with these matters. This consistent and quite remarkable feature of his letters, so self-evident when one reads them that it is apt to be overlooked, has already been noted. He constantly reminds the whole community of its obligations in these areas and calls upon every member to fulfill them.[31] His letters are uniformly addressed to the local groups as a whole rather than to any authorities within them, and the expression "brethren" is constantly on his lips—not least in places where organizational matters are being discussed. Clearly, all who belong to the community share responsibility for its practical operation.

For welfare

All were also responsible for each other's welfare. This involves self-examination on the part of individual members as well as alertness to the needs of others. They are all to "bear one another's burdens," "have the same care for one another," "look not only to (their) own interests but also to the interests of others," "encourage one another and to build one another up."[32] Appeals of this kind occur repeatedly in Paul's letters and indicate how fundamental a theme this was for him.

For discipline

Responsibility for the discipline of offending members also lies firmly with other believers. When someone has a legal grievance against another, and it cannot be settled personally, someone in the community should resolve the issue, not an outsider (1 Cor 6:1–6). If one of the members succumbs unwittingly to a self-destructive course of action others should "restore him in a spirit of gentleness," looking to themselves, however, lest they "too be tempted" (Gal 6:1). When an action detrimentally affects the life of the community anyone aware of this should bring the matter to its attention; however, there must be at least two, if possible three, involved so that it may be substantiated by more than one witness.[33] Only if the defendant refuses to listen and

---

[31] E.g., 1 Cor 11:33–34a; 14:39–40; 16:2–3.
[32] Gal 5:2; 1 Cor 12:25; Phil 2:4; 1 Thess 5:11.
[33] 2 Cor 13:1; cf. 1 Cor 1:11.

deliberately continues to disrupt the community are the members to "note" and "avoid" that person, especially at the communal meal.[34] If the person fails to respond more dramatic steps
become necessary.[35] Where, as in 1 Cor 5, the error is repugnant
even by pagan standards and the offender remains unrepentant,
the community as a whole should assemble together, recognize
the presence of evil amongst them, and "deliver the person to
Satan" as executor of God's chastisement (1 Cor 5:3–5). This
strange expression could mean that they are to disown the offender, i.e., completely withdraw from all contact. Or, on the
analogy of the Ananias and Sapphira incident in Acts 5, it could
signify their calling down a "death sentence," i.e., a prayer for
judgment to take place. Either way, the object of this extreme
form of disciplinary action is the person's ultimate welfare. This
(if 2 Cor 2 refers to the same case as 1 Cor 5) may lead to a quicker
change of attitude on the part of the offender.

For growth

This leads to a consideration of the way in which the community deepened its Christian commitment and determined its
future development. We have seen how gifts were distributed to
every member of the community by the Spirit and that through
their mutual sharing these were exercised amongst them. Guidance on matters affecting the community's life was principally
granted to members when they met together to discern what God
required of them. They received this guidance from the Spirit
through their exercise of gifts of knowledge, revelation, wisdom,
and so on. In all this Paul never tires of insisting that every
member of the community has the responsibility to impart the
particular insights they have been given. All are called to "instruct
one another," to "speak God's word . . . so that all may learn and
all be encouraged," and to "teach and admonish one another in
all wisdom," for it is through "speaking the truth in love" that they
are to "grow up in every way into him who is the head, even
Christ.[36] Thus, the most characteristic setting in which the community received guidance was when Christians assembled to

---

[34]2 Thess 2:14; 1 Cor 5:11.
[35]1 Cor 16:22; Rom 16:17.
[36]Rom 15:14; 1 Cor 14:31; Col 3:16; Eph 4:15.

share and evaluate the gifts given to them. Here, in a variety of complementary ways, guidance was conveyed through each to all and through all to each.

Both nurture and discipline within the congregation, then, should arise spontaneously from the concern of every member for the quality of its life and the involvement of every member in decisions affecting the whole.

CONCLUSION

With respect to each of these areas of community life, responsibility lies with every member to play their particular part in the leadership of the community. Rather than being the task of one person or a select group, leadership is a corporate affair devolving in some measure upon all. The principle of equality was, of course, deeply embedded in Greek legal and political thought and was important to a certain degree in social relations. It was also strongly emphasized in Stoicism, which deduced the theoretical equality of all from the possession of reason by all. Paul's approach differs from these formulations. He grounds equality in a divine act rather than in some aspect of the human personality and extends it into a more intimate conception of communal life. Even so, for Paul equality was subservient to the more fundamental idea of unity. For this reason the idea of equality itself could never become a leading motif in his thought.

14

—⚬⚬⚬—

SERVICE AND
ITS RECOGNITION

Although all members of the community participate in its gatherings and are responsible for its affairs, some individuals do so more than others. Examples of this have already been given in various areas of corporate life and can now be grouped together. For example, people like Aquila and Priscilla (1 Cor 16:19; Rom 16:3–5) or Nympha (Col 4:15) had a special hand in arranging the affairs of the churches that met in their homes. Gaius, as "host" to the "whole church" in Corinth, had practical responsibilities to perform (Rom 16:23). In the area of pastoral care we have the cryptic reference to a "true yoke fellow" who is to help two women at Philippi come to a common agreement in the Lord (Phil 4:2–3).

These references are some of the infrequent places in Paul's writings where he does not address his remarks to the whole church. A few other examples are: when Paul speaks in turn to husbands and wives, parents and children, slaves and masters in Col 3; or to the married, single, and separated in 1 Cor 7; or to Jews and Gentiles, weak and strong in Rom 1–2; 14–15. There are other instances of some individuals called to specialized service. Paul envisages the presence in Corinth of "wise" people who could solve legal disputes between members of the community (1 Cor 6:5). In the discussion of *charisma*, we noted the distinction between the regular ministry of "prophets" and "teachers" (1 Cor 12:29) and the occasional prophesying and teaching in which all members of the community engaged.

My reason for not systematically taking up these references before is that, whatever Paul may say about the role of particular individuals within the community, his emphasis is on the responsibility of all. We will now investigate terms used by Paul to describe the administrative, pastoral, and directive aspects of the church's life. We shall also look at some accompanying remarks that throw light on the role played by people involved in these activities.

TWO CLASSES WITHIN THE COMMUNITY

As a prelude to this, we may note that Paul makes a broad distinction between those among his readers who are more and less mature. Earlier we alluded to Paul's statement that "if a person is overtaken in any trespass, you who are spiritual should restore such a one in a spirit of gentleness" (Gal 6:1). In a number of other places he differentiates between those who are strong and those who are worldly or weak in their Christian understanding.[1] He regards these not as two levels of membership within the community but as varying stages of maturity. Some, because of their sinfulness, remain immature in their attitudes long after they should have progressed beyond them. Paul urges them to rectify this state of affairs. Others, because of their background, pass through an initial stage of immaturity. For a period, Paul willingly accommodates his teaching to them. Spiritual growth, precisely because it involves intellectual and moral growth, is a gradual affair, even though some are able to get on the right wavelength in a shorter period of time. Only when those capable of deeper insight and more consistent behavior fail to develop spiritual maturity does the discrepancy between them and other members of the community become unhealthy. Maturity is the aim of all and Paul nowhere limits its achievement to an elite.

---

[1] Cf. 1 Cor 2:14–3:4; Rom 14:1–15:7.

In the meantime, those who have advanced furthest along the path towards maturity ought to assist those who still have some distance to travel. Such people must watch themselves lest they too slip back into less responsible patterns of behavior (Gal 6:1b). Those who are more mature should be grateful for what they have been able to attain (Phil 3:15–16). Within this group, which may have been encouragingly large in many of his churches, even if disappointingly small in others, Paul singles out some who have more specific tasks to perform.

THOSE WITH SPECIAL TASKS IN THE COMMUNITY

We turn now to the terms Paul uses to describe the mature people who have particular functions in the community. When his letters are examined in order of composition, some interesting features emerge.

The first reference to such people occurs in 1 Thess 5:12. No title is mentioned, nor does Paul identify any positions held. Instead we have three particles used to define three tasks in the community, viz., *kopiontas, proistamenous,* and *nouthetountas.* These are the ones who "labor among you," "give aid to you," and "admonish you." (The NRSV translates the second of these as "those who . . . have charge of you in the Lord." However, the translation, "he who gives aid," is preferable.) Though the term appears occasionally in the papyri for official persons in voluntary associations, religious as well as secular, it is unlikely to have that more technical force here. This is clear from the use of its participial rather than noun form, its positioning between the two other terms, and the general meaning of the verb in the NT. Together these three words simply indicate the effort expended by such people in carrying out their tasks, the supportive character of their work, and the note of exhortation and warning appropriate to it. Because those "who give aid" in the Roman social system were those in a position to confer benefits upon others, we may have reference here to people who came from the more socially advantaged level of the Thessalonian community. Nevertheless what is in view here is not official positions within the community but special functions.

In the list of ministries and gifts at the end of 1 Cor 12, we find two different terms, *antilempseis* and *kuberneseis*. Here, unlike 1 Thess 5, we have nouns being used rather than participles, but they still describe functions rather than persons or positions. In Paul's list only the first three items—apostles, prophets, and teachers (1 Cor 12:28)—have specific persons in view; the remainder, *antilempseis* and *kuberneseis* among them, are applicable to any. For this reason, we must depart again from the RSV rendering of these words as "heads" and "administrators." Instead, they simply mean the rendering of assistance and the giving of direction in a less personalized way. (It is difficult to think of words in the plural that could be used as more exact translations of their Greek counterparts: "helpful deeds" and "practical initiatives" are about as close as one can get.) Once again these terms are not technical in character. Certainly no official positions in the church are in view. Their application to functions rather than the persons engaged in them, their ranking so far down the list of gifts and, perhaps, their occurrence only here in the NT, all support this.

Later in this same letter Paul recommends the household of Stephanas to the Corinthian community (1 Cor 16:15–18). He describes them as the *aparche*, firstfruits, of the gospel in Asia. In the church, "they devoted (or appointed) themselves to the service (*eis diakonian*) of the saints." Here we have the very general term for "service" whose wide range of meaning we have already discussed. Nothing suggests that the word *diakonia* has any technical meaning here. The community's function is not to ordain such people but rather to recognize the value of their service. Paul goes on to say that acknowledgment is due not only to Stephanas and his household, but also "to everyone who works and toils with them" (in the Greek *sunergounti kai kopionti*). The participial form of these words and the broad way in which Paul alludes to these people preclude the possibility that any formal position is involved. The reference to "firstfruits," however, may suggest that the initial converts in a given locality became both the nucleus around which a new community was established and key participants in consolidating it. And the fact that Stephanas possessed a household—Fortunatus and Archaicus may have been two of his slaves—indicates again that a more socially eminent group in the community fulfilled these pastoral functions.

Galatians has little to offer on this topic—only Paul's injunction that those who learn should display some generosity to those who teach (*katechountes*—Gal 6:6). Here we have the participial construction; a specific title or position is not in mind. The exhortation to the beneficiaries to "share all good things" with those who benefit them does not, as commonly stated, indicate that a paid ministry existed at this time. Certainly Paul establishes in this verse the principle of reimbursement, as he does elsewhere. Of the Gentiles' debt to the Jews he says that those who "have come to share in their spiritual blessings . . . ought also to be of service to them in material blessings" (Rom 15:27, RSV). Or again, speaking of his own work, he asks, "If we have sown spiritual good among you, is it too much if we reap your material benefits?" (1 Cor 9:11, RSV). The basic principle here, stemming from a commandment of the Lord, is that "those who proclaim the gospel should get their living by the gospel" (9:14), though this is not a right that Paul insists on (9:15–18). But in such passages Paul has in mind his communities' debt to him or to the Jerusalem church—the two sources of the gospel message. Most probably his comment in Galatians has one of these sources in mind as well. The more general expression, "all good things," may not even mean primarily material possessions but simply the expression of fellowship between receiver and giver.

In the list of gifts provided by Paul in Rom 12 we have reference to someone described as "giving aid," *proistamenos* (Rom 12:8). This occurs in the participial form, though here with more emphasis on the person involved in the activity. The NRSV translation "the leader" is quite untrue to the spirit of the Greek. In 1 Thessalonians Paul mentions the vigor ("zeal" in Rom 12) with which such work should be undertaken. The construction used clearly demonstrates that no formal office is in view, despite its more direct personal reference and its position (between references to those who make financial contributions and act mercifully).

Paul uses two other words later in Romans when he endorses Phoebe, the traveler from Cenchreae. She is called a deacon, *diakonos* (16:1), of the church at Cenchreae and a *prostatis*, helper (16:2), of many, including Paul himself. This second term, which probably relates to her being a "patron" of the Pauline mission rather than any specific activity by her in the local church, will be looked at more carefully in the following chapter. The other term provides us with the first clear application of the noun *diakonos* (the word has the same form for masculine and for feminine) to a member of a local gathering. But it would be premature to conclude from this that Phoebe held some official position in the church. She has simply distinguished herself by her helpfulness, though (as the word *prostatis* hints) the social level she occupied may well have enabled her to do this. The nominal form of the term could suggest that a more precise terminology is developing in Paul's communities or in his own thinking about them.

Very frequently a basis for the idea of office is thought to be in Paul's greetings to "bishops" and "deacons" in Philippians and in the mention of pastors (*poimenes*) and Archippus' ministry (*diakonia*) in Ephesians and Colossians respectively. In Philippians, names are used to distinguish two groups of people from the rest of the community (Phil 1:1). Yet the "saints" have precedence over "guardians" (*episkopoi*) and "servants" (*diakonoi*)—a strange order if the latter were the chief officeholders in the church. Also, and this applies to the words in Ephesians (*poimenes* and *didaskaloi*) as well,[2] the Greek has no definite article with these terms. This means that they are not being treated as titles. Maybe only one group of people is in view. Further, with the sole exception of the reference to the "true yokefellow" whose task is to settle a personal dispute, in Ephesians, Philippians, and Colossians Paul always addresses the whole community. Nowhere does he entrust special responsibilities to any single group vis-à-vis the remainder. True, certain individuals are singled out in Philippians on account of the gifts they have brought from the community to Paul (Phil 4:18), but this is a different matter (and will be treated more fully in a moment).

In any case the terms *episkopos* and *diakonos* themselves should be freed of the ecclesiastical connotations they have for us today, for they are not essentially different from the various other pastoral terms Paul uses. No real evidence exists to suggest that these terms had any technical meaning at the time. This is confirmed by the fact that in the second century Ignatius and Polycarp know of no episcopal pattern in the church at Philippi. In Colossians, Archippus, who appears to be a member of another socially prestigious household, is charged to fulfill the ministry (*diakonia*) that he has received from the Lord (Col 4:17). Though this is the very general term for ministry, it is a ministry to which Christ, not the church, appointed him. The church community's task is to encourage him to exercise it.

The conclusions we have drawn from these terms is reinforced by the thrust of the comments accompanying them. In

---

[2] Eph 4:11; cf. 1 Thess 5:12; 1 Cor 16:16.

1 Thess 5, the members should "respect" and "esteem very highly in love" Stephanas and his household, not because of any official position they have been granted within the community, nor, for that matter, because of any social position they may have occupied outside it, but "because of their work" (1 Thess 5:12–13)—on account of the way they have functioned within it. It is significant that, after saying this, Paul goes on to speak to the wider church (some commentators take the word "brethren" here to apply to the smaller group Paul has just mentioned, but this is most unlikely) and exhorts *everyone* to "admonish the idle, encourage the faint-hearted, help the weak, be patient with all" (5:14). Pastoral responsibility can never remain the preserve of a select few but always exists as an obligation upon every member of the community—even if some have a more advantageous position or a greater gift for it and so can devote themselves more energetically to the task.

This is confirmed by the reference to Stephanas and his household in 1 Cor 16. They had not been appointed to any position in the church; their prominence in Paul's eyes arose from the way they had freely "devoted (or appointed) themselves" to helping others (v. 15). The community is to "recognize" and "order itself under" such people because of this "work" and "labor" they have performed (vv. 16, 18). Only a few verses before we find Paul reminding all the members of the community that they too should be "abounding in the work of the Lord, knowing that your labor is not in vain" (15:58), just as here "everyone who works and labors" (16:16) should receive the same acknowledgment as that due to Stephanas and his household.

SOME RESIDUAL PROBLEMS

The link between "pastors" and "instructors"

The relationship between the workers discussed in 1 Thessalonians and 1 Corinthians and the prophets and teachers in these churches is unclear. In view of their work of admonition mentioned in 1 Thessalonians some link could be presumed, yet the list of gifts and ministries in 1 Cor 12 distinguishes those involved in prophecy and teaching from those involved in other helpful and practical activities. Not until Eph 4 do we find teachers and pastors closely linked. Even there the term "pastor" (*poimenes*) may be simply a metaphor whose content is defined by the following "teacher" (*didaskalos*).[3] In any case, the prophets remain in a group by themselves. So we must not assume that prophetic and teaching gifts on the one hand and pastoral contributions on the other were necessarily combined in the one person.

The reason for this may well lie in the specifically charismatic basis of the first and the partially social foundation of the second. (Not that these two categories should be set off against one another; we saw earlier how Paul embraces "natural" capacities and "social" advantages within his concept of what is charismatic.) Also we need to remind ourselves that *all* members of the church are called upon to prophesy and teach in some measure and that those who have a special ministry of this kind are not to be listened to uncritically. Evaluation of the prophet's message comes explicitly into view in 1 Cor 14. The need to test the teacher's instruction follows from Paul's warning to disown false teaching when it infiltrates the community.[4] The teacher's acceptance by the community corresponds to the degree with which the teacher genuinely speaks on God's behalf.

The question of "ordination"

In none of the above passages do we find Paul suggesting that people have undergone ordination to the ministries they fulfill. There are places where Acts records that Paul and Barnabas "appointed elders . . . in every church," with prayer and fasting (Acts 14:23). This process of appointment probably took place through the laying on of hands, as it did elsewhere. But in these references in Acts we find that, either through the word of a prophet in the assembly (13:3) or through the discerning choice of all the members (6:1–6), people were chosen with a view to their fitness for the task. Hands were then laid upon them as a tangible sign of fellowship and prayer, not as a mechanism for the creation of a ministry or imparting of special grace. In Acts 14:23, Luke mentions that "elders" were appointed in this way.[5] However, outside the Pastorals (see later), Paul never uses the term *presbuteros*, elder, in his letters. Luke uses the term *episkopos* once to refer to elders (20:28), but this is probably a later standardization of Paul's more fluid terminology.

---

[3] Cf. 2 Bar. 77:13–16.
[4] 1 Cor 14:6–9; Rom 16:17–18.
[5] Cf. Acts 20:17.

The origin of "eldership"

In view of suggestions that the notion of eldership was drawn from the synagogue, it should be noted that there is no evidence whatever for the synagogue having this type of position. The Jewish sources mention no such group. The one reference in the NT that describes Jewish elders has the elders of the city in view, not office holders in the synagogue (Luke 7:3). (In secular Greek *presbuteros* simply meant "senior man"—at least outside Egypt. Just possibly Luke understood it this way in Acts. If he did, then Paul appointed some "elders" to a particular responsibility, not some people to the position of elder.) As we have seen, Paul does not use the term "elder" in his undisputed letters.

The word *episkopos* served a wide range of purposes in non-biblical Greek, being applied to men and women overseeing various activities or other people, philosophers examining and testing their hearers,[6] and, most relevantly, officeholders in voluntary societies. However, the term never refers to any precise function. The positions held are always of a minor kind. Biblical Greek uses the word freely but knows no clearly defined office bearing that title.[7] In any case, Paul's understanding of "oversight" grew out of his view of gift, service, and work. This transformed the meaning of any terms he might have borrowed from the surrounding culture.

CONCLUSION

Surveying these passages as a whole, we conclude that the varied and imprecise terminology used by Paul, its comparatively infrequent and unemphatic occurrence in his letters, and the thrust of his surrounding remarks, all confirm the view that formal positions within the communities are nowhere in mind. We have noted a gradual move towards a more specific and personal, rather than general and functional, terminology. However, considering the small amount of evidence we have for such, this should not be overstressed. Since variations in terminology may at times

---

[6] Epictetus, *Dissertationes* 3.22.97. Plutarch, *De Solone* 19.1.
[7] E.g., Neh 11:9; 2 Kings 11:15; 1 Macc 1:51. Cf. Philo, *Dreams* 2.186. Josephus, *Antiquities* 12.254.

reflect local usage in the communities (influenced perhaps by the backgrounds from which their adherents came), it would be unwise to generalize from the appearance of *episkopos* in Philippians or *diakonos* in Philippians and Romans.

We cannot say, then, that Paul's communities were hierarchical in structure. He did not vest authority in one person, or in a group of people, over the remaining members. On the other hand his communities were not egalitarian. He did not vest authority in all equally nor did his communities select or call certain people to act on their behalf in some democratic fashion. Paul's communities were instead theocratic in structure. Because God gave to each individual within the community some contribution for its welfare, there is a strong democratic tendency. Everyone participates authoritatively in its activities. Because the Spirit distributes gifts and advantages unequally, so that some have more to contribute than others, there is also an element of differentiation. But neither the democratic nor the differentiating note is given a formal structure. Instead they are transformed through their subordination to the charismatic and, if I may coin the term, "diaconic" principle.

Significant persons are present in Paul's communities. Their authority comes from the ministry discharged by them in the community rather than from their status outside it or position within it, and it is not an irrevocable possession. Insofar as all Christians discharge a ministry through the exercise of the gifts they have been given or the advantages they have acquired, authority resides not only in the core contributors but in everyone without exception. While there are some whom God speaks or acts authoritatively through more frequently than others, their authority does not differ in principle from that which accrues in some measure to all. We have here a *participatory society* in which authority is dispersed throughout the whole membership. For all the democratic tendencies present in the synagogue and, to a lesser extent, in Qumran, nothing quite like it existed in contemporary Judaism or Hellenism. (Compare the earlier examination of authority figures in these communities and the cults.) But are there not figures outside Paul's participatory society, viz., its apostolic founder, his associates, and others involved in apostolic activity, who have a qualitatively different kind authority over it? As we consider this question, the essential character of the authority present in all these ministries will come into clearer focus.

15

—∽—

PAUL AND HIS CO-WORKERS

Who were the influential people in the communities founded by Paul? How did they achieve their influence? Prominent persons emerge in Paul's churches, but their authority does not stem from any special status or office so much as from the special gifts they have and their exercise of them. Well-known figures who exist outside the churches in Paul's mission also play a part in their foundation and continuing life. We must gain a clearer understanding of exactly who was involved in the mission and on what terms. We must also obtain a precise definition of its charter, particularly with respect to the communities founded by Paul's mission. This will enable us in chapter sixteen to consider the role played by those involved permanently in local churches yet having some connection with Paul's work, as well as that played by Paul's hand-picked associates in the mission. Since neither Paul nor Luke discuss these matters in a systematic way, information about them has to be gleaned from passing comments on the activities of the mission or from passages dealing primarily with other matters.

PAUL'S CO-WORKERS

Paul began his missionary work as a companion apostle and assistant (Acts 13:2–4) and later became the senior member (Acts

13:13ff.).[1] On the second journey he chose his own assistant (15:40) and then broadened the membership of his mission by the recruitment of additional personnel, beginning with Timothy (16:1–3). He began by relying upon his rabbinic status and using synagogues as platforms for his message.[2] Over time, his approach developed into one that was more in line with the methods of those who may be called the "Sophists" of his time. Utilizing his Roman citizenship and social position, he gained an entrance into certain levels of the Hellenistic social elite. (Paul's family subsidized his education in Jerusalem and received citizenship in Tarsus. Since both of these required substantial property and status, Paul's family must have met the requirements of the social elite.)

In the Eastern provinces, the Hellenistic social elite comprised members of the commercial and administrative classes more than, as in Rome itself, of the traditional aristocracy. Such people were sometimes already sympathetic towards or connected with the local synagogue. It was from this base that Paul frequently communicated his message, made his converts, and established his churches.[3]

Unlike the "Sophists" and the rabbis (who only in the second century exercised a trade alongside their teaching), Paul generally worked with his hands in the places where he stayed and used his earnings to help support his colleagues, who increased in number, as well as pay for his own needs.[4] (Presumably Paul's family did not financially support his conversion to Christianity.) Paul was essentially a part-time, not a full-time, missionary, carrying on his evangelistic and pastoral activities alongside the practice of his trade. This makes his achievements all the more extraordinary. However, at times he could not work—when he was imprisoned, for example, or constantly on the move.

Financial supporters

At this point the hospitality and financial help of Paul's supporters became necessary. From his writings we can single out

---

[1] See also Acts 11:25, 30; 12:25; 13:7.
[2] Acts 13:5, 14; 14:1 et al.; 17:1, 10, 17; 18:4, 19; 19:8.
[3] Acts 16:15; 17:4–7, 12; 18:5–7; Rom 16:2, 4, 23; Phil 4:2–3; Phlm 7 (cf. v. 22). See also Acts 19:31; Phil 4:22.
[4] 2 Thess 3:6–9; 1 Cor 9:3–6; Acts 18:3; 20:33–35. Cf. *m. 'Ab.* 2.2; 3.21. See also Cicero, *De Officiis* 1.150. Cf. Dio Chrysostom, *Orationes* 3.123ff.

as many as forty persons who were actual or potential sponsors of his activities; his letters abound with thanks for their generosity. Through the exercise of hospitality and granting of financial aid, they enabled him to carry out his work freely in the new areas he entered, and they often aided him when he ran afoul of the authorities or was imprisoned for his efforts.

Working associates

Paul's writings also reveal a second group of people who helped his ministry: his colleagues or working associates. A number of these came and went from local churches, sometimes rendering particular services to him—bringing financial assistance (Phil 4:18), greetings from his churches,[5] appeals for his help (1 Cor 1:11)—and sometimes undertaking return services to the groups they had come from (Phil 2:25–30). Others were more or less permanent members of his entourage, attending him in a secretarial way (Rom 16:22), or medical capacity (Col 4:14), or being deployed to carry out specific and limited tasks vis-à-vis local churches that he could not fulfill, e.g., carrying letters and/or verbal messages[6] and overseeing the collection for the Jerusalem poor.[7] Though Paul on occasions was forced to deal with situations alone, most of the time he had a circle of colleagues around him. In contrast to his patrons, who (with one or two exceptions) were fixed local sponsors, these temporarily or permanently journeyed with him and actively participated in the work.

Race, Class, and Gender Distinctions

As we have done already with the composition of Paul's communities, we must now examine the way in which the traditional race, class, and gender distinctions affected the membership of his missionary work.

---

[5] 1 Cor 16:17–18; Col 1:7–8; 4:12.
[6] 1 Thess 3:6; 1 Cor 4:17; 2 Cor 7:6–15; Phil 2:19–23; Col 4:7–9; Eph 6:21–22.
[7] 1 Cor 16:3; 2 Cor 8:16–23.

Jews and Gentiles

Among the forty or so persons mentioned as Paul's possible patrons we have only one or two Jewish Christians explicitly named, e.g., Crispus (Acts 18:8); however, the majority of those directly involved in his work are Jewish converts to Christianity. According to Acts, Paul begins his mission among the Gentiles with Barnabas and his cousin Mark, all three Jews of the Dispersion, the latter two from Cyprus (Acts 4:36; Col 4:10). After his break with Barnabas, Paul takes Silas, a distinguished member of the church at Jerusalem (Acts 15:22, 40) with him. On this second journey he also recruits Timothy, who, though he has a Greek father, was raised by his Jewish mother in the religion of her forebears (16:1). At Corinth the party is enlarged by the addition of Aquila and Priscilla, the former from Pontus and the latter probably from either there or Rome (18:1–2). On his third missionary tour we have first mention of a full Gentile, Erastus, the city treasurer from Corinth,[8] (unless Luke, who joined them at Troas on the previous trip, is such—Acts 16:10). Among Paul's "co-workers," Lucius, Jason, Sosipater (Rom 16:21), and probably Sosthenes and Jesus Justus (1 Cor 1:1), were all Jews. Aristarchus was also one of Paul's kinsmen

From this point on it becomes increasingly difficult to identify the racial origin of the people associated with Paul, viz., at Ephesus—Gaius and Aristarchus (Acts 19:29); on the return journey through Macedonia—Sopater, Secundus, Tychicus, another Gaius, and Trophimus (20:4). Others whose race is difficult to determine are mentioned at various points in Paul's letters.

The declining Jewish Christian membership in his mission is reflected in his regretful admission in Colossians that Aristarchus, Mark, and Jesus Justus "are the only men of the circumcision among my fellow workers for the kingdom of God" (Col 4:10–11, RSV). The predominance of Jewish Christians in the early days of the mission should not cause us to overlook the comparable participation of Gentiles, notably Titus[9] and Tychicus.[10] Interestingly, the three most active members in the work appear to have been Silas, a Jew, Timothy, a half-Jew and half-Greek, and

---

[8] Acts 19:22; cf. Rom 16:23.
[9] Gal 2:1–5; 2 Cor 2:12–13; 7:6, 13; 8:6, 16, 18, 23; 12:18.
[10] Acts 20:4; Col 4:7; Eph 6:21.

Titus, a Greek. The increasing ratio of Gentile converts involved in the mission as it progresses has already been noted.

Slaves

Were slaves included among those accompanying Paul? Only in one instance can we be certain this took place, viz., the celebrated case of the runaway slave Onesimus.[11] Although Paul eventually returns him to his master Philemon, he nowhere suggests that the presence of Onesimus was inappropriate. In his letter to Philemon, Paul clearly wishes to have Onesimus back (Phlm 13). He even hints that Philemon might exceed Paul's desire (v. 21), perhaps by freeing Onesimus from his service so that he would be free to assist Paul.

This raises an interesting, if speculative, point. In many ways the most unexpected aspect of Paul's mission in this area may be that there is no suggestion that he brought with him or obtained slaves or servants to undertake the various practical arrangements that his missionary enterprise involved. The Acts of the Apostles and Paul's letters indicate that, by virtue of his family background and Roman citizenship, he was a person of some status and thus would normally be expected to have his own slaves with him on extensive travels.

Women

We can now turn to Paul's attitude to women as it comes to expression in the course of his apostolic mission. His first and second journeys start with an all-male group. Not until Paul crosses from Asia into Macedonia do women begin to feature in the story in a significant way. At Philippi, a Roman colony where apparently there was no synagogue, Paul and his colleagues sought out Jews and Gentile "god-fearers" who might be gathered for prayer by the river. As a result of this encounter, Lydia, a woman from Thyatira engaged in commercial activity, was converted, together with her household (Acts 16:13–15). She not only opened her home to the apostle and his assistants but also became host to the new church there (v. 40). From this point on we find frequent reference to the adherence of "leading women

---

[11] Col 4:8–9; Phlm 10ff.

among the Greeks" to the apostle's cause, for example, at Thessalonica (17:4), Berea (v. 12), and Athens (v. 34).

At Corinth, he made the acquaintance of a couple who went on to play an important role in his activities: Aquila and Prisca (or less formally, Priscilla), who had been exiled from Rome by Claudius' decree in AD 49–50 (Acts 18:1–3). Paul and especially Luke usually mention Priscilla first, perhaps because her status was superior to her husband's.[12] (Possibly she belonged by birth or manumission to the *gens Acilia*, an influential family among the Roman nobility.) Rather than being confined to domestic duties, Priscilla is involved alongside her husband in the family business. In view of their later practice at Ephesus and Rome (1 Cor 16:19; Rom 16:3), they were probably hosts to one of the infant churches in Corinth. When Paul returned to Asia, they came with him as "co-workers" in his mission,[13] so from this point on Paul's missionary party includes women as well as men. When certain deficiencies became apparent at Ephesus in the teaching of an itinerant Jewish Christian, Apollos, both wife and husband (she is again named first) are involved in setting him straight (Acts 18:27). Priscilla's basis for doing this lay in her calling as a "fellowworker" with Paul. This couple appears once more amongst the greetings at the end of Paul's letter to the Romans, where they are described as people to whom not only Paul "but also all the churches of the Gentiles give thanks" (Rom 16:4).

There are many other women who were co-workers with Paul. Mary is a woman who has "labored" strenuously amongst the Romans (Rom 16:5). Since Paul elsewhere uses the term "laborer" in connection with "fellow-worker" (1 Cor 16:16) and as a description of his own apostolic work,[14] she may have been independently involved in Christian mission. Two other women, similarly engaged in Rome, are "those workers in the Lord, Tryphaena and Tryphosa," probably two sisters (Rom 16:12). Then, at the head of this list of greetings, Paul commends his "sister" Phoebe who he says "has been a helper of many and of myself as well" (v. 2). Outside this list in Romans, Paul refers to two Philippian women, Euodia and Syntyche, who "labored side by side" with him in the gospel along with the rest of his "co-workers" (Phil

---

[12]Acts 18:18, 26; Rom 16:3.
[13]Acts 18:18; cf. Rom 16:3.
[14]Gal 4:11; Phil 2:16; Col 2:29.

2:2–4). Mary, Tryphaena, and Tryphosa (and perhaps Euodia and Syntyche) are examples of unmarried or widowed women acting as missionary "workers" in a localized setting. It is more than likely that Junias (Rom 6:7) is a female apostle (at least that is how the early commentators interpreted the reference to her). If women do not occupy as prominent a place as men in Paul's missionary apparatus, they nevertheless play an important part within it and contribute significantly to the spread of Christianity in the early years of its expansion.

PAUL'S PRACTICE IN HIS SOCIAL CONTEXT

Little can be said about the social background to Paul's practice of combining Jews and Gentiles in his mission or about his apparently preferring to travel unattended by slaves. Although Jews and non-Jews interacted in various areas of daily life, particularly in more Hellenized upper class circles, there does not seem to be any real precedent for their collaborating to propagate religious ideas. We have noted earlier the spread of the mystery cults through citizens from the cults' homeland and through adherents from other lands and cultures. But we do not know of any attempt to do this along the lines of Paul's mission, with reliance upon a team of colleagues from different religious and national backgrounds. As for traveling unattended, it seems that itinerant teachers and miracle-workers were normally accompanied by servants—Paul's contemporary Apollonius of Tyana is an example—who were employed to carry out various secretarial and practical duties. The Cynics are the exception; they prided themselves on journeying without slaves.[15] So while Paul's practice in many ways cuts across the normal procedures of his day, it did have some parallels.

More can be said about the role of women in various public activities. Among the later rabbis who composed the Mishnah this question was very easily settled: women were not permitted to engage in any real public activity. This attitude is reflected in earlier Jewish writings as well. Unmarried women especially were

---

[15] Philostratus, *Apollonius* 1.18. But see Epictetus, *Dissertationes* 4.22, 45–47.

advised to stay within the borders of their house and not venture outside them.[16] Married women had to cover themselves when they went out so that they would not be observed by those with whom they might come into contact. Failure to comply with this placed the husband under an obligation to divorce his wife.[17] Conversation with anyone in public was also frowned upon (John 4:27). (A notorious exception was Beruriah, the daughter of Rabbi Meir.) While stricter attitudes may have prevailed after AD 70 the principle "Talk not much with womankind" was enunciated a century and a half before Jesus. Since this applied to one's own wife, how much more should it govern one's relationship with another's![18]

Concerning women's attendance at meetings, Philo writes:

> market places and council halls, law courts and gatherings, and meetings where a large number of people are assembled—in short all public life with its discussion and deeds, in times of peace and war—are proper for men. It is suitable for women to stay indoors and to live in retirement, limited by the middle door [to the men's apartments] for the young girls and the outer door for married women.[19]

The Gospels show that women did not customarily converse with strangers.[20] But in many ways, the ideals of the Jewish Dispersion recorded by Philo were more rigid than the practice of Jewish women. In Jewish towns women frequently had to assist their husbands in their craft or profession, at the point of sale as well as during production.[21] As the Gospels indicate, women occasionally prophesied in the Temple, moved freely about Jerusalem, and (unless Jesus' presence provoked untraditional behavior) also entertained visiting teachers and listened to instruction.[22] They seem to have caused no surprise as they followed Jesus around the countryside (Luke 8:1–3; Matt 20:20). In rural areas especially, women traveled from one place to another, assisted in the fields,

---

[16]Philo, *Flaccus* 11, 89. Cf. Ecclus 42:11–12; 2 Macc 3:19; 3 Macc 1:18–19.

[17]*m. Ket.* 7.6.

[18]*m. 'Ab.* 1.5. Cf. earlier Ecclus 9:9.

[19]Philo, *Special Laws* 3.169.

[20]Luke 1:39–40, 8:19–21, 43; John 4:7. *m. Ket.* 1.10; *m. Yeb.* 15.2; *m. Eduy.* 1.12, but see John 4:27.

[21]*m. Ket.* 9.4.

[22]Luke 2:36–38; 4:39; 10:38–42; 11:27–28; John 11:20; 12:2.

drew water from the village well, sold goods at the door, served at tables, and were less concerned with the stricter urban proprieties of dress. Amongst the aristocracy even more freedom was permitted (e.g., Matt 14:6). Practices in the middle of the first century were certainly more free and less uniform than the later rabbinic writings suggest.

The Greeks' prevailing attitudes on the public role of women were not dissimilar. Women had been traditionally disqualified from political life and, until their marriage, daughters were generally confined to the home.[23] Daughters certainly attended festivals, funerals, and the like, and married women attended civic speeches and religious rituals, went shopping and walking, etc.[24] Yet discussion of moral and other matters was primarily a masculine pastime from which as a rule the women were excluded. When her husband had guests, a wife would retire to her own quarters, since it was only the *hetairai*, or courtesans, who participated openly in such activities.[25] Yet Acts suggests that women could participate in commercial life, at least in places like Corinth, and move freely from one province to another (Acts 18:3).

In Roman life this restriction did not apply, though in company the wife was expected to support her husband and not disagree with him.[26] This may have been the case elsewhere, especially in the Greek cities of the East.[27] In both Rome and the East there existed wider opportunities for women to engage in public life. Roman noblewomen were able to move around more freely in public than their Greek counterparts, to receive some education in moral and other subjects, and to belong to women's societies.[28] Some indirectly exerted considerable influence upon the course of political affairs.[29] In Macedonia, married and widowed women openly participated in commercial life, both inside and outside their native cities, as the evidence from Acts demonstrates (Acts 16:14–15). On occasion some received special honorific grants of full citizenship. They could also occasionally

---

[23]Xenophon, *Oeconomicus* 8.10.

[24]Aristophanes, *Frogs* 1346–1351.

[25]Sallust, *Bellum Catilinae* 23.3f.; 28.2.

[26]Plutarch, *Advice on Marriage* 19, 32, 48. Seneca, *Ad Helvium* 17.2–5.

[27]Cf. Rom 16:1; Acts 18:26.

[28]Livy, *History* 3.44ff. Pliny, *Epistulae* 4.19.1–5 (cf. Plutarch, *De Pompeio* 55.1). Ovid, *Ars Amatoria* 3.634–642.

[29]E.g., Sallust, *Bellum Catilinae* 24.3; 25.5. Tacitus, *Annals* 1.3–14.

instigate judicial proceedings and, in some places, become magistrates. We have two examples of women who accompanied a semi-itinerant philosopher or teacher/exorcist, though this practice seems to be most exceptional.[30] So free women in such areas were far from living secluded and subordinate lives.

CONCLUSION

As with the composition of his churches, Paul's mission in part contradicted, in part reflected, and in part extended the various crosscurrents of national, social, and gender cooperation in his day. The Jewish/Gentile identity of his colleagues seems to have been his most adventurous practice, though his apparent refusal to be attended by slaves was also unusual, at least in Hellenistic circles, less so considering Paul's Jewish background. We have ample evidence of the prominent part played by women in the advancement of his mission, particularly on Macedonian and Roman soil. While this reflects the greater freedom enjoyed by women in such areas, it also testifies to Paul's flexibility of practice where that would not lead to offence. His approach resulted in the elevation of women to a place in religious work for which we have little contemporary parallel.

---

[30] Diogenes Laertius 6.96 (Crates and Hipparchia). Justin Martyr, *First Apology* 26 (Simon Magus and Helena) if reliable.

16

—m—

THE MISSION
AND THE CHURCHES

We have seen that Paul's work existed as a separate entity with a life of its own alongside the local churches founded and supported by it. But just as Paul's apostolic career has a history that is independent of the communities fathered by him, the reverse is also true. His communities tended to move away from close dependence on Paul. In fact, clear differences existed between Paul's mission and the churches at the level of the principles upon which they operated. The precise points where these differences occur can now be plotted.

At first sight the structure of Paul's mission has certain *similarities* with that of the churches founded by him. So, for example: (a) there is an extensive use of family terminology between those involved in the work, viz., father (Phil 2:22), son (Phlm 10), brother,[1] sister (Rom 16:1; Phlm 2); (b) there are gifts and ministries in evidence among the group, viz., apostles (Gal 1:1 et. al.), prophets,[2] evangelism (2 Cor 8:18, 20), serving (2 Cor 8:20), healing (Acts 28:8–9); and (c) there is a strong note of

---

[1] 1 Thess 3:2; 1 Cor 1:1; 16:12, 20; 2 Cor 1:1; 2:13; 8:18, 22, 23; Phil 2:25; 4:21; Col 1:1; 4:7–9; Phlm 1, 20; Eph 6:21.
[2] 2 Cor 8:23; Rom 16:7; Acts 15:32.

equality present among its members, indicated by Paul's way of referring to them as fellow-workers,[3] fellow-soldiers (Phil 2:25; Phlm 2), fellow-servants (Col 4:7), and by the types of people represented, viz., Jews and Gentiles, men and women, slaves and free. Alongside these similarities, however, exist some real *differences* between the work and the churches.

DIFFERENCES BETWEEN PAUL'S MISSION AND HIS CHURCHES

Character

In the first place, Paul's whole operation has a specialized character. It exists for a specific and limited purpose. Unlike the churches, its basis lies not just in Jesus' death and resurrection and the Spirit's fruit and gifts. Nor is its goal primarily the welding together of its members into a common life. Like the members of the churches, members of Paul's mission must possess gifts and the maturity that goes with them. Experience of Christ and the Spirit, however, are not in themselves sufficient to qualify someone for inclusion in the mission. Paul's mission is unique. It is itinerant, not local, and does not constitute itself chiefly by gathering. It is constantly on the move and is more marked by the dispersion of its members than by their assembling. This does not mean that those involved in it never "churched" together. In some measure that must have happened among those who were traveling together, especially when no local churches were in the vicinity. But this was not the main purpose of the group.

Function

In the second place, nowhere do we find any hint of the "body" metaphor, so frequently used of the church, being applied to this group. Those involved in Paul's mission were not primarily participating in a common life—though that certainly did also occur—but rather sharing in a common task. Hence the descrip-

---

[3] 1 Cor 3:9; 16:16; 2 Cor 8:23; Rom 16:3, 9, 21; Phil 2:25; Col 4:11; Phlm 1.

tion *ergon*, work, which lies at the root of so much of Paul's thinking about this.[4] The members were more other-directed than inner-directed. Paradoxically, this may have led to their sharing "all things in common" more than the communities founded by them. For example, whatever Paul earned at his trade seems to have gone into funding his missionary enterprise (Acts 20:34); gifts from his churches were presumably treated in the same way (Phil 4:14–16). The "work" may be viewed as a sort of mobile commune in which all resources are pooled. Unlike the churches, however, it has as its focal point not a *group* of people but *one* person: Paul himself. They were drawn into the orbit of Paul's own ministry and became an extension of it. So this work has as its basis Paul's commission and certain relevant gifts that can help fulfill it and has as its purpose the preaching of the gospel and the establishing of churches. In contrast, the churches have as their foundation the message preached by Paul and the reality of the spirit and have as their goal the growing harmony and maturity of all who belong to them.

Gifts

In the third place, despite the variety of gifts represented in the mission, not all those listed by Paul as occurring in congregational contexts are present. Most prominent are those gifts that can be aimed towards outsiders rather than the Christian group. What we have here is a *concentration* of gifts, with the most significant ones disproportionately present. Paul's entourage consists essentially of a group of specialists, whose gifts have to do with the most fundamental areas of religious life. Evangelism, rather than edification, is the primary task—even though, as churches are founded in various places, edification of church members also takes place. The activities of Paul's workers are directed outside the group to a different circle; they frequently exercise their gifts outside the home in places where people gather, e.g., religious buildings, lecture halls, debating forums, market places, etc. Some in the church had similar gifts for commending the Christian message to outsiders, and these were also chiefly employed outside the local gathering (Col 1:7). On a smaller scale their activities would run parallel to Paul's work, related to the church

---

[4] Gal 6:4; 1 Cor 3:13–15; 9:1; 16:10; Phil 2:30.

from which they had come but not strictly "church" activities. Both the churches and Paul's mission had some members with evangelistic gifts that were exercised in similar ways. The main difference between the two groups is that Paul and those centered around him, his mission, had a much larger focus on evangelistic gifts, to the exclusion of the many other gifts seen in the churches.

Authority

Fourthly, for all that he says about the cooperative nature of his work, Paul himself was not only the main influence in the group but the one around whose personal authority its activities centered. Paul regarded his ministry to the Gentiles as divinely granted and, after his break with Barnabas, assumed a position of authority among his assistants that he did not allow those in the churches subsequently founded by him to have. There were always several leading figures in his communities,[5] so that a system of checks and balances existed between them. But there is only one Paul. And whereas it is ultimately the whole congregation, including its apostle, in whom authority resides, in his work Paul appears quite definitely to be "in charge." So, for example, he is the one who "sends" or "leaves" his colleagues to engage in various activities[6] and who generally seems to decide what the next step will be throughout the journeyings of the group.[7]

There are only two occasions where Paul is not treated as the authority. The first one is when Barnabas refused to comply with Paul's insistence that Mark should not come with them (Acts 15:36–41). Because Barnabas had been the senior member of the duo, this disagreement resulted in the establishing of two separate missionary works. The second occasion is when Apollos, having been urged by Paul to visit Corinth "with the other brethren," declined to do so since "it was not at all his will to go now" (1 Cor 16:12). Since Apollos was engaged independently in evangelistic activity he did not come under Paul's authority. That Paul wanted Barnabas and Apollos to yield to his wishes does not mean that he was authoritarian in manner or that consultation

---

[5] 1 Thess 5:12–13; Phil 1:1; cf. Acts 13:1–2.
[6] 1 Thess 3:2; 1 Cor 4:17; 2 Cor 8:18ff.; Phil 2:19, 23, 25, 28; Col 4:8–9; Phlm 12; Eph 6:22.
[7] Cf. Acts 16:9; 18:1, 18–21; 19:21; 20:13, 16–17 et al.

with his fellow-workers was absent. The nature of Paul's relationship with his colleagues and the consideration of both Paul's desires and those of his colleagues is beautifully displayed in his exclamation to the Corinthians: "But thanks be to God who puts the same earnest care for you into the heart of Titus. For he not only accepted our appeal, but being himself very earnest he is going to you of his own accord."[8]

INTER-RELATIONSHIP BETWEEN PAUL'S MISSION AND HIS CHURCHES

Mutual participation

Despite their different orientations, the "work" and the "churches" participate in each others' activities in various ways. Paul and those involved in other missions seek to nurture the small communities they have founded and lead them to Christian adulthood. They carry out this responsibility by making personal visits of longer or shorter duration, writing letters to help them with their problems, sending emissaries as their personal representatives, and praying constantly for their welfare and progress.[9] But always Paul is moving on, "making it [his] ambition to preach the gospel, not where Christ has already been named, lest [he] build on someone else's foundation."[10]

For their part, the churches seek to forward the pioneering work in which Paul and other apostles are engaged. They fulfill this in the following ways: by *transmitting* the Spirit's call of one of their members to the work of evangelism and *commissioning* that person to whom the Spirit has given the gift for the task (Acts 13:1–3); by *participating* in the work that results, whether as members of the sponsoring church or of churches founded by the mission, through forwarding financial aid (Phil 4:14–16), praying for its success,[11] and maintaining personal contact through letters or

---

[8] 2 Cor 8:16, 17, RSV; see also 2 Cor 8:6; 9:5; 12:18; Phil 4:2.
[9] 1 Thess 1:2ff.; 2 Thess 1:3ff.; 3:1ff.; 1 Cor 1:4ff.; 2 Cor 1:3ff.; 13:9; Rom 1:8ff.; Phil 1:3ff.; Col 1:3ff.
[10] Rom 15:20; cf. 2 Cor 10:13–16.
[11] 1 Thess 5:25; 2 Cor 1:11; Rom 15:30–32; Phil 1:19–20; Col 4:18; Eph 6:18–20.

visits;[12] by *assembling* to hear from those involved in the work everything that had taken place[13] and *sending* representatives to other churches to defend their activities when they come under suspicion (Acts 15:1ff.). In all these ways they actually "participate" in the apostolic mission and are members of it. This provides the model for their involvement in any evangelistic work.

The principles upon which Paul's mission operated do not in all respects conform to those he impressed upon the churches that he founded. Some overlap occurs but, as has been shown, there is a quite intentional divergence between them. The two groups are interdependent and assist one another in their work, but the purpose for which each exists, the skills upon which each depends, and the authority through which each lives are not identical. This once again prompts the question: did the churches founded by Paul really possess as independent a life as his mission had apart from them? How subservient were the churches to him, his associates, and other apostles? To answer this question we must compare the role of leading local members temporarily or intermittently caught up in Paul's missionary work with the role of permanent colleagues chosen by Paul who have only an occasional contact with particular local churches.

Local co-workers

The first group, the local members, comprises those instrumental in founding a church and maintaining personal contact with Paul as it developed. Since they engaged in these activities they were also involved in his work. That is why he speaks of them as "fellow-workers" and "laborers." Participating in church is one thing, commencing a church is another; the latter quite possibly depended upon a prior call, either directly from God or mediated through Paul. Stephanas and his household almost certainly fell into this category (1 Cor 16:15). So too Philemon, Apphia, and Archippus (Phlm 1). This group also includes others who, like Epaphras, independently evangelized their own home cities and founded communities but then maintained contact with Paul (Col 1:7; 4:12). For this reason Paul designates Epaphras a "fellow-slave" and "servant."

---

[12] 1 Cor 1:11; 7:1; 16:17–18; Phil 2:25; 4:18; Col 1:17 et al.
[13] Acts 14:26; 18:22–23.

Although the communities did not elect representatives to lead their gatherings, from time to time they did set aside certain people to perform particular extramural tasks on their behalf. When certain functions had to be fulfilled elsewhere it was impracticable for the community as a whole to carry them out. Instead, it deputized one or more members for tasks such as a journey to Paul taking monetary aid or news of the community's progress. Epaphroditus carried out this task on behalf of the community at Philippi. Paul describes him as his "fellow-worker" and "soldier" and as the Philippians' "apostle" and "servant" (Phil 2:25). Another example is those people "accredited by letter," who assisted in carrying the collection to Jerusalem—something Paul also refers to as a "work" (2 Cor 8:19). In this instance, there is only a temporary and limited commission to fulfill.

All such people, insists Paul, are to be given their due honor by the communities who commissioned them or whom they represent, not because of any superior position or rank they possess, but on account of the helpful services they perform. So with Epaphroditus in mind, Paul encourages his readers to "honor such people. For he nearly died for the work of Christ, risking his life to complete your service to me."[14] We find here a further application of the principle of recognition that underlies Paul's whole approach to servanthood within the community. The worth of these people and the acknowledgment they should enjoy are determined by the quality of their labors, not by any inherent status.

Itinerant colleagues

We turn to the second group, Paul's intermediate colleagues. Outside the Pastorals (which will be discussed separately later) we do not have a great deal of evidence about the position of Paul's co-workers in the communities where they spend time. Paul certainly instructs the churches to graciously receive such people when they are in the vicinity. But when he commends them, he does so based on the nature and quality of their work, not the position they hold in his missionary organization or have by right.

For example, when Timothy is sent by Paul to Corinth to remind the community of his message, his position in the church

---

[14]Phil 2:29–30; cf. 1 Cor 16:17–18; 2 Cor 8:9; Col 4:13.

on arrival is not automatically guaranteed by his connection with Paul's mission. Paul has to urge them to "put him at ease" among them and "not to despise him" since "he is doing the work of the Lord as I am" (1 Cor 16:10–11a). He should be accepted because he performs the mission God has given him to fulfill. Doubts also existed about the way the same community would accept Titus, but Paul's mind was eventually "set at rest" when he heard that they had received him with the respect due to him on account of his work (2 Cor 7:13–15).

The sending of Tychicus to Colossae, Timothy to Philippi and Thessalonica, and Titus to Corinth again illustrates the temporary commission such associates of Paul have. Their worth is endorsed on the grounds of their activities and sense of commitment to the task. He reminds the Corinthians that Titus is his "partner and fellow-worker in your service" who, "being very earnest," journeys to them "of his own accord" (8:17, 23). Of Timothy Paul says, "I have no one like him, who will be genuinely anxious for your welfare" and goes on to add, "But Timothy's worth you know, how as a son with a father he has served with me in the gospel."[15] He describes Tychicus as "a beloved brother and faithful minister and fellow servant in the Lord" and says that he has "sent him for this very purpose" (Col 4:7–8). Paul consistently appeals to their faithful performance of the work entrusted to them, not to any honorific position they have been given. The authority these people exercise when they visit the local communities does not differ in principle from that of residents in the community who have special functions to fulfill.

PAUL'S MISSION COMPARED TO OTHER ITINERANT ACTIVITY WORK

Generally

At this point we can sum up what has been said about the structure and character of Paul's missionary work and compare this with other kinds of itinerant activity in Jewish and Graeco-Roman circles around the same time. Traveling was quite widely

---

[15] Phil 2:19–23, RSV; cf. 1 Thess 3:1–8.

undertaken in the first century, if mainly by those in business or by the well-to-do. We have already noted that philosophic "missionaries" toured the ancient world disseminating their views. Stoic and Cynic philosophers in particular sometimes operated in this way, their travels and methods being celebrated in historical romances[16] and derided in satirical essays.[17] We know from Acts that Jewish exorcists traveled around the synagogues of the Dispersion (Acts 19:13–15), while the Gospels tell us that (individual?) Pharisees journeyed by land and sea to make Gentile converts (Matt 23:15). Just how frequently any of this took place is hard to say; there is little evidence to draw upon. However, there are precedents for the sort of traveling and preaching activity in which Paul was involved.

Is there any parallel to the size of his missionary apparatus or to the complex network of relationships built up around it? So far as one can trust the evidence, Cynic philosophers like Diogenes seem to have moved around mainly as individual teachers. Some itinerants, such as the "prophet" Alexander, traveled with a single partner. Others who journeyed with a group, like Apollonius, did so with "disciples," a "scribe," and "secretary," not with genuine co-workers.[18] The "Sophists" sought payment for their services, a right Paul consistently declined to press. Paul's "search and destroy" visit to Damascus may suggest that Pharisees traveled with ancillary help to assist them, but this may be affected by his working under the high priest's direction (Acts 9:7). Apart from the NT, we do not really have any evidence for Pharisaic proselytizing in the Diaspora. On Jewish territory outside Judaea, according to the Gospels, Pharisees generally appear in a group.[19]

In general, Paul's enlistment of full and part-time helpers on his later missionary journeys, at times swelling his company of co-workers substantially, has no parallel in the field of contemporary religious propagation. This could also be said of his mission's continuing close involvement—through messengers, letters, and prayers—in the communities founded by it, and their participation—through visits, letters, gifts, and prayers—in

---

[16] E.g., Philostratus, *Apollonius of Tyana*.

[17] E.g., Lucian, *The False Prophet*.

[18] See Dio Chrysostom, *Orationes* 8–9. Lucian, *False Prophet* 6. Philostratus, *Apollonius* 1.18; 4.37–38; 8.19, 21, 24. (Demetrius in 4.25 and 42.31 was originally independent.)

[19] Mark 2:24; 3:6; 8:11; 10:2; Luke 5:17; 13:31; 15:2; 16:14; 17:20.

its ongoing work. The new dynamic in the Christian message and the new quality of life created by it apparently could not be contained within conventional itinerant activities, whether religious or philosophic.

A specific case

The encouragement, collection, and transport of financial aid from the Gentile churches for the poor among the saints in Jerusalem was an important aspect of Paul's work.[20] This requires closer inspection because it possesses, externally at least, some parallels with another Jewish institution. The similarities between this and the annual payment of the Temple tax (Matt 17:24–27) throughout the Dispersion have frequently been noted. Both involved extensive itinerant activity, the creation of groups to oversee the collection and payment, and the acknowledgment of Jerusalem as a distinctive religious center.

But there are significant differences. Paul's collection has a specific basis, for it expresses the gratefulness of the Gentile churches for the foundational preaching in Jerusalem. It is also a cosmopolitan affair in that it involves both Jews and non-Jews in giving. Additionally, it possesses a social objective in its aim to alleviate the needs of the poor. All this marks it off from the legal and cultic character of the Temple tax. There are other differences between these two collections. One is voluntary, the other compulsory. One is gathered in individual homes, the other at central collecting points. One is paid to those within the Jerusalem community for charitable disbursement, the other to the Temple authorities. So again, we have only general parallels between these two institutions. Though Paul may have modeled this aspect of his work upon the Temple tax payment, it differs from the Jewish institution at most levels of its operation.

CONCLUSION

Not only is Paul's conception of the *ekklesia* distinctive, but his conception of the *ergon* is as well. These two, the church and the work, should never be confused, as they generally have been

---

[20] 1 Cor 16:1–4; 2 Cor 8–9; Rom 15:24ff.; cf. Gal 2:8–10; Acts 11:27–30.

in subsequent Christian thinking. Paul views his missionary operation not as an *ekklesia* but rather as something existing independently alongside the scattered Christian communities. Only in a secondary way does it provide the organizational link between the local churches, suggesting the basis for a wider conception of *ekklesia* of a "denominational" kind. Paul's mission is a grouping of specialists identified by their gifts, backed up by a set of sponsoring families and communities, with a specific function and structure. Its purpose is first the preaching of the gospel and the founding of churches, and then the provision of assistance so that they may reach maturity. While this clearly involves interrelationship with the local communities, Paul's work is essentially a service organization whose members have personal, not structural, links with the communities and seek to develop rather than dominate or regulate.

17

—m—

THE NATURE OF PAUL'S
AUTHORITY

From the authority of Paul's wider and narrower circle of co-workers, we turn to the authority of the apostle himself in relation to others. Before we look at this in connection with his communities, his relationship with three other groups must be considered: his authority over his immediate colleagues, his position with respect to the original apostles in Jerusalem, and his attitude towards other "apostles" who sought to undermine his work. This will prepare the ground for a detailed examination of his involvement in the churches he founded. Throughout this discussion the underlying nature of the authority to which even the apostle is subject will gradually come into focus, though this will be more fully explored in the following chapter.

PAUL'S AUTHORITY OVER
HIS IMMEDIATE COLLEAGUES

We have already discussed Paul's relationship with such colleagues as Timothy and Titus. He undoubtedly held the pre-eminent place in his work and was chiefly responsible for decisions affecting the movements of his companions. Yet he does not appear to have acted in an authoritarian manner, as if his function was simply to command and theirs only to obey. The presence of a personal rather than formal framework of authority emerges from the familial way he portrays their relationship. Emphasis is also laid on the voluntary nature of their response to his requests. So much for what we have seen to be the case.

Relevant for identifying more precisely the nature of his authority is a model of authority and delegation that is of Jewish origin, the institution of the *shaliach*, i.e., official "messenger" or "representative." Much of the discussion engendered by this term has centered around the issue of Paul's commissioning by Christ. But it really has more relevance to understanding Paul's relationship with his delegated co-workers. The *shaliach* was, after all, commissioned by people, not God, and was required to carry out tasks on their behalf.

The *shaliach* is a messenger with a specific limited task to perform. Outside the boundaries of that commission he has no authority. He has importance only so far as he represents the one who sends him and faithfully carries out his will. He is viewed really as an extension of that person.[1] The *shaliach* institution concerns not the messenger but the one who commissions him. It shows no interest in the one who is sent, viz., as a person in his own right. This provides some parallel to the relationship between Paul and his immediate or occasional colleagues, whose ministry partly involved relaying instructions to the communities from their apostle.

We shall look at the significance attached to their words and the precise character of his authority extended to them as his "*shaliach*" shortly. But his co-workers have additional functions to perform when they are traveling among the churches. They have a ministry to exercise in their *own* right, in accordance with the individual gifts they have been given by God. Paul acknowledges this by mentioning them alongside himself when referring to his initial work of apostleship (2 Cor 5:11ff.). On other occasions he takes pains to stress the particular contribution each has made to the advance of the gospel and their assistance of the churches (8:17). He eagerly desires them to be welcomed and received by

---

[1] *m. Ber.* 5.5; see *m. Gitt.* 3.6; 4.1; *m. Kidd.* 2.1; *m. Yom.* 1.15; *m. B. M.* 1.3, 4; 2.2.

his communities for their own sake and given liberty to minister among them.[2] This does not imply that Paul's colleagues had the kind of heightened self-conscious authority that characterized the wandering Cynic philosophers,[3] or, in a more muted way, that was exhibited by their Stoic counterparts. There was a subordination to Paul, though one that was voluntary[4] and "familiar" rather than formal in character.[5] So once again this aspect of his mission cannot be understood simply in terms of parallels found in Jewish or Hellenistic circles.

PAUL'S RELATIONSHIP TO
THE ORIGINAL APOSTLES

Other apostolic missions existed apart from Paul's and had their own commission to fulfill. Peter had been entrusted with "the gospel to the circumcised" prior to Paul's call to go to the Gentiles (Gal 2:7). Apollos also seems to have concentrated primarily upon the Jews (Acts 18:24–28). But both Peter and Apollos also contributed occasionally to the life of churches not founded by them. This raises the question of their authority when they visited Paul's communities. Paul's own practice is illuminating here. He claims no privileged status within communities that he has not himself founded, even when he personally knows many of the people. He comes to these as a distinguished visitor seeking an audience rather than as one who holds a special right of entry. He does not assume any airs of superiority in writing to them but addresses them as equals. If he regards himself as having certain gifts he can confer on them, they in turn have others from which he will benefit (Rom 1:11–12). Though he is "bold" enough to say certain things to them, it is by way of "reminder" that he does so and on the grounds of his general commission as an apostle to the Gentiles (15:15–16), the limits of which he is especially conscious (2 Cor 10:13–16).

---

[2] 1 Cor 16:10–11; 2 Cor 8:22, 24; Phil 2:20–22, 25–28; Col 4:7, 12–13.
[3] Epictetus, *Dissertationes* 3.22, 41ff.
[4] Cf. 2 Cor 8:17.
[5] 1 Cor 4:17; Phil 2:22.

Paul appears to regard in the same light the relationship between other apostles and the churches he had founded. We know that Peter and Apollos had visited Corinth, and Paul is happy to endorse and encourage their ministry.[6] He is always insistent, however, that the community must *test* the contributions made by such people against the foundation upon which they were built.[7] Elsewhere he lays down the principle that they should not allow visitors to go beyond the "terms of commission" they have been given by God (2 Cor 10:15). Certainly the founding apostles in Jerusalem are not accorded any privileged position in relation to Paul's congregations. Though others regard them as "pillars" of the Christian movement, Paul appears quite unconcerned about their status (Gal 2:6, 9). He is willing to challenge them when fundamental principles are at stake and sets his experience before his churches as an indicator of what their own attitudes should be (Gal 2:4–20). He regards the collection for the Jerusalem believers as an expression of his communities' gratefulness to the Jerusalem church, not as a token of their subordination.[8]

Paul's Attitude to Other "Apostles"

Apart from these figures, there are other so-called apostles who also spend time with the communities he has founded. Particularly in Galatia and at Corinth this was occurring with disturbing results. These apostles are not, in Paul's view, genuine apostles but only counterfeits of whom his church should beware. He is extremely scornful of those "false" (2 Cor 11:13) or, as he ironically describes them, "superior" apostles (12:11), who go beyond the boundaries of their commission and give themselves a position in local churches to which they have no right. Such people, he says, "commend themselves" (10:12, 18), "compare themselves with one another" (10:12), and "boast beyond the limits in other people's labors" (10:15). In order that the churches "may make much of them" (Gal 4:17) they "put on airs," "take

---

[6] 1 Cor 3:5–9, 21–23; 16:12.
[7] Gal 1:9; cf. 1 Cor 4:10–15.
[8] 2 Cor 9:11–13; Rom 15:26–27.

advantage" of others, "prey" upon them, and in effect, "make slaves" of those they should be serving.[9]

Though on one or two occasions Paul dares to "boast" (2 Cor 11:20) about his authority, he does this only because he has been forced to show how, if he wished, he could outdo their claims (11:21ff.). He does not really believe in this way of proceeding (12:1), and on those rare occasions when he boasts, he "commends" himself for different reasons (2 Cor 6:4) than those of the people who "pride themselves on a person's position and not on their heart" (2 Cor 5:12). He totally rejects his opponents' approach and insists that it is not the people who commend themselves that are accepted but the people "whom the Lord commends" (2 Cor 11:18). Thus if Paul is to boast of anything, he will boast of his "weaknesses" so that "the power of Christ" (12:6), rather than his own prowess, may be seen to be at work. Instead of "taking advantage" (12:17) of his communities, he forgoes his rightful claim upon them even when it has the backing of a word of Jesus (1 Cor 9:14–15); he "gives himself up to death" (2 Cor 4:11), and he "suffers" for them (1:6–7). Since for him life "is Christ," he "will not venture to speak of anything except what Christ has wrought" (Rom 15:18, RSV) through him. All this is summed up in his assertion that "what we preach is not ourselves, but Jesus Christ as Lord, with ourselves as your servants for Jesus' sake" (2 Cor 4:5, RSV). That is the essence and, as we shall now see, the criterion of his involvement in the life of his communities.

PAUL'S AUTHORITY WITHIN HIS CHURCHES

What kind of authority is it that he possesses vis-à-vis his churches? Significantly, the word *exousia*, "authority," does not greatly help us here. Paul uses it fewer than a dozen times in his writings, mostly as something he refuses to exercise even when it has the support of Jesus' express command.[10] The only two occasions on which he refers to it positively are in contexts where the false apostles in Corinth have left him with no other choice

---

[9] 2 Cor 1:12ff.; 10:8; 11:1ff.

[10] 1 Thess 2:6; 2 Thess 3:9; 1 Cor 9:4ff. (3 times), 12, 18; and especially 1 Cor 9:14.

(2 Cor 10:8; 13:10). To understand his position in the communities founded by him we have to look elsewhere. Paul views his relationship with his churches primarily in terms drawn from family life—e.g., as the "father" who conceived them, as the "mother" who bore them, or as the "nurse" who cared for them[11]— rather than through analogies from the legal, administrative, political, or even religious sphere. But a permanent dependence of the communities upon him as of child to parent (or parent surrogate) is not what he has in mind. On the contrary, Paul continually encourages his churches to grow up to maturity (or adulthood) in their thinking and behavior. Although, because of his fundamental role in their foundation (1 Cor 4:15) and eschatological presentation to Christ,[12] apostle and community are indissolubly tied together from beginning to end, he never suggests that this maturity would lead to a severance of their relationship. Rather, Paul's model is the parent's relationship to an *adult* child rather than to an *infant* child. The distinction between these has not been sufficiently noted in discussions of Paul's authority within his churches.

In the early days of a community's existence a heavy burden lies upon the apostle to put his converts on a firm footing with God and one another. But from the very beginning Paul recognizes their self-sufficiency in the Spirit, even though in some areas they may still need his assistance.[13] In his first letter to the Thessalonians, he acknowledges that "concerning love of the brethren you have no need to have any one write to you, for you yourselves have been taught by God to love one another; and indeed you do love all the brethren throughout Macedonia" (1 Thess 4:9–10, RSV). When he exhorts them to continue to love all the brethren, Paul is merely expressing his continuing concern for their welfare. But when he goes on to add that "we would not have you ignorant, brethren, concerning those who are asleep" (1 Thess 4:13ff., RSV), he opens up a subject on which they need further tuition, tuition that he has a responsibility to give. To a community he has not founded he declares himself "satisfied about you, my brethren, that you yourselves are full of goodness, filled with all knowledge, and able to instruct one another" (Rom 15:14, RSV). He then adds,

---

[11] 1 Cor 4:14–15; cf. 2 Cor 12:14; 1 Thess 2:11 (father); Gal 4:19 (mother); 1 Thess 2:7; cf. 1 Cor 3:2 (nurse).

[12] 1 Thess 2:19; cf. 2 Cor 1:14; Phil 4:1.

[13] 1 Thess 4:8; Gal 2:3–5; 1 Cor 2:12–16; Rom 8:9–14.

"But on some points I have written to you very boldly by way of reminder, because of the grace given me by God" (Rom 15:15, RSV). Interestingly the term "reminder" here covers not only what they well know but also further inferences drawn from it that they may not have been familiar with. But more of that in a moment.

Striking in all this is the way Paul encourages his communities to a deeper point of view, recalls them from a false direction, or simply reminds them of things they already know and practice. The terms he employs are most frequently words of exhortation and appeal rather than command or decree. By far the most common term is *parakalein*, "appeal," which is used some twenty-three times in his writings.[14] This parallels the use of the term *peitho*, "persuade" or "convince," in contexts where his preaching to outsiders is in view.[15] Both outside the churches and within them Paul seeks the voluntary decision of his hearers. He highly prizes their full consent and commitment to what he has to say. Often he attempts to win this in the most passionate way; "urging" rather than simply "asking"[16] them or "speaking" to them.[17] We could even conclude that Paul seeks to "compel" his hearers and readers to transform their way of life without compulsion.

Significantly, Paul never employs the very strong term of command, *epitage*, for his own instructions. The three occasions when he does use the noun he has only an opinion to offer, and in the one place where the verb occurs, he refuses to speak in such terms.[18] True, we occasionally find in his letters such terms as *diatassein*, "direct," and *parangellein*, "charge" or "command," but neither of these are used in any strongly legislative way. The particular passages where the first term occurs suggest that there was a regularity about many of the guidelines Paul laid down in his churches and that he expected his converts to abide by them.[19] The second term, *parangellein*, is one used in much the same sense, viz., "instructions" (1 Cor 11:17). Apart from his statement, "to the married I give charge . . . " (7:10), the remaining five

---

[14]E.g., 1 Thess 2:11; 4:1, 10; 5:14; 2 Thess 3:12; 1 Cor 1:10; 4:16; 16:16; 2 Cor 5:20; 6:1; 10:1; 13:11; Rom 12:1; 15:30; 16:17; Phil 4:2; Eph 4:1.
[15]2 Cor 5:11; cf. Acts 13:43; 17:4; 18:4; 19:8, 26; 26:28; 28:23, 24.
[16]1 Thess 4:1; 5:12; 2 Thess 2:1; Eph 3:20.
[17]Gal 1:9; 5:2, 16; 1 Cor 7:8, 12; Rom 12:3; 15:8; Phil 4:4; Col 2:4; Eph 4:17.
[18]1 Cor 7:6, 25; 2 Cor 8:8; Phlm 8.
[19]1 Cor 11:34; 16:1.

occurrences are in 1 and 2 Thessalonians—four coming from the one passage in the second letter.[20] All but one example of this, plus a third term, *entole* (meaning "commandment" or "instruction"), are confined to 1 Corinthians[21] and the two Thessalonian letters.[22]

It is significant that in these three letters, together with Galatians, Paul adopts his most authoritative tone. This must not be ignored, for in these churches serious departures from basic teachings are present. Paul employs the strongest possible language to bring their members to their senses. The most dramatic example of this occurs in 1 Corinthians when Paul says quite bluntly "what I am writing to you is a command of the Lord" (1 Cor 14:37, RSV). Yet even here he desires that people should "acknowledge" and "recognize" it (1 Cor 14:37–38). Failure to do so does not result in forcible exclusion from the community, just nonrecognition of the person concerned. Compare too his strong injunction to the Thessalonians that "whoever rejects this rejects not human authority but God" (1 Thess 4:8, NRSV), "this" being an instruction, given "through the Lord Jesus." His reminder that it is "God" who "gives his holy Spirit to you" once again indicates that the truth of his statements should be self-evident to them.

All this is an exception to the general rule that Paul prefers not to speak in terms of a commanding authority; elsewhere in his letters language of this type is absent. When he writes to churches who have exhibited a mature stance on most matters and a genuine concern for his welfare, a different spirit is present. Paul's letter to the Philippians is an excellent example of this. Though it contains admonitions of various kinds, these are not conveyed in the strong language that we find in 1 Corinthians and 2 Thessalonians. He reiterates things the Philippians already know and do but, as he says, "to write the same things is not irksome to me, and it is safe for you" (Phil 3:1). His warm letter to Philemon also catches the spirit of Paul's general approach. "Though I am bold enough in Christ to command you to do what is required," he says, "yet for love's sake I prefer to appeal to you" (Phlm 8–9, RSV). Even his expressed boldness to command stems from his new freedom "in Christ" rather than some "legal right."

---

[20] 2 Thess 3:4–12; 1 Thess 4:11 (cf. 4:2).
[21] 1 Cor 7:19; 14:37.
[22] Except Col 4:10.

THE HEART OF THE MATTER

Two statements, both to troublesome communities, reveal the heart of Paul's attitude. In the first of these statements he tells the Corinthians, "We do not lord it *over* your faith; we work *with* you for your joy" (2 Cor 1:24). The apostle—for all his divine call, diverse gifts, and founding labors—does not set himself in a hierarchical position above his communities or act in an authoritarian manner towards them. He refuses to do this since Christ, not he, is their master (4:5). As himself subject to Christ, Paul stands *with* them in all that he does. That is why he talks elsewhere of his belonging to the church, not of the church belonging to him.[23] He does not issue his approvals, encouragements, instructions, warnings, and censures in isolation from the community but as one who stands within it, surrounded by all the gifts and ministries the Spirit has granted its members. Even at a distance he can envisage them assembling together with his spirit present in their midst (1 Cor 5:3; Col 2:5). Paul constantly forms new compound words with the prefix *sun-*, "with" or "co-," to emphasize his fellowship with his communities.[24] He identifies with them in their weaknesses and strengths, their struggles and labors, their sufferings and consolations, their prayers and thanksgiving, their rejoicings and victories. When he speaks to them, he speaks always as one of them, even when he has the severest things to say. So in the second of these statements he writes to the Galatians, "Brethren, I beseech you, become as I am, for I also have become as you are" (Gal 4:12, RSV).

There are profound reasons for Paul's identifying with his communities in this way and addressing them as he does. Did not Christ identify himself with those he came to aid in the most far-reaching way? Paul writes that God sent "his own Son in the likeness of sinful flesh and for sin, . . . condemned sin in the flesh."[25] "For our sake he made him to be sin who knew no sin, so that in him we might become the righteousness of God. *Working together with him*, then, we entreat you not to accept the grace of

---

[23] 1 Cor 5:2, 3; 12:28.
[24] 1 Cor 12:26; Rom 1:12; 15:32; 16:9, 21; Phil 1:7; 2:2, 17, 25; 3:17; Col 4:11; Eph 2:19, 21, 22; 3:6; 4:16.
[25] Rom 8:3, RSV.

God in vain."[26] In this respect Paul not only proclaims the gospel message and all that flows from it but *embodies* it, conveying its life through both his words and his deeds. Christ's identification with humankind also affects the manner in which Paul can speak to his converts. For God draws people not through the exercise of power, but through the demonstration of "weakness"—or so it seems from a human point of view—in the cross (1 Cor 1:20–24). But then "God's weakness is stronger than human strength" (1:25). Because of Christ's humility Paul cannot imperiously "command" his readers. When he addresses his communities he does so in "weakness," "fear," and "trembling" (2:3). In doing this he is speaking "in demonstration of the Spirit and power" (v. 5). Christ "was crucified in weakness," he says, "but lives by the power of God. For we are weak in him, but in dealing with you we shall live with him by the power of God" (2 Cor 13:4, RSV). In the death of Jesus, Paul finds an understanding of his own authority with the churches he was called to serve.

---

[26] 2 Cor 5:21–6:1, RSV.

18

—⚎—

THE EXERCISE OF PAUL'S
AUTHORITY

Paul exercises authority among his communities by persuading them to accept his point of view. He does not try to coerce his converts. His persuasion is based on his capacity to convince them, by word and example, that he desires for them only what the gospel requires.

THE RELATIONSHIP BETWEEN
AUTHORITY AND FREEDOM

Paul's approach to authority did not develop independently of his understanding of freedom but arose in close association with it. He strongly affirms the freedom within which his communities already stand through the gospel he preached (Gal 5:1, 13). He does not place limits upon freedom, drawing lines around his converts and only little by little allowing them to expand into new areas of experience. From the beginning they have freedom in Christ as full and complete as it could be (2 Cor 3:3, 17). Paul's task is to help them discover the real dimensions of that freedom and discern false versions of it that others might press upon them (1 Cor 3:21–23). Their freedom is a reality to be appropriated, not a possibility to which they must be gradually introduced. For this reason his instructions to his converts are generally couched in terms of appeal and exhortation rather than command and decree. Even when he threatens to come to them with a "rod of iron" and "punish" or "not spare" his readers, it is the "rod," "punishment," and "severity" of God's word that he intends to lay upon them, not that of some worldly power that enforces their submission to Paul's will (2 Cor 10:3–6).

In any case he would prefer to come to them "with love in a spirit of gentleness."[1] This explains why, precisely when he fears he may have to take a severe course of action, he hesitates and holds himself at a distance, allowing the Corinthians time to become aware of real situation and alter their attitude accordingly. Subsequently accused of vacillating in his plans, Paul replies:

> it was to spare you that I refrained from coming to Corinth. . . . For I made up my mind not to make you another painful visit. . . . And I wrote as I did, so that when I came I might not suffer pain from those who should have made me rejoice, for I felt sure of all of you, that my joy would be the joy of you all. (2 Cor 1:23; 2:1, 3, RSV)

As he says elsewhere, the "authority that the Lord has given" him is for "building up and not for tearing down."[2] Nothing is gained by conformity to his point of view unless they see the truth and embrace it for themselves. A nominal obedience does not result in any real growth in understanding or living.

Paul's approach to authority relates to his view of freedom in another respect as well. We saw earlier that for him liberty involves independence from certain things and for others; however, this becomes possible only through dependence upon Christ. The experience of freedom begins through submission to another and only on this basis can it continue. We saw also that the life of freedom involves interdependence, particularly with those who belong to the Christian community, resulting in a mutual serving of one another. This interrelationship is the natural expression of Christian freedom and is the only context within which it can grow

---

[1] 1 Cor 4:21; cf. 2 Cor 10:3–6.
[2] 2 Cor 10:8; cf. 13:10.

to maturity. We have a real paradox here, for it is precisely through increasing service to Christ and to others that the Christian becomes progressively more free. This helps us to understand several references to "obedience" that occur in Paul's letters.

Paul requests the Philippians "as you have always obeyed, so now, not only as in my presence but much more in my absence" (Phil 2:12, RSV). In one sense this may be seen as God's work, but in another as their own. Paul here is asking for obedience not to himself so much as to the gospel, which requires them to "work out (their) own salvation with fear and trembling" (2:12b, RSV). He says this more explicitly to the Thessalonians who, when they received the gospel from him " . . . accepted it not as a human word but as what it really is, God's word" (1 Thess 2:13, NRSV). The "obedience" he has won "from the Gentiles" (mentioned several times in Romans) also has as its object "the gospel of Christ."[3] The "obedience" of the Corinthians (resulting from Titus' visit among them) led to their now standing "firm in the faith." It followed the "repentance that leads to salvation" (occasioned by Paul's earlier letter), though Paul also notes how with "fear and trembling" they received Titus among them.

Paul writes to the Corinthians to find whether "they are obedient" in everything,[4] to ask the Thessalonians "to obey what we say in this letter,"[5] and to reveal to Philemon that he is "confident of [Philemon's] obedience" (Phlm 21). But here we need to remind ourselves that at the basis of Paul's instructions to his communities lies a call to "remembrance" and that behind all his appeals is an acknowledgment of their possession of the Spirit.[6] Not only things he has already taught them but even new teaching can be presented to them in this context. Whatever he says, whether already expressed or yet to be communicated, has its root in the foundation on which their community rests. When a question of conflict arises, he deals with it by drawing their attention to that common starting point and tracing out its consequences for the specific issue at hand.[7]

---

[3] Rom 15:18; cf. 1:5; 16:17–19, 26.
[4] 2 Cor 2:9; cf. 10:6.
[5] Cf. here 2 Thess 3:14.
[6] 1 Thess 4:8; 1 Cor 2:12ff.; Phlm 19–20.
[7] See ch. 8, n. 16; also 1 Thess 4:13ff.; Gal 3:1ff.; 1 Cor 1:17ff.; 2 Cor 5:11ff.; Rom 6:15ff.; Phil 3:2ff.; Col 2:8ff.; Eph 5:1ff.

THE ULTIMATE AUTHORITY OF THE GOSPEL

This leads us to the heart of the matter. What is the ultimate authority to which not only individual Christians, but their communities, and even the apostle, are subject? This "foundation," or "common starting point," is the source of Paul's authority. It is nothing less than the *euangelion*, "gospel," that he has been called to preach, embody in his life, and hand over to his communities.[8] Only as he remains faithful to that gospel in word and life does he or any other apostle possess its authority and deserve recognition from others. While he endorses the freedom of other apostles to build on the foundation he has laid, Paul also insists that his communities test the contributions made by such people against that foundation itself, as he himself has done (Gal 1:9; 2:11–21). The original apostles, he maintains, had nothing to add to his gospel but simply confirmed its legitimacy (2:6). His churches should evaluate his own subsequent teaching by that same criterion. Paul makes this quite explicit. "If we ourselves," he says, "or even an angel from heaven, should preach a gospel at variance with the gospel we preached to you, let him be anathema" (1:8). The church has the right and power to excommunicate its own apostle if he radically departs from the gospel!

Interesting to note here is how Paul from time to time consciously distinguishes his own inferences from the words of Jesus. In doing so he appeals for consideration on the basis of his trustworthy functioning in previous situations, not on a claim to his apostolic status or infallibility (1 Cor 7:25). Although it is clear that he thinks the Spirit has guided him (7:40), he has left the way open for his communities to see how he arrived at his conclusions and to judge whether they are legitimate deductions from their gospel premise.

The gospel itself, as key passages in his writings demonstrate, concerns God's saving activity on our behalf.[9] This has been most clearly revealed in Jesus' death and resurrection, presence and return, and in the reconciliation this has effected.[10] At its heart is "the word of the cross" (1 Cor 1:18). But it is also a living

---

[8] E.g., 1 Cor 1:17; 9:19–23; 15:1–3.
[9] 1 Thess 1:5, 9–10; Col 1:26–27.
[10] 1 Cor 15:3–4; 2 Cor 5:18–19 et al.

and growing reality in the world, transforming people and establishing colonies among them. This takes place through the
Spirit[11] who comes from God (1 Cor 2:12). The gospel is not just
a word or a message but rather a "life" and a "person" (Rom 10:14).
This remains true whether we think of Christ around whom it
centers, the apostle through whom it is transmitted, or the individual in whose life it takes root. True, the *words* spoken by each
are crucial, for without them there might not be understanding of
what they bring. But no less crucial is what they *do*, particularly
the suffering they endure, for in this the heart of what they bring
is revealed (1 Thess 1:6).

Christ is both the content of the gospel and the source of its
continuing potency. Not only is he defined by the preaching but
also his presence is actualized in it. Not only is he the objective
authority to whom they point but also he is the subjective authority in whose power they operate. And the Spirit is none other than
the power of the living Christ here and now.[12] This two-sided
reality explains how Paul can speak of the "tradition" passed on
by him as something received from Christ, not mere human
beings, even though much of it was handed over to him by earlier
apostles.[13] It also means that Paul exhibits Christ's authority when
he who is only an "earthly vessel" (2 Cor 4:7) faithfully fulfills, in
word and deed, in preaching and living, and in communicating
and suffering the ministry to which he has been commissioned.

This close connection between the apostle and the gospel
becomes even more emphatic when Paul talks about "my"[14] or
"our"[15] gospel. This does not refer to the interpretation he placed
upon the gospel for the Gentiles, but to his involvement in it
through his preaching and its effects on his communities. The
dynamism of the gospel is more in view here than its content.
Paul further expresses the connection between the two through
his understanding of "tradition." He attached his own initial experience of Christ to the traditions handed on to him by earlier
apostles (1 Cor 15:8–10). He also regards the "tradition" as becoming "gospel" in only two ways: when someone interprets it
through preaching, and when it subsequently becomes a living

---

[11] 1 Thess 1:5; 1 Cor 2:4; 2 Cor 3:6.
[12] 2 Cor 3:17; cf. Gal 1:12 with 1:16.
[13] 1 Cor 11:23; 15:3.
[14] Rom 2:16; 16:28; cf. Gal 1:11; 2:2.
[15] 1 Thess 1:5; 2:14.

experience for others.[16] The virtual equivalence of the two in his thinking comes to dramatic clarity when he exhorts people to imitate him. "You became imitators of us and the Lord," he reminds the Thessalonians (1 Thess 1:6). "I urge you," he says to the Corinthians, "become imitators of me," even "as I am of Christ" (1 Cor 4:6; 11:1). "Become as I am," he beseeches the Galatians (Gal 4:12). "Join in imitating me," he encourages the Philippians (Phil 3:17).

Paul regards himself as closely identified with the gospel, as constructively involved in the tradition, and as a clear reflection of Christ. Even so he is not the only one who can be spoken of in this way. The Philippians are to imitate "those who so live as you have an example in us" (Phil 3:17, RSV), and the Thessalonians have already become "imitators of the churches of God in Judaea" who suffered from their countrymen as Christ himself had done (1 Thess 2:14–15). Paul can move so freely between Christ, himself, and certain of his converts precisely because he urges obedience primarily not to himself or his instructions but to the gospel in all its ramifications. This gospel has become transparent in him and in some of his readers. All this applies, in some measure or other, to any member of the community who genuinely reflects the fruit of the Spirit. This is why Christians are to submit to one another in the community; in some degree each is the bearer to the other of the word and life of Christ. All, as Paul crystallizes it, are to "be subject to one another out of reverence" (Eph 5:21), and, as Luther so beautifully expresses it, are "to be a sort of Christ to one another." But we may go further. Since, according to Paul, the gospel about Christ was prefigured in the earlier OT scriptures (Gal 3:8) and elaborated in subsequent gospel and apostolic traditions (2 Thess 2:15; 3:6), it stands as the criterion by which all are to be evaluated, and the power by which all are to live.

THE DISTINCTIVENESS OF PAUL'S APPROACH TO AUTHORITY

Drawing together the various threads of Paul's approach to authority, we conclude that:

---

[16] 1 Cor 15:1–3; cf. 11:2, 23; Rom 6:17.

1.   all authority stems from God the Father as revealed in his Son Jesus Christ and is mediated by their Spirit;

2.   in the prophetic history of Israel, as recorded in the OT scriptures, and in the apostolic development of the church, this authority was decisively present; but the person and the work of Jesus Christ and the message about him enshrined in the apostolic writings are the definitive expression of God's will and are normative for all that precedes and follows;

3.   through the Spirit, God continues to speak and work authoritatively, not through coercion of people's personalities but by convincing their minds of the truth and warming their hearts with love so that they freely embrace it;

4.   authority is exercised through the service of others in word and deed, not through their domination, and Jesus is the example par excellence of the way this takes place, since "though he was in the form of God, [he] did not count equality with God a thing to be grasped, but emptied himself, taking the form of a servant . . . " (Phil 2:6–7, RSV);

5.   authority is conveyed in this way primarily through the apostles, who still live in their writings, and in differing measure through all Christians, who are instruments of Christ's authority when they manifest Christ to one another according to the ministries given them by the Spirit.

This understanding of authority can be distinguished from other first-century approaches. For example, the authority based on the *sacerdotal rights* of the priesthood was communicated by succession of election from one generation of chosen men to another (as among the Essenes and Qumran community). Other approaches had their authority centered around a sacred curriculum of *written and oral traditions* preserved and extended by an accredited series of teachers (as among the Rabbis and Scribes). In other groups the authority arose from the *individual experience* of those who had been mystically enlightened or who had rationally grasped the truth (as in the mystery religions and Stoicism) and who, by virtue of that experience alone, were regarded as qualified transmitters of it. Although some of Paul's terminology overlaps with what one finds among these various groups—for example the talk of "traditions," the making of "commands," the expectation of "obedience"—these words are not central to his understanding of authority. The real differences lie in the *content*, for though they all ultimately grounded authority in the divinity worshipped, the means by which authority is conveyed and the character of authority differ markedly.

Attempts to find a model for the type of authority Paul possessed in the Jewish *shaliach* institution have already been briefly addressed. If any parallels exist, the relationship between Paul and his colleagues provides a more relevant field for comparison, though even there only formal similarities come to light. There is an additional problem here and it accentuates the difficulty of drawing Paul into the discussion. Jewish missionaries or prophets are never described in *shaliach* terms even by the rabbis. Though the word is used of those engaged in the collection of the Temple tax for Jerusalem, this may reflect post-AD 70 practice. Paul oversaw his collection, but the responsibility for carrying it out largely lay with his associates. Since the earliest written evidence for the *shaliach* institution comes from the middle of the second century, the form in which it has been discussed might not have existed before the destruction of the Temple in AD 70.

More points of contact can be found between Paul's view of apostleship and the self-understanding of the Cynic philosopher, at least as depicted by Epictetus. Both are conscious of a divine call and commission.[17] Both see their task in terms of seeing God and teaching people.[18] Both celebrate freedom and wish others to enter into it.[19] Both are willing to suffer in the pursuit of their vocation.[20] Both are engrossed in their calling.[21] Still there are real differences: the idea of apostleship is not as clearly articulated among the Cynics; there is no eschatological edge to their proclamation; self-exertion rather than grace is in the foreground; and suffering is more an exemplary work than something inherent in their vocation. In certain respects the Cynics were also individualists, with no sense of a localized community. Although they

---

[17] Epictetus, *Dissertationes* 3.22.23. Cf. Gal 1:1.

[18] Epictetus, *Dissertationes* 3.22.24f. 1 Cor 1:4, 15; cf. Rom 1:14.

[19] Epictetus, *Dissertationes* 3.22.48, 96f. Cf. Gal 5:13; 1 Cor 9:1; 2 Cor 13:12f.

[20] Epictetus, *Dissertationes* 3.24.113f. Cf. 2 Cor 4:10.

[21] Epictetus, *Dissertationes* 3.22.94f. Cf. 2 Cor 11:27f.

propagated the idea of universal friendship, they did not see the need for more intensive forms of community life.

CONCLUSION

Paul's understanding of his calling, and the idea of authority inherent in it, cannot be fully paralleled in the activities of the Jewish *shaliach* or the Cynic philosopher. His understanding has more in common with the prophetic vocation of some of his OT forerunners. But the unique character of the Christ whom he preaches and embodies and the new freedom of community life generated by the gospel have both left their distinctive mark upon him. Paul's apostolic authority was a gift, given by Christ on the Damascus road for use in the communities he founded through the power of the Spirit. Ultimately Paul owed his idea of community not to any cultural precedent but to the instruction and example of Christ himself.

—m—

CONCLUSION

We have come to the end of our investigation of Paul's idea of community. Before we conclude, something should be said about the practicability of his view. There can be no doubt that his communities failed to express fully the ideals of common life he held out before them and that Paul was aware of this. But it would be a mistake to represent his approach to community as idealistic. While it differs from alternative views of community during his time, even other Christian ones, and bypasses the more structured frameworks in which most of them operated, it does not stem from an unrealistic utopian viewpoint. It resulted from a sober estimate of his churches' potential "in the Lord" through the agency of "his Spirit."

No one is more realistic than Paul in dealing with the frailties and failures of human relationships. Yet he continually sets before his communities a vision of what their common life should, and one day will, be. He sees this as simply the consequence of the life that is in them and therefore as the reality they should strive to realize. His view of community unfolds necessarily out of his understanding of the gospel and the way that gospel is geared to the real contradictions of human existence. All the way through this study we have seen how Paul develops his view of community directly from fundamental gospel realities. Christ's radical words, "Who are my brethren?" and "When two or three gather together there am I in the midst of them," lie behind Paul's approach to community relations and assemblings. Christ's sacrificial service stands as the model and motive for those who have special responsibilities in the community, including Paul himself. Christ's resurrection power acts as the source of the community's unity and as the dynamic behind the gifts and ministries exercised within the community. Paul's understanding of community is nothing less than the gospel itself in corporate form!

His organization of community life contains no detailed confession or code to subscribe to, no liturgical order to govern their meetings, no clerical leadership to control its affairs. This does not mean that Paul was unconcerned about right belief and conduct, order and decency in church, stability and unity within and between his communities. Nor does it mean that statements of faith, principles of conduct, criteria for assembling, distinctions between members, and tangible expressions of fellowship did not exist within them. But none of these were secured by the formal means mentioned above. Despite this apparent absence of all institutional means of support, we should not imagine that Paul's work was provisional and incomplete. It was not a series of interim measures intended to be superseded by more concrete arrangements, even though others after Paul felt the need to develop more formal structures for the church. In the writings of the following period there occur a series of minor shifts of emphasis that began to alter his understanding of community.

In the Introduction we noted that Paul's idea of community was not only the most detailed but also the most developed and profound in the NT times. The superiority of Paul's view is no less apparent if one compares it with the Christian literature of the succeeding centuries. In addition, Paul may be the first individual to formulate and implement an idea of religious community not subservient to those two fundamental institutions of ancient society: the family and the state. There are religious communities that possessed a relatively or completely independent status, but they antedate Paul by several centuries. About some of these we have very little information, though others left a more permanent record. As we have seen, Stoics were interested in the idea of community, but their discussions tended to remain at the abstract level. The Dead Sea community was a concrete reality, whose self-understanding and practices were carefully committed to writing by the members themselves. But the Qumran sect left a composite rather than personal record and its outlook was more political in nature.

There is a further side to Paul's understanding of community, namely the historically significant role it has played in the development of Christian thought and practice and in the formation of more general social theory. We do not need to say much about the first. The seminal importance of Paul's ideas for the view of the church held by Augustine in late antiquity, Calvin and the Anabaptists in the time of the Reformation, and, in the last century, various movements for the reform of ecclesiastical and missionary structures, is well known. The rediscovery of Paul's approach to community has periodically broken traditional thinking about the church and challenged institutional practice.

Less recognized is Paul's contribution to more general social thought. For example, many of the basic elements in Augustine's social teaching—one of the foundational contributions to Western social thought—have their origin in Paul's writings. Augustine was a more systematic thinker than Paul and was responsible for creatively elaborating ideas from a number of sources. But commentators too often have credited him with originating certain social ideas and principles that were actually drawn from Paul's writings. One particular example is Augustine's highly developed organic view of society, which has its basis in Pauline ideas.

A modern example of Paul's continuing wider influence is provided by Max Weber's adoption of the concept of *charisma*. Its value in the clarification of early Christian ideas of authority had been impressed upon him by a reading of Rudolf Sohm's work on church history and law, Sohm himself having taken the term directly from Paul. Weber gave it a wider sociological relevance and in certain significant respects also altered its meaning. But the roots of his concept and, though Sohm did not see it, the basis for its wider social application lie in the Pauline writings themselves.

Paul's historical significance does not stop here. While in view of a changed cultural situation his actual *practices* are not always applicable today, the *principles* underlying them continue to attract the attention of those actively seeking community. His understanding of community raises serious questions both for established ecclesiastical structures that claim a historical link with Paul and for counterculture groups that ardently promise "community" to those who join them. The former have excluded many of Paul's basic insights into the nature of community and frozen others into a rigid form. The latter lack the foundation in the gospel, which alone can give the fullest cohesion and depth to their efforts.

Paul's approach to community has stimulated the creation of alternatives to ecclesiastical structures and counterculture groups, e.g., house churches and basic Christian communities, and at times these have been accompanied by a contemporary version of Paul's work to complement and enhance their activities. It has also spurred the development of cell groups and charismatic fellowships within traditional and newer church structures—though these rarely result in reappraisal, along Pauline lines, of the ecclesiastical institutions in which they operate. Obviously, the principles underlying Paul's idea of community remain as revolutionary and challenging in the twentieth century as they were in the first.

APPENDIX:
THE DRIFT OF THE PASTORALS

When did the drift away from Paul's idea of community begin? While some have located the movement from Paul's view only in the postapostolic writings of the succeeding period, others have discerned its roots in the NT itself, even in writings attributed to or descriptive of Paul himself. In the Introduction we noted the doubts surrounding Ephesians, Acts, and the Pastorals.

EPHESIANS

The decision to include Ephesians within the treatment of Paul seems in retrospect to be warranted. Although at a few points different terms are used (e.g., *doma* instead of *charisma*), some new developments occur (e.g., its theology of racial integration), and stronger emphases can be detected (e.g., the church built on the foundation of the apostles and prophets), the extent and character of their usage do not require, though they may permit, a non-Pauline view of its authorship.

ACTS

We have also freely used Luke's account of Paul throughout our discussion, since it contains much valuable historical information about the background and nature of Paul's activities. It has considerable detail on the composition, movements, and consequences of his mission, but it has very little direct material on Paul's understanding and practice of community. Where it does illuminate this, it frequently supports and extends what we find in Paul's letters, e.g., the household basis of his churches, the personal links between them, the informality of their gatherings. In certain matters we find a preservation of pre-Pauline attitudes, viz., concentration on the more extraordinary works of the Spirit and more prosaic descriptions of the communities as "disciples" or "believers," though in other matters a reflection of post-Pauline views begins to appear, i.e., the greater use of *ekklesia* for the community rather than for the gathering, the tendency to standardize Paul's terminology of leadership through references to elders, and the portrayal of Paul as more accommodating to the Jerusalem authorities than his letters would suggest. But none of these make Luke the purveyor of "early Catholicism" that many have claimed him to be or preclude him from being helpful to our examination of Paul's idea of community.

THE PASTORALS

What then of the Pastorals? To compare 1–2 Timothy and Titus with the undisputed letters of Paul, we will look in turn at their conception of *ekklesia* and metaphors of community, their view of gifts and order, their depiction of class and leadership in the community, and their understanding of the authority of Paul and his colleagues.

Conception of ekklesia and metaphors of community

The local sense of *ekklesia* still seems to be preserved in the Pastorals (1 Tim 3:5; 5:16), though in one place a more generic sense is present (3:15). But the notion of "gathering" no longer appears in the foreground; *ekklesia* is virtually a synonym for the community. The language of family relationships, seen in the undisputed letters of Paul, also occurs in the Pastorals. Indeed, the church is expressly described as "the household of God" (1 Tim 3:15). Along with occasional reference to the "brethren" (4:6; 6:2), which are proportionately less frequent than in any other Pauline letter except Ephesians, we have the striking advice to Timothy not to "rebuke an older man but exhort him as you would a father; treat younger men like brothers, older women like mothers, younger women like sisters . . . " (5:1–2, RSV).

Interestingly enough, the community is never described in the letters as a "body" though this idea is also absent from the (late) letter to the Philippians. The building metaphor occurs in the Pastorals but in a more static form than elsewhere. Though the church is the property of "the living God," its function is that of "the pillar and bulwark of the truth" (3:15).

So while the terms used in the Pastorals are generally similar to those in the other letters, overall we are presented with a less dynamic view of the Christian community. However, we do not have here, as some have suggested, a sacramental view of the church. Baptism and the Lord's Supper are not so much as mentioned, let alone aggrandized in any way.

View of gifts and order

The term *charisma* also turns up in the letters to Timothy, though only with reference to Timothy himself, not to members of the community in general (1 Tim 4:14; 2 Tim 1:6). Certainly many of the functions that are mentioned are described as *charismata* in the undisputed letters of Paul (e.g., prophecy,[1] teaching,[2] exhortation,[3] pastoral care,[4] service,[5] giving aid,[6]) but they are not called gifts and there is less emphasis on mutual ministry. False teaching must be tested, though the responsibility for this devolves on the genuine teachers (2 Tim 2:2; Tit 1:9–11) and only indirectly on the community at large.

---

[1] 1 Tim 1:1; 4:14; Tit 1:12.
[2] 1 Tim 4:13; 2 Tim 2:2; Tit 1:9; 2:1 et al.
[3] 1 Tim 4:13; 5:1; Tit 2:2ff.; 2:15.
[4] 1 Tim 3:5.
[5] 1 Tim 3:10, 11.
[6] 1 Tim 5:25.

The term *agape*[7] occurs in these letters, but nowhere describes the ethos within which members carry out all their communal responsibilities as it does in Paul's undisputed letters. Only three times do we have any reference to the Spirit.[8] There are three allusions to "prophecies": two to predictive utterances related to Timothy's commissioning for his task and one to a pagan prophet from Crete. None refer to any ongoing activity in the life of the community.[9] Teaching now occupies the primary position, along with exhortation. Mention of the more spectacular gifts, such as healings, miracles, or glossolalia, is lacking. Since there is a similar silence in Romans, perhaps too much should not be made of this. However, unlike Romans, the Pastorals do not even touch upon the apostolic exercise of these gifts.[10] So, despite some of the language held in common with the other letters, we appear to be in the presence of a less dynamic approach to gifts and a less participatory view of community. The charismatic dimension seems to have diminished in importance, though it has not altogether disappeared.

Depiction of class and leadership

The functions talked about in these letters do require the involvement of more than just the prominent people in the community. Pastoral and teaching responsibilities are confined to the more mature members of the congregation,[11] but widows are also encouraged to engage in a similar ministry among women (Tit 2:3–4). Younger men, and probably their wives, can carry out tasks appropriate to deacons (1 Tim 3:8–13). Any two or three members of the church can bring a charge of irresponsibility against an elder (5:19).

The role of women suffers more restrictions. Women are expressly prohibited from teaching and exercising authority over their husbands (1 Tim 2:12), whereas Colossians speaks of the relative freedom for all to teach and admonish one another (Col 3:16). The restriction upon women is buttressed in the Pastorals

---

[7] 1 Tim 1:5; 2:15; 4:12; 6:11; 2 Tim 1:7; 2:22; 3:10; Tit 2:2; cf. 1 Tim 1:14; 2:13.

[8] 1 Tim 4:1; 2 Tim 1:14; Tit 3:5.

[9] 1 Tim 1:18; 4:14; Tit 1:12.

[10] Cf. Rom 15:19.

[11] 1 Tim 3:1–7; Tit 1:5–12.

by an appeal to their responsibility for the Fall (1 Tim 2:14), while in the undisputed letters Eve's weakness is seen as a warning to all and Adam's responsibility is more firmly in the foreground.[12] On the other hand, the strong word *authentein* suggests that what is at issue in First Timothy is the excessive use of authority, that is domination, by women over men. So we could have here a particular situation in which "Paul's" words are to be interpreted as a corrective to, not as a denial of, the public ministry of women.

In these writings the *episkopos*, "bishop," casts a longer shadow over various aspects of the community's life—organizational arrangements; pastoral care and discipline; community guidance, advancement, and protection—than any figure mentioned in the other letters. Yet the language of function rather than office still dominates the Pastorals, for it is a *task* (1 Tim 3:1), not an "office" (as in the RSV). It is those who "labor" in exhortation and teaching who deserve honor (5:17). The qualifications laid down for those appointed to such a ministry indicate that this took place only after they had shown themselves worthy of such work. Yet the description of such work as "noble" (3:1) and the emphasis on "respectability" (3:7), more than sacrificial service, have a different atmosphere than comparable descriptions in other Pauline epistles.[13]

These two tendencies towards high esteem are also present in the remarks concerning deacons. Although their work is portrayed in functional terms (1 Tim 3:13) and prior testing is required (3:10), they acquire a "good" standing or rank for themselves if they perform well. Personal moral requirements are stressed at the expense of charismatic endowments. Still, there is nothing here that approaches an ordination procedure in the later sense[14] and, although a succession of elders is envisaged, it is one of teaching rather than office (2 Tim 2:2). In other words, to talk of the institutionalization of the ministry in the Pastorals is to exaggerate.

Understanding of Paul's and his colleagues' authority

Precisely what role do Timothy and Titus have? They are essentially the apostle's representatives, reminding the churches

---

[12]2 Cor 11:3; Rom 5:15ff.
[13]Contrast 1 Cor 16:15.
[14] 1 Tim 4:14 (commissioning); 5:22 (reacceptance); 2 Tim 1:6 (baptism).

of his teaching and practice and acting towards the communities as Paul would if he were present. Their association with Paul does not in itself gain them full recognition. They have to work for that, not by assuming control or asserting their privileged status, but by "taking heed" of themselves and their teaching and by setting "the believers an example in speech and conduct" (1 Tim 5:13, 16). Their ministry should revolve mainly around exhortation, and they are to develop family relationships with people rather than exert formal power over them.[15] Nowhere is this clearer than in the instruction "the Lord's servant must not strive, but be gentle towards all, apt to teach, patient, in meekness instructing his opponents" (2 Tim 2:24–25).

Yet certain tendencies lead in a different direction. The note of command, viz., the use of *parangellein* to command, features more strongly here,[16] and terms for rebuke occur more often than in the other letters.[17] For the first time such people also "preach" to these communities (2 Tim 4:2)—something that Paul does elsewhere only to nonbelievers. One cannot escape the impression that Timothy and Titus also play a more prominent part in community activities. While there are similar kinds of disciplinary action in other NT books,[18] the apostle's associates are strongly involved in administering it,[19] as with the appointment of *episkopoi* from among the elders (Tit 1:5). But they do not exercise the functions of monarchical bishops as some have suggested; the reference to hands being laid upon them has nothing to do with later ordination procedures. Rather, we have here a parallel to the setting aside of Barnabas and Paul for their missionary work by the prophets and teachers at Antioch.

The portrait of Paul in these writings has real similarities with that found in the less disputed materials. The centrality of the gospel in his experience and work,[20] his relationship with his colleagues,[21] the approach to discipline[22]—all have much in com-

---

[15]E.g., 1 Tim 5:1–2; 2 Tim 4:2.
[16]1 Tim 1:3; 4:11; 5:7; 6:13, 17; cf. 1 Tim 1:5, 18.
[17]1 Tim 5:20; 2 Tim 4:2; Tit 1:13; 2:15 but contrast 1 Tim 5:1.
[18]1 Tim 1:3–4; 5:19–20; 2 Tim 4:3; Tit 1:9–16; 3:9–11.
[19]1 Tim 1:3; 5:20–22; Tit 3:10.
[20]E.g., 1 Tim 1:12–17; 2:3–7; 3:14–16; 4:9–10; 6:11–16; 2 Tim 1:8–12; 2:8–13; Tit 2:11–14; 3:3–8.
[21]1 Tim 1:2, 18; 2 Tim 1:2; 2:1; Tit 1:4.
[22]Cf. n. 15.

mon. Yet alongside the gospel an increased importance is given to "sound doctrine"[23] and the "sacred writings."[24] Again, this could be due to the particular circumstances in these churches. Along with the note of appeal and exhortation there is an increased tendency for "commands" and "rebukes" to be issued on Paul's behalf and there is a more significant role granted to his associates. In dealing with refractory members, "Paul" unilaterally excludes two people rather than consult with the community they belong to (1 Tim 1:20). Yet despite a lack of emphasis upon the Spirit and the formalization of ways in which "Paul" speaks about himself, e.g., not only as an apostle but also as a "herald" and "teacher,"[25] distinctive marks of the apostle do pervade the work, nowhere more so than in the place suffering occupies in his work.[26]

CONCLUSION

What are we to make of all this? Real similarities exist between the Pastorals and the other letters of Paul, as do a number of clear differences. All too often the differences have been either exaggerated or overlooked. The content of the Pastorals is neither as far from nor as close to what we find in the other letters as scholars frequently suggest. Can the differences between them be explained by their later composition and altered historical situation? Possibly. The differences between the earlier letters of Paul and the Captivity letters have been understood in this way.

However, the differences here are greater than those between earlier Pauline letters and the Captivity letters. Not only are the divergences between the Pastorals and other Pauline correspondence (including Ephesians) greater in number, they are also more apparent. There are additional differences to the ones I have identified. The Pastorals have novel themes, unique

---

[23] 1 Tim 1:3, 10; 4:6, 11, 13, 16; 5:17; 6:1, 3; 2 Tim 2:2; 3:10, 14; 4:2–3; Tit 1:9; 2:1, 10.
[24] 1 Tim 4:13; 2 Tim 3:16.
[25] 1 Tim 2:7; 2 Tim 1:11.
[26] 2 Tim 1:11–12; 2:8–9; 3:10–12.

style and vocabulary, and improbable statements such as: "For this I was appointed a preacher and apostle (I *am telling the truth*, I *am not lying*), a teacher of the Gentiles in faith and truth" (1 Tim 2:7, RSV). Ultimately, readers must judge for themselves in this matter. It is a close call. But even if these letters were written by a follower of Paul, not the apostle himself, they are still canonical and still relevant to church life today, especially to situations encompassing tendencies and problems similar to those these letters address.

BIBLIOGRAPHY

Since, as the table of contents shows, the topics treated in adjoining chapters are thematically related, I have arranged this bibliography accordingly. I have restricted the number of entries under each heading to no more than twenty articles or books so as to keep the list concise. Extensive bibliographic material can be found in a number of them. No reference is made to standard dictionaries and encyclopedias, though there are many that contain fine discussions of important terms, e.g., the *Theological Dictionary of the New Testament*, the *Interpreter's Dictionary of the Bible*, the *Encyclopaedia Biblica*, the *Encyclopaedia Judaica*, and now the *Anchor Bible Dictionary*. Commentaries are also omitted, but should be consulted on central passages—as should the standard lexicons on New Testament Greek literary, papyrological, and epigraphical usage for any serious study of the key terms. Only works written in, or translated into, English are included.

Many basic texts on this subject remain untranslated, especially from German. Anyone who wishes to investigate these will find ample reference to them in the footnotes of the works cited in the following bibliography. Various articles in the *Reallexikon für Antike und Christentum*, which have wide-ranging bibliographies, are also essential reading. Specialists may be interested to hear of unpublished dissertations by C. Hill on "A Sociology of the New Testament Church" and K. Hemphill on "Paul's Concept of

Charisma," available from Nottingham (U.K.) and Cambridge (U.K.) Universities respectively and of the enlightening, expansive list of writings dealing with Paul's social and intellectual environment contained in E. A. Judge's article on "St. Paul and Classical Society," *Jahrbuch für Antike und Christentum* 15 (1972) 19–36.

CHAPTERS ONE AND TWO

1. The Social and Religious Setting
2. The Arrival of Radical Freedom

Barrett, C. K., ed. *The New Testament Background: Selected Documents.* Rev. and Exp. ed. San Francisco: Harper & Row, 1989.

Benko, S., and J. J. O'Rourke, eds. *Early Church History: The Roman Empire as the Setting of Primitive Christianity.* London: Oliphants, 1971.

Branick, V. *The House Church in the Writings of Paul.* Wilmington, Del.: Michael Glazier, 1989.

Cumont, F. *Oriental Religions in Roman Paganism.* New York: Dover, 1956.

Drane, J. *Paul: Libertine or Legalist?* London: SPCK, 1975.

Gager, J. G. *Kingdom and Community: The Social World of Early Christianity.* Englewood Cliffs, N.J.: Prentice-Hall, 1975.

Furnish, V. P. *Theology and Ethics in Paul.* Nashville and New York: Abingdon, 1968.

Halliday, W. *The Pagan Background to Early Christianity.* New York: Cooper Square, 1925.

Judge, E. A. *The Social Pattern of Christian Groups in the First Century.* London: Tyndale, 1960.

Longenecker, R. N. *Paul: Apostle of Liberty.* New York: Harper & Row, 1964.

Martin, D. B. *Slavery as Salvation: The Metaphor of Slavery in Pauline Christianity.* New Haven: Yale University Press, 1990.

McMullen, R. *Roman Social Relations: 50 B.C. to A.D. 284.* New Haven: Yale University Press, 1974.

Meeks, W. A. *The First Urban Christians: The Social World of the Apostle Paul.* New Haven: Yale University Press, 1983.

Moore, G. F. *Judaism in the First Three Centuries of the Christian Era.* 2 vols. New York: Schocken, 1971.

Morris, L. L. *The Apostolic Preaching of the Cross.* Grand Rapids: Eerdmans, 1955.

Neyrey, J. H., ed. *The Social World of Luke–Acts: Models for Interpretation.* Peabody, Mass.: Hendrickson, 1991.

Nock, A. D. *Conversion: The Old and New in Religion from Alexander the Great to Augustine of Hyppo.* New York: Oxford University Press, 1933. Reprint. Brown Classics in Judaica. Lanham, Md.: University Press of America, 1988.

Sampley, J. P. *Pauline Partnership in Christ: Christian Community and Commitment in the Light of Roman Law.* Philadelphia: Fortress, 1980.

Sandmel, S. *The First Christian Century in Judaism and Christianity: Certainties and Uncertainties.* New York: Oxford University Press, 1969.

Stambaugh, J. E., and D. L. Balch. *The New Testament in its Social Environment.* Philadelphia: Westminster, 1986.

Tod, M. N. "Clubs and Societies in the Greek World." In *Sidelights on Greek History.* Pages 71–96. London: Oxford University Press, 1932.

CHAPTERS THREE AND FOUR

3. Church as Household Gathering
4. Church as Heavenly Reality

Baldry, H. C. *The Unity of Mankind in Greek Thought.* New York: Cambridge University Press, 1965.

Barton, S. C., and G. E. Horsley. "A Hellenistic Cult Group and the New Testament Churches." *Jahrbuch für Antike und Christentum* 24 (1981) 7–41.

Branick, V. *The House Church in the Writings of Paul.* Wilmington, Del.: Michael Glazier, 1989.

Campbell, J. Y. "The Origin and Meaning of the Christian Use of the Word 'ΕΚΚΛΗΣΙΑ.'" In *Three New Testament Studies.* Pages 41–54. Brill: Leiden, 1965.

Cerfaux, L. *The Church and the Theology of St. Paul.* London: Herder & Herder, 1959.

Downey, G. *A History of Antioch in Syria.* Princeton: Princeton University Press, 1961.

Elliot, J. H. "Philemon and House Churches." *Bible Today* 22 (1984) 145–50.

PAUL'S IDEA OF COMMUNITY

Filson, F. V. "The Significance of the Early House Churches." *Journal of Biblical Literature* 58 (1939) 105–12.

Fiorenza, E. Schussler. *In Memory of Her: A Feminist Theological Reconstruction of Christian Origins.* New York: Crossroads, 1987.

Gärtner, B. *Temple and Community in Qumran and the New Testament.* New York: Cambridge University Press, 1965.

Goguel, M. *The Primitive Church.* London: Allen & Unwin, 1964.

Green, M. *Evangelism in the Early Church.* London: Hodder & Stoughton, 1970.

Jewett, R. "Tenement Churches and Communal Meals in the Early Church: The Implications of a Form-Critical Analysis of 2 Thessalonians 3:10." *Biblical Research* 38 (1993) 23–43.

Judge, E. A., and G. S. R. Thomas. "The Origin of the Church at Rome: A New Solution?" *Reformed Theological Review* 25 (1966) 81–94.

Judge, E. A. "Contemporary Political Models for the Interrelations of New Testament Churches." *Reformed Theological Review* 22 (1963) 65–76.

Malherbe, A. J. "House Churches and Their Problems." *Social Aspects of Early Christianity.* 2d ed. Pages 60–91. Philadelphia: Fortress, 1983.

Murphy-O'Connor, J. *St. Paul's Corinth: Texts and Archeology.* Wilmington, Del.: Michael Glazier, 1983.

Panikulam, G. *Koinonia: A Dynamic Exposition of Christian Life.* Rome: Biblical Institute Press, 1979.

Peterson, Joan M. "House-Churches in Rome." *Vigiliae Christianae* 23 (1969) 264–72.

La Piana, G. "Foreign Groups in Rome during the First Century of the Empire." *Harvard Theological Review* 20 (1927) 183–354.

Verner, D. C. *The Household of God: The Social World of the Pastoral Epistles.* Chico, Calif.: Scholars, 1983.

CHAPTERS FIVE AND SIX

5. The Community as a Loving Family
6. The Community as a Functional Body

Barrett, C. K., ed. *The New Testament Background: Selected Documents.* Rev. and Exp. ed. San Francisco: Harper & Row, 1989.

Barth, M. "A Chapter on the Church: The Body of Christ." *Interpretation* 12 (1958) 131–56.

Best, E. *One Body in Christ*. London: SPCK, 1955.

Bonhoeffer, D. *Sanctorum Communio*. London: Collins, 1963.

Bornkamm, G. "The More Excellent Way." In *Early Christian Experience*. Pages 180–93. London: SCM Press, 1969.

Campbell, J. Y. "KOINONIA and its Cognates in the New Testament." In *Three New Testament Studies*. Pages 1–28. Leiden: Brill, 1965.

Cerfaux, L. *The Church in the Theology of St. Paul*. New York: Herder & Herder, 1959.

de Boer, P. A. H. *Fatherhood and Motherhood in Israelite and Judaean Piety*. Leiden: Brill, 1974.

Doohan, H. *Paul's Vision of Church*. Wilmington, Del.: Michael Glazier, 1989.

Furnish, V. P. *The Love-Command in the New Testament*. Nashville and New York: Abingdon, 1972.

Gundry, R. H. *Soma in the New Testament*. London: Cambridge University Press, 1976.

Kruse, C. *New Testament Models for Ministry: Jesus and Paul*. Nashville: Thomas Nelson, 1989.

Lincoln, A. T. *Paradise Now and Not Yet*. New York: Cambridge University Press, 1981.

Martin, R. P. *The Family and Fellowship*. Grand Rapids: Eerdmans, 1979.

McDermott, M. "The Biblical Doctrine of KOINONIA." *Biblische Zeitschrift* 19 (1975) 64–77.

Minear, P. S. *Images of the Church in the New Testament*. Philadelphia: Westminster, 1960.

Neyrey, J. H. *Paul, In Other Words: A Cultural Reading of his Letters*. Louisville: Westminster, 1990.

O'Brien, P. "The Church as a Heavenly and Eschatological Entity." In *The Church in the Bible and the World*. Edited by D. A. Carson. Exeter: Paternoster, 1987.

Robinson, J. A. T. *The Body*. London: SCM, 1952.

Sampley, J. P. *And the Two Shall Become One Flesh*. New York: Cambridge University Press, 1971.

Schweizer, E. *The Church as the Body of Christ*. Richmond: John Knox, 1964.

CHAPTERS SEVEN AND EIGHT

7. Intellectual Elements in Growth
8. Physical Expressions of Fellowship

Barrett, C. K. *Church, Ministry and Sacraments in the New Testament.* Exeter: Paternoster, 1985.

Bornkamm, G. "Faith and Reason in Paul." In *Early Christian Experience.* Pages 29–46. New York: Harper & Row, 1969.

Cullmann, O., and F. Leenhardt. *Essays on the Lord's Supper.* London: Lutterworth, 1958.

Doohan, H. *Paul's Vision of Church.* Wilmington, Del.: Michael Glazier, 1989.

E. Ferguson, "Laying on of hands: its significance in ordination." *Journal of Theological Studies* 26 (1975) 1–12;

_____. "Selection and Institution to Office in Roman, Greek, Jewish and Christian Antiquity." *Theologische Zeitschrift* 30 (1974) 273–84.

Harvey, A. E. "Elders." *Journal of Theological Studies* 25 (1974) 315–32.

Jeremias, J. *The Eucharistic Words of Jesus.* Philadelphia: Fortress, 1977.

Jewett, R. "Tenement Churches and Pauline Love Feasts." *Quarterly Review* Spring (1994) 43–58.

Johnson, L. T. *Sharing Possessions: Mandate and Symbol of Faith.* Philadelphia: Fortress, 1991.

Kemmler, D. *Faith and Human Reason: A Study of Paul's Preaching as Illustrated by 1–2 Thessalonians and Acts 17:2–4.* Leiden: Brill, 1975.

Kennedy, H. A. A. *St. Paul and the Mystery Religions.* London: Hodder & Stoughton, 1913.

Koenig, J. *New Testament Hospitality: Partnership With Strangers as Promise and Mission.* Philadelphia: Fortress, 1985.

Moule, C. F. D. *Worship in the New Testament.* London: Lutterworth, 1961.

Murphy-O'Connor, J. *Paul on Preaching.* New York: Sheed & Ward, 1964.

_____. "Eucharist and Community in First Corinthians." *Worship* 50 (1976) 370–385; 51 (1977) 56–69.

Neyrey, J. H. *Paul, In Other Words: A Cultural Reading of his Letters.* Louisville: Westminster, 1990.

Nock, A. D. *Early Gentile Christianity and its Hellenistic Background*. New York: Harper & Row, 1964.

Robinson, D. W. B. "Towards a Definition of Baptism." *Reformed Theological Review* 24 (1975) 1–15.

Schnackenburg, R. "Christian Adulthood According to the Apostle Paul." *Catholic Biblical Quarterly* 25 (1963) 354–70.

Stendahl, K., ed. *The Scrolls and the New Testament*. London: SCM, 1953.

Wagner, G. *Pauline Baptism and the Pagan Mysteries*. Edinburgh and London: Oliver & Boyd, 1967.

CHAPTERS NINE AND TEN

9. Gifts and Ministry
10. Charisma and Order

Bornkamm, G. "On the Understanding of Worship." In *Early Christian Experience*. Pages 161–79. New York: Harper & Row, 1969.

Bourke, M. M. "Reflections on Church Order in the New Testament." *Catholic Biblical Quarterly* 30 (1969) 493–511.

Campenhausen, H. von. *Ecclesiastical Authority and Spiritual Power in the Church of the First Three Centuries*. London: A. & C. Black, 1969.

_____. "The Problem of Order in Early Christianity and the Ancient Church." In *Tradition and Life in the Church*. Pages 123–40. London; Collins, 1968.

Carson, D. A. *Showing the Spirit: A Theological Exposition of 1 Corinthians 12–14*. Sydney: Anzea, 1988.

Cullmann, O. *Early Christian Worship*. London: SCM, 1953.

Delling, G. *Worship in the New Testament*. Philadelphia, Westminster, 1962.

Dunn, J. D. G. *Jesus and the Spirit*. Philadelphia: Westminster, 1975.

_____. "The Responsible Congregation." In *Charisma und Agape* (1 *Kor*. 12–14). Edited by P. Benoit. Pages 201–69. Rome: St. Paul, 1984.

Ellis, E. E. "Spiritual Gifts in the Pauline Community." In *Prophecy and Hermeneutic in Early Christianity*. Pages 30–44. Grand Rapids: Eerdmans, 1984.

Hahn, F. *Worship in the New Testament*. Philadelphia: Fortress, 1973.

Käsemann, E. "Worship in Everyday Life: A note on Romans 12." In *New Testament Questions of Today*. Pages 188–95. Philadelphia: Fortress, 1969.

_____. "The Cry for Liberty in the Worship of the Church." In *Perspectives on Paul*. Pages 122–37. Philadelphia: Fortress, 1971.

Koenig, J. *Charismata: God's Gifts for God's People*. Philadelphia: Westminster, 1978.

Kruse, C. *New Testament Models of Ministry: Jesus and Paul*. Nashville: Thomas Nelson, 1983.

Lindsay, T. M. *The Church and the Ministry in the Early Centuries*. London: Hodder & Stoughton, 1902.

Oesterley, W. O. E. *The Jewish Background of the Christian Liturgy*. Gloucester: Peter Smith, 1964.

Peterson, D. "The Biblical Concept of Edification." In *Church, Worship and the Local Congregation*. Edited by B. Webb. Pages 45–58. Sydney: Lancer, 1987.

Schweizer, E. *Church Order in the New Testament*. Naperville, Ill.: Allenson, 1961.

_____. "The Service of Worship: An Exposition of 1 Corinthians." *Neotestamentica* 14. Pages 333–43. Zurich: Zwingli, 1964.

CHAPTERS ELEVEN AND TWELVE

11. Unity in Diversity among the Members
12. The Contribution of Women in Church

Atkins, R. A., Jr. *Egalitarian Community: Ethnography and Exegesis*. Tuscaloosa: University of Alabama Press, 1991.

Balsdon, J. P. V. D. *Roman Women: Their History and Habits*. Westport, Conn.: Greenwood, 1962.

Bartchy, S. S. **ΜΑΛΛΟΝ ΧΡΗΣΑΙ**: *First Century Slavery and the Interpretation of 1 Corinthians 7:21*. Missoula, Mont.: Society for Biblical Literature, 1973.

_____. "Power, Submission and Sexual Identity Among the Early Christians." In *Essays on New Testament Christianity*. Edited by C. R. Wetzei. Pages 50–80. Cincinnati: Standard, 1978.

Caird, G. B. "Paul and Women's Liberty." Manson Memorial Lecture, University of Manchester, 1971.

Dix, G. *Jew and Greek: A Study in the Primitive Church*. New York: Harper, 1953.

Ellis, E. E. "Paul and the Eschatological Woman." In *Pauline Theology: Ministry and Society*. Pages 53–86. Grand Rapids: Eerdmans, 1989.

Fiorenza, E. Schussler. *In Memory of Her: A Feminist Theological Reconstruction of Early Christian Origins.* New York: Crossroad, 1987.

Harnack, A. *The Mission and Expansion of Christianity.* Vol. 2. New York: Putnam, 1905.

Hayter, M. *The New Eve in Christ.* Grand Rapids: Eerdmans, 1987.

Heyob, S. *The Cult of Isis among Women in the Graeco-Roman World.* Leiden: Brill, 1975.

Hooker, M. D. "Authority on her head: 1 Cor. 11:10." *New Testament Studies* 10 (1963–4) 410–16.

Jeremias, J. *Jerusalem in the Time of Jesus.* Philadelphia: Fortress, 1969.

Keener, C. S. *Paul, Women, and Wives: Marriage and Women's Ministry in the Letters of Paul.* Peabody, Mass.: Hendrickson, 1992.

Loewe, R. *The Social Position of Women in Judaism.* London: SPCK, 1966.

MacMullen, R. *Roman Social Relations, 50 BC to AD 284.* New Haven: Yale University Press, 1974.

Malherbe, A. J. *Social Aspects of Early Christianity.* 2d Edition. Philadelphia: Fortress, 1983.

Pomeroy, S. B. *Goddesses, Whores, Wives, Slaves: Women in Classical Antiquity.* New York: Schocken, 1976.

Witherington, B., Jr. *Women in the Earliest Churches.* New York: Cambridge University Press, 1988.

Walker, W. O., Jr. "1 Corinthians 11.2–16 and Paul's Views Regarding Women." *Journal of Biblical Literature* 94 (1975) 94–110.

Chapters Thirteen and Fourteen

13. Participation and Its Responsibilities
14. Service and Its Recognition

Barrett, C. K. *Church, Ministry, and Sacraments in the New Testament.* Exeter: Paternoster, 1985.

Branick, V. *The House Church in the Writings of Paul.* Wilmington, Del.: Michael Glazier, 1989.

Campenhausen, H. von. *Ecclesiastical Authority and Spiritual Power in the Church of the First Three Centuries.* London: A. & C. Black, 1969.

Collins, J. N. *DIAKONIA: Re-interpreting the Ancient Sources.* Oxford: Blackwell, 1990.

Doohan, H. *Leadership in Paul.* Wilmington, Del.: Michael Glazier, 1984.

Dunn, J. D. G. *Jesus and the Spirit*. Philadelphia: Westminster, 1975.

Forkman, G. *The Limits of Religious Community*. Lund: Gleerup, 1972.

Giles, K. *Patterns of Ministry among the First Christians*. San Francisco: Harper & Row, 1991.

Goguel, M. *The Primitive Church*. London: Allen & Unwin, 1964.

Goppelt, L. *Apostolic and Post-apostolic Times*. New York: Harper & Row, 1970.

Hall, D. R. "Pauline Church Discipline." *Tyndale Bulletin* 22 (1969) 3–26.

Holmberg, B. *Paul and Power: The Structure of Authority in the Primitive Church as Reflected in the Pauline Epistles*. Lund: Gleerup, 1978.

Käsemann, E. "Ministry and Community in the New Testament." In *Essays on New Testament Themes*. Pages 63–94. London: SCM, 1964.

Kruse, C. *New Testament Models for Ministry: Jesus and Paul*. Nashville: Thomas Nelson, 1983.

Martin, D. B. *Slavery as Salvation: The Metaphor of Slavery in Pauline Christianity*. New Haven: Yale University Press, 1990.

Powell, D. "Ordo Presbyterii." *Journal of Theological Studies* 26 (1975) 290–328.

Sabourin, L. *Priesthood: A Comparative Study*. Leiden: Brill, 1973.

Schweizer, E. *Church Order in the New Testament*. Naperville, Ill.: Allenson, 1961.

Stanley, D. M. "Authority in the Church: A New Testament Reality." *Catholic Biblical Quarterly* 29 (1967) 555–73.

Warkentin, A. *Ordination: A Biblical Historical View*. Grand Rapids: Eerdmans, 1982.

CHAPTERS FIFTEEN AND SIXTEEN

15. Paul and His Co-Workers
16. The Mission and the Churches

Allen, R. *Missionary Methods: St. Paul's or Ours?* Grand Rapids: Eerdmans, 1962.

Beardslee, W. *Human Achievement and Divine Vocation in the Message of Paul*. London: SCM, 1961.

Bowersock, G. W. *Greek Sophists in the Roman Empire*. Oxford: Clarendon, 1969.

Bruce, F. F. *The Pauline Circle*. Grand Rapids: Eerdmans, 1985.

Collins, J. N. DIAKONIA: Re-interpreting the Ancient Sources. Oxford: Blackwell, 1990.

Deissmann, A. Paul: A Study in Social and Religious History. New York: Harper, 1957.

Ellis, E. E. "Paul and his Co-Workers." New Testament Studies 17 (1971) 437–52.

Fiorenza, E. Schussler. "Women in the Pre-Pauline and Pauline Churches." Union Seminary Quarterly Review 33 (1978) 153–66.

Green, M. Evangelism in the Early Church. London: Hodder & Stoughton, 1970.

Hanson, A. T. The Pioneer Ministry. London: SCM, 1961.

Harnack, A. The Mission and Expansion of Christianity in the First Three Centuries. Vol. 1. New York: Putnam, 1905.

Holmberg, B. Paul and Power: The Structure of Authority in the Primitive Church as Reflected in the Pauline Epistles. Philadelphia: Fortress, 1980.

Jewett, R. J. Christian Tolerance: Paul's Message to the Modern Church. Philadelphia: Westminster, 1982.

Judge, E. A. "The Early Christians as a Scholastic Community II." Journal of Religious History 2 (1961) 125–37.

MacDonald, M. Y. The Pauline Churches: A Socio-Historical Study of Institutionalization in the Pauline and Deutero-Pauline Writings. New York: Cambridge University Press, 1988.

Nickle, K. F. The Collection. Naperville, Ill.: Allenson, 1966.

Redlich, E. B. St. Paul and His Contemporaries. London: Hodder & Stoughton, 1913.

Robinson, D. W. B. "The Doctrine of the Church and its Implications for Evangelism." Interchange 15 (1974) 156–62.

Witherington, B., Jr. Women in the Earliest Churches. New York: Cambridge University Press, 1988.

Chapters Seventeen and Eighteen

17. The Nature of Paul's Authority
18. The Exercise of Paul's Authority

Barrett, C. K. The Signs of an Apostle. London: Epworth, 1970.

Best, E. Paul and his Converts. Edinburgh: T. & T. Clark, 1988.

Bruce, F. F. "Paul and Jerusalem." Tyndale Bulletin 19 (1968) 3–25.

Doohan, H. *Leadership in Paul.* Wilmington, Del.: Michael Glazier, 1984.

Dunn, J. D. G. *Jesus and the Spirit.* Philadelphia: Westminster, 1975.

Giles, K. *Patterns of Ministry among the First Christians.* San Francisco: Harper & Row, 1991.

Grassi, J. *The Secret of Paul the Apostle.* New York: Orbis, 1980.

Hay, D. "Paul's Indifference to Authority." *Journal of Biblical Literature* 88 (1969) 36–44.

Holmberg, B. *Paul and Power: The Structure of Authority in the Primitive Church as Reflected in the Pauline Epistles.* Lund: Gleerup, 1978.

Judge, E. A. "St. Paul and Classical Society." *Jahrbuch für Antike und Christentum* 15 (1972) 19–36.

Kirk, A. "Apostleship Since Rengstorf." *New Testament Studies* 21 (1975) 249–64.

Kruse, C. *New Testament Models for Ministry: Jesus and Paul.* Nashville: Nelson, 1985.

Malherbe, A. *Paul and the Thessalonians: The Philosophic Tradition of Pastoral Care.* Philadelphia: Fortress, 1987.

Munck, J. *Paul and the Salvation of Mankind.* Paperback Edition. Atlanta: John Knox, 1977.

Munro, W. *Authority in Peter and Paul.* New York: Cambridge University Press, 1983.

Schmithals, W. *The Office of Apostle in the Early Church.* New York: Abingdon, 1969.

Schnackenburg, R. "Apostles before and during St. Paul's Time." In *Apostolic History and the Gospel.* Edited by W. W. Gasque and R. P. Martin. Pages 287–303. Exeter: Paternoster, 1970,

Schütz, J. H. *Paul and the Anatomy of Apostolic Authority.* New York: Cambridge University Press, 1975.

Tinsley, E. J. *The Imitation of God in Christ.* London: SCM, 1960.

Young, F., and D. F. Ford. *Meaning and Truth in 2 Corinthians.* Grand Rapids: Eerdmans, 1987.

GLOSSARY

Adonis   A fertility and vegetation god, whose cult was brought from Cyprus to Athens in the first century BC and existed only in conjunction with the rites of Aphrodite.

Alexander   The object of a satire entitled *The False Prophet* by the author Lucian, Alexander originated a new form of the cult of Asclepius, the healing god, during the middle of the second century AD in Asia.

Apollonius of Tyana   A contemporary of Paul, an ascetic itinerant teacher and miracle worker from Cappadocia, whose real and legendary exploits are celebrated in the early third century *Life* by Philostratus.

Apuleius   A Latin poet, philosopher, and author, born ca. AD 123, whose "novel" *The Metamorphoses* (more popularly *The Golden Ass*) contains a first-hand account, in fictional form, of rites associated with Isis.

Aristophanes   The great classic poet-dramatist of the fifth and fourth century BC, whose surviving plays include *Lysistrata*, *The Birds*, *The Frogs*, and others.

Attis   Youthful partner of the Phrygian goddess Cybele, he remained a subordinate part of her cult as it spread to Greece
and Rome, but gained official recognition by Claudius and,
in AD 150, equal honors.

Cicero   Famous first-century BC Roman philosopher, politician,
orator, and man of letters, whose views contain both Platonist and Stoic elements.

Crates   Wandering Greek Cynic philosopher ca. 365–285 BC who
led a life of voluntary poverty and humanitarian actions after
his conversion.

Cybele   The great Phrygian mother-goddess, whose cult became
known in Greece in the late third century BC.

Cynics   Idiosyncratic followers of the principles laid down by the
fourth-century philosopher Diogenes of Sinope, who practiced poverty, rejected conventions, and deliberately shocked
their contemporaries.

Dio Chrysostom   First-century Greek orator, philosopher and writer
who, like others during his time, combined Stoic and Cynic
ideals and, more the exception here, spent much of his later
life as an exiled wandering preacher.

Diogenes Laertius   Author of an early third-century AD survey of the
lives and teachings of the ancient Greek philosophers, about
whose own circumstances nothing is known.

Dionysiac festivals   Dramatic sensual rituals incorporated into the
city-state cult in Athens in the classical period, centered
around the god of emotional religion who stemmed from
Thrace or Phrygia.

Eleusinian mysteries   An old agrarian cult, integrated into the Athenian state-cult in the sixth century, involving various rites,
processions, initiations, etc.

Epictetus   Stoic philosopher ca. AD 55 to 135, originally a slave and
student of Musonius Rufus, who before his banishment by
Domitian in AD 80 taught successfully in Rome and left

behind moral discourses, a manual *Encheiridion*, and some fragments containing his views.

Epicureans Followers of late fourth and early third-century BC Greek moral and natural philosopher, always a minority group, who favored the simple, communal life, taught that the gods no longer intervened in human affairs, and elaborated a particular cosmology and science.

Essenes Monastic urban and rural groups in Judaea and elsewhere, who rejected Greek cultural intrusions and demanded a strict keeping of the Law.

Eusebius of Caesarea The first church historian, author of the *Ecclesiastical History* spanning more than three centuries, who was also Bishop of Caesarea and a moderate supporter of Arius.

Gnosticism Second-century AD phenomenon, comprising Jewish, Hellenistic, Oriental, and especially Christian elements, stressing the importance of esoteric knowledge and repudiation of the body for attaining salvation.

Helena According to tradition, the partner of Simon Magus in his Gnostic transformation and miraculous dissemination of early "Christianity."

Hipparchia Convert of early Cynic philosopher, Crates, who later married her teacher and accompanied him on his travels.

Ignatius Influential Syrian Christian bishop, martyred by the Romans in the early second century AD, whose last letters to various churches and fellow-bishop Polycarp insist on a monoministerial ecclesiastical structure.

Isis and Serapis Egyptian goddess and her husband; from the fourth and particularly second century BC, she became a leading goddess in the Greek and Roman world, eventually gaining official recognition and a wide following.

Josephus Jewish general in revolt against Rome, AD 66–70, who went over to the Romans and proceeded to write in Greek an apologetic account of the war, history of the Jews (the *Antiq-uities*), and account of his life.

Justin Martyr   Christian apologist in Rome during the second century AD, whose writings discuss Jewish skepticism about
Christianity, Roman calumnies against Christians, and Pla-
tonic philosophical views.

Lucian   Prolific Athenian writer ca. AD 120–180, who perfected a
special dialogue form and used it to great effect against
alleged religious "imposters" and "fanatics."

Mishnah   Collection of rabbinic legal traditions, some predating
Christianity, which were set down in writing in the early third
century AD.

Mithras   Ancient Persian god, whose masculine religion spread
throughout the Roman world via the army and business
classes, from the late first century AD, but never really gained
widespread popularity.

Musonius Rufus   Enlightened Stoic philosopher, born 30 AD, who
spent most of his time in Rome; unfortunately only fragments of his works remain.

Origen   One of the most famous early Christian "fathers," latter
judged to be heretical, who continued Clement's fusion of
Christianity and philosophy in Alexandria and Caesarea during the third century AD and also defended Christianity against
pagan attacks.

Orphism   Archaic Greek religious movement, distinguished by having a personal founder, fraternal character, and sacred texts
that had an intermittent following in the classical and later
ages.

Pharisees   Devout, law-centered Jewish group, originating in oppo-
sition to Hellenistic intrusions in second century BC, which
gained increasing popular respect and after the war of AD
66–70 dominated Jewish religious life.

Philo Alexandrian Jew, ca. 30 BC—AD 45, who developed a highly sophisticated apologia for Judaism in his many philosophical writings, most of which took the form of allegorical biblical commentaries.

Philostratus Member of the philosophical circle patronized by the early third-century emperor, Septimius Severus, and his wife, Julia Domna; also the author of various philosophical "lives," including that of Apollonius of Tyana.

Platonism Philosophical tradition stemming from Plato that underwent a revival in the first century BC, but did not become widely influential again in its own right till the second century AD.

Plutarch Born ca. AD 50 and died ca. AD 120, Plutarch was an eclectic philosopher-writer, theological interpreter of the Isis mysteries, and biographer of famous Greeks and Romans.

Posidonius One of the architects of the first-century BC Stoic revival, rejuvenating it through the infusion of Platonist elements, especially imprinting it with a more transcendental emphasis.

Qumran Well-known monastic community by the Dead Sea, the finding of whose writings threw light not only on its own "Essene-like" character but on first century BC and AD Judaism in general.

Seneca Important Roman philosopher and statesman of the first century AD, author of ethical treatises, epistles, dialogues, tragedies, and prose works, and representative of a more personal Stoicism.

Simon Magus Samaritan pseudo-Christian in Acts, who, according to later traditions, was the originator of a heretical form of Christianity with strong Gnostic leanings.

Sophists Virtuoso orators drawn from the ranks of the educated elite, who were involved in education, law, and politics. They often secured a large public following.

Stoicism   Philosophical school founded by Zeno in Athens about 300 BC which, by the first century AD, largely dominated intellectual life with its pantheistic world view, emphasis upon reason, cosmopolitan outlook, and disciplined emotional life.

Teacher of Righteousness   Leader, though not founder, of the Qumran community at some stage during the second century BC, renowned as an interpreter of the Law and the Prophets.

Thucydides   Famous Greek historian, author of the account of the war between Athens and Sparta, 431–404 BC, which is one of the seminal historical works.

Tibullus   First-century BC Latin poet, of whose life little is known, mainly remembered for the quality of his few surviving elegies.

Xenophon   Early Greek historian, living mostly in Athens or Sparta, ca. 428–354 BC, who composed many other works and later achieved considerable popularity among the Romans.

INDEX OF ANCIENT SOURCES